Marcus Joseph Wright

General Scott

Marcus Joseph Wright

General Scott

ISBN/EAN: 9783337124816

Printed in Europe, USA, Canada, Australia, Japan

Cover: Foto ©Andreas Hilbeck / pixelio.de

More available books at **www.hansebooks.com**

Great Commanders

EDITED BY JAMES GRANT WILSON

GENERAL SCOTT

GREAT COMMANDERS

GENERAL SCOTT

BY

General MARCUS J. WRIGHT

NEW YORK
D. APPLETON AND COMPANY
1894

COPYRIGHT, 1893,
BY D. APPLETON AND COMPANY.

All rights reserved.

PREFACE.

In the preparation of this volume the author has consulted and used with freedom the following-named works: History of the Mexican War, by General Cadmus M. Wilcox; Autobiography of General Scott; Life of General Scott, by Edward D. Mansfield; Life of General Scott, by David Hunter Strother; Life of General Scott, by J. T. Headley; History of the Mexican War, by John S. Jenkins; Anecdotes of the Civil War, by General E. D. Townsend; Sketches of Illustrious Soldiers, by General James Grant Wilson; Fifty Years' Observation of Men and Things, by General E. D. Keyes; Reminiscences of Thurlow Weed, and Historical Register of the United States Army, by F. B. Heitman.

My thanks are due to Mr. David Fitzgerald, Librarian of the War Department; Mr. Andrew H. Allen, Librarian of the State Department; and Colonel John B. Brownlow, for many courtesies. I am specially indebted to Mr. John N. Oliver, of Washington city, for valuable assistance rendered me.

M. J. W.

WASHINGTON, *August, 1893.*

CONTENTS.

CHAPTER I.

Parentage and birth of Scott—Precocity—Enters William and Mary College—Leaves college and commences the study of law with Judge Robinson—Attends the trial of Burr at Richmond—Impressment of American seamen and proclamation of President Jefferson—Joins the Petersburg troop—Leaves for Charleston—Returns to Petersburg—Appointed captain of artillery—Trial of General Wilkinson—Scott sends in his resignation, but withdraws it and returns to Natchez—Is court-martialed—On staff duty at New Orleans—Declaration of war with Great Britain—General Wade Hampton and the Secretary of War—Hull's surrender—Storming of Queenstown—March to Lewiston—Scott's appeal to the officers and soldiers—Indians fire on a flag of truce—Incident with a Caledonian priest—Letter in relation to Irish prisoners sent home to be tried for treason 1

CHAPTER II.

Scott ordered to Philadelphia—Appointed adjutant general with the rank of colonel—Becomes chief of staff to General Dearborn—Death of General Pike—Leads the advance on Fort Niagara—Anecdote of Scott and a British colonel—Commands the expedition to Burlington Heights—March for Sacket's Harbor—Meets a force at Cornwall—Retreat of Wilkinson—Scott appointed brigadier general—Attack on and surrender of Fort Erie—Battle

of Chippewa—Lundy's Lane and wounding of Scott—
Retreat of the army to Black Rock—Fort Erie—Visits
Europe 23

CHAPTER III.

Is received and entertained by prominent civilians and military men in Europe—Marries Miss Mayo—Offspring—Thanks of Congress—Thanks of the Virginia Legislature voted, and also a sword—Controversy with General Andrew Jackson and correspondence—Prepares general regulations for the army and militia—Controversy with General Gaines and the War Department about rank—In command of the Eastern Division—War with the Sac and Fox Indians—Black Hawk—Cholera breaks out among the troops 41

CHAPTER IV.

Troubles in South Carolina growing out of the tariff acts apprehended, and General Scott sent South—Action of the nullifiers—Instructions in case of an outbreak—Action of the South Carolina Legislature 60

CHAPTER V.

Events that led to the war in Florida—Treaty of Camp Moultrie and its stipulations—Complaints of Indians and whites—Treaty of Payne's Landing—Objections of the Indians to complying with the latter treaty—Councils and talks with the Seminoles—Assiola—Murder of mail carrier Dalton—Murder of Charley Amathla—Dade's massacre—Murder of General Thompson and others—General Clinch—Depredations by the Indians on the whites and by the latter on the Indians—Volunteers—Military departments of Gaines and Scott . . . 72

CHAPTER VI.

Review of the army by General Gaines—Arrival of General Gaines at Fort King—Lieutenant Izard mortally wounded—Correspondence between General Gaines and Clinch—General Scott ordered to command in Florida—Disadvantages under which he labored—Preparations for movements—Commencement of hostilities against the Indians 103

CHAPTER VII.

Scott prefers complaint against General Jesup—Court of inquiry ordered by the President—Scott fully exonerated by the court—Complaints of citizens—Difficulties of the campaign—Speech in Congress of Hon. Richard Biddle—Scott declines an invitation to a dinner in New York city—Resolutions of the subscribers—Scott is ordered to take charge of and remove the Cherokee Indians—Orders issued to troops and address to the Indians—Origin of the Cherokee Indian troubles—Collision threatened between Maine and New Brunswick, and Scott sent there—Correspondence with Lieutenant-Governor Harvey—Seizure of Navy Island by Van Rensselaer—Governor Marcy 122

CHAPTER VIII.

Annexation of Texas—Causes that led to annexation—Message of the President—General Scott's letters regarding William Henry Harrison—Efforts to reduce General Scott's pay—Letter to T. P. Atkinson on the slavery question—Battle of Palo Alto, and of Resaca de la Palma, Monterey, and Buena Vista—"The hasty plate of soup"—Scott's opinion of General Taylor—Scott ordered to Mexico—Proposal to revive the grade of lieutenant general, and to appoint Thomas H. Benton—Scott reaches the Brazos Santiago—Confidential dispatch from Scott to Taylor—Co-operation of the navy—Letters to the Secretary of War as to places of rendezvous—Arrival and landing at Vera Cruz, and its investment, siege, and capture—Letter to foreign consuls—Terms of surrender—Orders of General Scott after the surrender . . . 149

CHAPTER IX.

General Santa Anna arrives at Cerro Gordo—Engagement at Atalaya—General Orders No. 111—Reports from Jalapa—Report of engagement at Cerro Gordo—Occupation of Perote—Account of a Mexican historian—General Santa Anna's letter to General Arroya—Delay of the Government in sending re-enforcements—Danger of communications with Vera Cruz—Troops intended for Scott ordered to General Taylor—Colonel Childs appointed governor of Jalapa—Occupation of Puebla—Arrival of re-enforcements—Number of Scott's force . . . 175

CHAPTER X.

Movement toward the City of Mexico—The Duke of Wellington's comments—Movements of Santa Anna—A commission meets General Worth to treat for terms—Worth enters Puebla—Civil administration of the city not interfered with—Scott arrives at Puebla—Scott's address to the Mexicans after the battle of Cerro Gordo—Contreras—Reconnoissance of the *pedregal*—Defeat of the Mexicans at Contreras—Battle of Churubusco—Arrival of Nicholas P. Trist, commissioner—General Scott meets a deputation proposing an armistice—He addresses a communication to the head of the Mexican Government—Appointment of a commission to meet Mr. Trist—Major Lally—Meeting of Mr. Trist with the Mexican commissioners—Failure to agree—Armistice violated by the Mexicans and notice from General Scott—Santa Anna's insolent note—The latter calls a meeting of his principal officers—Molino del Rey—Chapultepec—Losses on both sides. 195

CHAPTER XI.

General Quitman's movements to San Antonio and Coyoacan—Movements of General Pillow—General reconnoissance by Scott—Chapultepec—Scott announces his line

of attack—Surrender of the Mexican General Bravo—
Preparations to move on the capital—Entry of General
Scott into the City of Mexico—General Quitman made
Military Governor—General Scott's orders—Movements
of Santa Anna—General Lane—American and Mexican
deserters—Orders as to collection of duties and civil
government 223

CHAPTER XII.

Scott's care for the welfare of his army — Account of the
money levied on Mexico—Last note to the Secretary
of War while commander in chief in Mexico—Army
asylums—Treaty of peace—Scott turns over the army to
General William O. Butler—Scott and Worth—Court of
inquiry on Worth—The "Leonidas" and "Tampico"
letters—Revised paragraph 650—Army regulations—General
Worth demands a court of inquiry and prefers
charges against Scott—Correspondence—General belief
as to Scott's removal command—The trial—Return
home of General Scott 254

CHAPTER XIII.

General Taylor nominated for the presidency—Thanks of
Congress to Scott, and a gold medal voted—Movement
to revive and confer upon Scott the brevet rank of lieutenant
general—Scott's views as to the annexation of
Canada—Candidate for President in 1852 and defeated
—Scott's diplomatic mission to Canada in 1859—Mutterings
of civil war—Letters and notes to President Buchanan—Arrives
in Washington, December 12, 1861—
Note to the Secretary of War—" Wayward sisters " letter
—Events preceding inauguration of Mr. Lincoln—Preparation
for the defense of Washington—Scott's loyalty—
Battle of Bull Run—Scott and McClellan—Free navigation
of the Mississippi River—Retirement of General
Scott and affecting incidents connected therewith—Message
of President Lincoln—McClellan on Scott—Mount

GENERAL SCOTT.

CHAPTER I.

Parentage and birth of Scott—Precocity—Enters William and Mary College—Leaves college and commences the study of law with Judge Robinson—Attends the trial of Burr at Richmond—Impressment of American seamen and proclamation of President Jefferson—Joins the Petersburg troop—Leaves for Charleston—Returns to Petersburg—Appointed captain of artillery—Trial of General Wilkinson—Scott sends in his resignation, but withdraws it and returns to Natchez—Is court-martialed—On staff duty at New Orleans—Declaration of war with Great Britain—General Wade Hampton and the Secretary of War—Hull's surrender—Storming of Queenstown—March to Lewiston—Scott's appeal to the officers and soldiers—Indians fire on a flag of truce—Incident with a Caledonian priest—Letter in relation to Irish prisoners sent home to be tried for treason.

WINFIELD SCOTT was born at Laurel Branch, the estate of his father, fourteen miles from Petersburg, Dinwiddie County, Virginia, June 13, 1786. His grandfather, James Scott, was a Scotchman of the Clan Buccleuch, and a follower of the Pretender to the throne of England, who, escaping from the defeat at Culloden, made his way to Virginia in 1746, where he settled. William, the son of this James, married Ann Mason, a native of Dinwiddie County and a neighbor of the Scott family. Winfield Scott was the issue of this marriage. There were an elder brother and two daughters. James [William] Scott died at an early age, when Winfield was but six years old. William, the father of Winfield, was a lieutenant and afterward captain in a Virginia company which served in the Revolutionary army. Eleven years after the father's death the mother died, leaving Winfield, at seventeen years old, to make his own way in the world.

At the death of his father, Winfield, being but six years old, was left to the charge of his mother, to whom he was devotedly attached. It is a well-warranted tradition of the county in which the Scott family resided, that the mother of General Scott was a woman of superior mind and great force of character. In acknowledging the inspiration from the lessons of that admirable parent for whatever of success he achieved, he was not unlike Andrew Jackson and the majority of the great men of the world. He wrote of her in his mature age as follows: "And if, in my now protracted career, I have achieved anything worthy of being written, anything that my countrymen are likely to honor in the next century, it is from the lessons of that admirable parent that I derived the inspiration."

In his seventh year he was ordered on a Sunday morning to get ready for church. Disobeying the order, he ran off and concealed himself, but was pursued, captured, and returned to his mother, who at once sent for a switch. The switch was a limb from a Lombardy poplar, and the precocious little truant, seeing this, quoted a verse from St. Matthew which was from a lesson he had but recently read to his mother. The quotation was as follows: "Every tree that bringeth not forth good fruit is hewn down, and cast into the fire." The quotation was so apt that the punishment was withheld, but the offender was not spared a very wholesome lesson.

General Scott's mother, Ann, was the daughter of Daniel Mason and Elizabeth Winfield, his wife, who was the daughter of John Winfield, a man of high standing and large wealth. From his mother's family he acquired his baptismal name of Winfield. John Winfield survived his daughter, and dying intestate, in 1774, Winfield Mason acquired by descent as the eldest male heir (the law of primogeniture then being the law of Virginia) the whole of a landed estate and a portion of the personal property. The principal part of this large inheritance was devised to Winfield Scott, but, the devisee having married again and had issue, the will was abrogated. The wife of Winfield Mason was the daughter of Dr. James Greenway, a near neighbor. He was born in England, near the borders of Scotland, and inherited his father's trade, that of a weaver. He was ambitious and studious, and giving all of his spare time to study, he became familiar with the Greek, Latin, French, and Italian languages. After his immigration to Virginia he prepared himself for the practice of medicine, and soon acquired a large and lucrative practice. He devoted much of his time to botany, and left a *hortus siccus* of forty folio volumes, in which he described the more interesting plants of Virginia and North Carolina. He was honored by memberships in several of the learned European societies, and was a correspondent of the celebrated Swedish naturalist Linnæus. He acquired such a knowledge of music as enabled him to become teacher to his own children.

James Hargrave, a Quaker, was one of young Scott's earliest teachers. He found his pupil to be a lad of easy excitement and greatly inclined to be belligerent. He tried very hard to tone him down and teach him to govern his temper. On one occasion young Scott, being in Petersburg and passing on a crowded street, found his Quaker teacher, who was a non-combatant, engaged in a dispute with a noted bully. Hargrave was the county surveyor, and this fellow charged him with running a false dividing line. When Scott heard the charge he felled the bully to the ground with one blow of his fist. He recovered and advanced on Scott, when Hargrave placed himself between them and received the blow intended for Scott; but the bully was again knocked to the ground by the strong arm of Scott. Many years afterward (in 1816) Scott met his Quaker friend and former teacher, who said to him: "Friend Winfield, I always told thee not to fight; but as thou wouldst fight, I am glad that thou wert not beaten."

His next instructor was James Ogilvie, a Scotchman, who was a man of extraordinary endowments and culture. Scott spent a year under his tutelage at Richmond, and entered, in 1805, William and Mary College. Here he gave special attention to the study of civil and international law, besides chemistry, natural and experimental philosophy, and common law. At about the age of nineteen he left William and Mary College and entered the law office of Judge David Robinson in Petersburg as a student.

Robinson had emigrated from Scotland to Virginia at the request of Scott's grandfather, who employed him as a private tutor in his family.

There were two other students in Mr. Robinson's office with Scott—Thomas Ruffin and John F. May. Ruffin became Chief Justice of the Supreme Court of North Carolina, and May the leading lawyer in southern Virginia. After he had received his license to practice he rode the circuit, and was engaged in a number of causes. He was present at the celebrated trial of Aaron Burr for treason, and was greatly impressed with Luther Martin, John Wickham, Benjamin Botts, and William Wirt, the leading lawyers in the case. Here he also met Commodore Truxton, General Andrew Jackson, Washington Irving, John Randolph, Littleton W. Tazewell, William B. Giles, John Taylor of Caroline, and other distinguished persons.

Aaron Burr was a native of Newark, N. J., and was the grandson of the celebrated Jonathan Edwards. He graduated at Princeton in September, 1772, and studied law, but in 1775 joined the American army near Boston. Accompanied Colonel Benedict Arnold in the expedition to Quebec, and acquired such reputation that he was made a major; afterward joined General Washington's staff, and subsequently was an aid to General Putnam. Promoted to the rank of lieutenant colonel, he commanded a detachment which defeated the British at Hackensack, and distinguished himself at Monmouth. Burr became Vice-President on the election of Jefferson as President, and was involved in a quarrel with Alexander Hamilton, and killed him in a duel at Weehawken, N. J., July 7, 1804. This affair was fatal to his future prospects. In 1805 he floated in a boat from Pittsburg to New Orleans. His purpose was supposed to be to collect an army and conquer

Mexico and Texas, and establish a government of which he should be the head. He purchased a large tract of land on the Wachita River, and made other arrangements looking to the consummation of his object. Colonel Burr was arrested and tried for treason in Richmond in 1807, but was acquitted. He died on Staten Island, September 14, 1836.

In May, 1807, the British frigate Leopard boarded the Chesapeake in Virginia waters and forcibly carried off some of her crew, who were claimed as British subjects. Mr. Jefferson, President of the United States, at once issued a proclamation prohibiting all British war vessels from entering our harbors. Great excitement was produced throughout the entire country. The day after the issuance of the President's proclamation the Petersburg (Va.) troop of cavalry tendered its services to the Government, and young Scott, riding twenty-five miles distant from Petersburg, enlisted as a member. He was placed in a detached camp near Lynn Haven Bay, opposite where the British squadron was at anchor. Sir Thomas Hardy was the ranking officer in command of several line of battle ships. Learning that an expedition from the squadron had gone out on an excursion, Scott, in charge of a small detachment, was sent to intercept them. He succeeded in capturing two midshipmen and six sailors, and brought them into camp. The capture was not approved by the authorities, and the prisoners were ordered to be released, and restored to Admiral Sir Thomas Hardy.

The prospect of a war with Great Britain had abated, and the affair of the Chesapeake being in train of settlement, Scott left Virginia in October,

GOES TO SOUTH CAROLINA.

1807, and proceeded to Charleston, S. C., with a view of engaging in the practice of law. The law of that State required a residence of twelve months before admission to the bar. Scott went to Columbia, where the Legislature was in session, and applied for a special act permitting him to practice. The application failed for want of time. He then proceeded to Charleston, with a view of office practice until he could be qualified for the usual practice in the courts; but the prospect of war being again imminent, he went to Washington, and on the application and recommendation of Hon. William B. Giles, of Virginia, President Jefferson promised him a captain's commission in the event of hostilities. No act of war occurring, he returned in March, 1808, to Petersburg, and resumed the practice of law in that circuit; but his life as a lawyer came suddenly to a close in the succeeding month of May, when he received from the President his commission as captain of artillery. He recruited his company in Petersburg and Richmond, and embarked from Norfolk to New Orleans, February 4, 1809.

It being thought that on the breaking out of hostilities the British would at once endeavor to invade Louisiana, a military force was sent to New Orleans under the command of General James Wilkinson. The discipline of the army became greatly impaired, and much sickness and many deaths occurred in this command. General Wilkinson was ordered to Washington for an investigation into his conduct as commanding officer, and General Wade Hampton succeeded to the command. The camp below New Orleans was broken up in June, 1809, and the troops were transferred to and encamped near Natchez.

General Wilkinson was charged with complicity with Aaron Burr, and with being in the pay of the Spanish Government, and was tried by court-martial; and although he was acquitted, there were many persons who believed him guilty, and among these was Captain Scott, who was present, as heretofore mentioned, at the trial of Burr, and participated in the strong feeling which it produced throughout the country.

The apparent lull in the war feeling having produced the impression that there would be no hostile movements, Captain Scott forwarded his resignation and sailed for Virginia, intending to re-engage in the practice of the law. Before his resignation had been accepted he received information that grave charges would be preferred against him should he return to the army at Natchez. This determined him to return at once to his post and meet the charges. Scott had openly given it as his opinion that General Wilkinson was equally guilty with Colonel Burr. Soon after his return he was arrested and tried by a court-martial at Washington, near Natchez, in January, 1810. The first charge was for "conduct unbecoming an officer and a gentleman," and the specification was "in withholding at sundry times men's money placed in his possession for their payment for the months of September and October." Another charge was "ungentlemanly and unofficer-like conduct," the specification being "In saying, between the 1st of December and the 1st of January, 1809-'10, at a public table in Washington, Mississippi Territory, that 'he never saw but two traitors—General Wilkinson and Burr—and that General Wilkinson was a liar and a scoundrel.'" This charge was based on the sixth article of war, which says: "Any officer who shall behave himself with contempt and disrespect toward his commanding officer shall be punished, according to the nature of the offense, by the judgment of a court-martial."

Captain Scott's defense to this charge was that General Wilkinson was not, at the time the words were charged to have been spoken, his commanding officer, that place being filled by General Wade Hampton. General Scott, in his Memoirs, says that some of Wilkinson's partisans had heard him say in an excited conversation that he knew, soon after Burr's trial, from his friends Mr. Randolph and Mr. Tazewell and others, members of the grand jury, who found the bill of indictment against Burr, that nothing but the influence of Mr. Jefferson had saved Wilkinson from being included in the same indictment, and that he believed Wilkinson to have been equally a traitor with Burr. He admits that the expression of that belief was not only imprudent, but no doubt at that time blamable. But this was not the declaration on which he was to be tried. This was uttered in New Orleans, the headquarters of General Wilkinson. The utterance on which he was tried, as will be seen, was made in Washington, Mississippi Territory, when General Wade Hampton was his commanding officer.

The finding of the Court on this charge was guilty, and that his conduct was unofficerlike. The facts in regard to the charge of retaining money belonging to the men of his command were, that prior to his departure for New Orleans he had recruited his company in Virginia, and, being remote from a paymaster or quartermaster, a sum of four hundred dollars was placed in his hands to be used in recruiting. Some of his vouchers were technically irregular, and at the time of his trial about fifty dollars was not covered by formal vouchers. This was the finding of the Court, but it expressly acquitted him of all fraudulent intentions. General Wilkinson nursed his wrath, and after the close of the war published an attack on General Scott. His own failure in the campaign of 1813, and especially his defeat at La Cale Mills, compared with Scott's brilliant campaign on the Niagara frontier in the following spring, may have induced this attack.

Captain Scott returned to Virginia after the trial, and under the advice of his friend, the distinguished lawyer and statesman, Benjamin Watkins Leigh, he devoted himself to the study of military works and of English attack. During the time mentioned he wrote a letter to Lewis Edwards, Esq., at Washington City, of which he following is a copy:

"PETERSBURG, *June, 1811.*

"DEAR SIR: I believe we have very little village news to give you, nor do I know what would please you in that way. Of myself—that person who has so large a space in every man's own imagination, and so small a one in the imagination of every other—I can say but little; perhaps less would please you more. Since my return to Virginia my time has been passed in easy transitions from pleasure to study, from study to pleasure; in my gayety forgetting the student, in the student forgetting my gayety.* I have generally been in the office of my friend Mr.

---

* "If idle, be not solitary; if solitary, be not idle." An apothegm of Burton paraphrased by Johnson, "My Motto."

Leigh, though not unmindful of the studies connected with my present profession; but you will easily conceive my military ardor has suffered abatement. Indeed, it is my design, as soon as circumstances will permit, to throw the feather out of my cap and resume it in my hand. Yet, should war come at last, my enthusiasm will be rekindled, and then who knows but that I may yet write my history with my sword?   Yours truly,
"WINFIELD SCOTT."

Scott rejoined the army at Baton Rouge, La., in 1811, and was soon appointed Judge Advocate on the trial of a colonel charged with gross negligence in discipline and administration. By dilatory pleas this officer had several times escaped justice, but on this trial he was found guilty and censured. In the winter of 1811–'12 Scott was frequently on staff duty with General Wade Hampton at New Orleans, and while there saw the first steam vessel that ever floated on the Mississippi.

On May 20, 1812, Captain Scott embarked at New Orleans for Washington *via* Baltimore, accompanying General Hampton and Lieutenant Charles K. Gardner. As the vessel on which they had taken passage entered near the Capes of Virginia it passed a British frigate lying off the bar. In a short time they met a Hampton pilot boat going out to sea. This was on June 29th, and this pilot boat bore dispatches to Mr. Mansfield, the British Minister at Washington, announcing that Congress had two days before declared war against Great Britain. The vessel bearing Captain Scott and his companions went aground about sixteen miles from Baltimore, and he and some others undertook the remainder of the journey on foot. At the end of the fourth mile they passed an enthusiastic militia meeting which had just received a copy of the declaration of war. Scott, having on a uniform, was made the hero of the occasion, and was chosen to read the declaration to the meeting. He was here offered a seat in a double gig to Baltimore, but the driver, who had become intoxicated, overturned the gig twice, when Scott took the reins and drove the latter part of the journey. On his arrival at Baltimore he received the pleasing intelligence that he had been appointed a lieutenant colonel in the United States army. He was then in his twenty-sixth year.

He went with General Hampton to Washington, where the general asked him to accompany him on an official visit to the Secretary of War. An unpleasant correspondence had a short time previously occurred between the general and the secretary, yet he felt it his duty to make the call. On General Hampton's name being announced to the secretary the latter appeared at the door and extended his hand, while General Hampton simply bowed and crossed his hands behind him. A conversation on official matters was held, at first formal and cold, but gradually terminating in one of a friendly character. When General Hampton rose to leave he extended to the secretary both of his hands; but it was now the latter's turn, and he bowed and placed his hands behind him. General Hampton sent a challenge to mortal combat, but mutual friends settled the matter without bloodshed, by requiring that Hampton should on the next morning present himself at the secretary's door with both hands extended in the

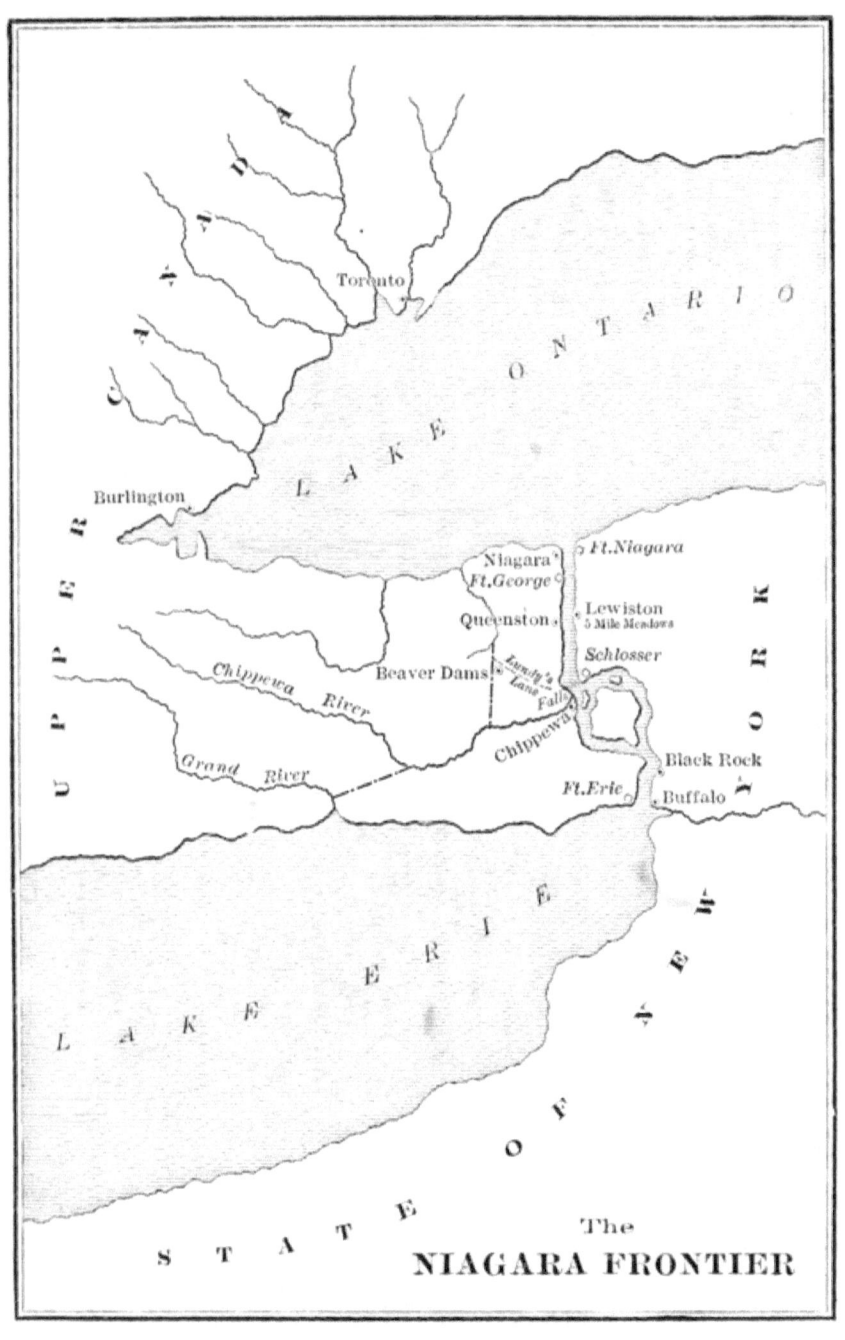

presence of the same persons who witnessed the former meeting. Colonel Scott was now ordered to Philadelphia to mobilize his regiment and organize a camp of instruction. On his own solicitation, he was soon afterward ordered to report to Brigadier-General Alexander Smyth, near Buffalo, N. Y.

The Congress of the United States made formal declaration of war against Great Britain and its dependencies June 18, 1812. In the month previous General William Hull had been appointed to the command of the northwestern army, intended for the invasion of Canada. This army arrived on the Maumee River on May 30th, and marching northward subsequently crossed over at Detroit. High hopes were entertained of the success of this expedition, and the bitterest disappointment and chagrin were manifested throughout the country when it was learned that Hull had surrendered his entire command to the British General Brock on August 14th. The regiment to which Colonel Scott was assigned was the Second Artillery. Colonel George Izard and he arrived on the Niagara frontier with the companies of Nathan Towson and James Nelson Barker. He was posted at Black Rock for the protection of the navy yard there established.

An expedition had been planned by Lieutenant Elliott, of the navy, for the capture or destruction of two armed British brigs which were lying under the guns of Fort Erie. On October 8th Colonel Scott detached Captain Towson and a portion of his company to report to Elliott. On the morning of the 9th the Adams was taken by Elliott and Lieutenant Isaac Roach, and the Caledonia was captured by Captain Towson. In passing down the river the

Adams drifted into the British channel and ran aground under the British guns. The enemy endeavored to recapture her, but were successfully resisted by Colonel Scott. This was his first experience under fire, and he was complimented for his skill and gallantry. The Caledonia was afterward a part of Commodore Perry's fleet on Lake Erie. The Adams, having drifted aground, was burned to prevent recapture.

The northwestern army at this time consisted of about ten thousand troops. General Henry Dearborn held command near Plattsburg and Greenbush, and was the commanding officer of all the forces on the northern frontier. A portion of his army was camped at Lewistown under the command of General Stephen Van Rensselaer, of New York. General Alexander Smyth was at Buffalo with some fifteen hundred regular troops. Besides these, there were small detachments at Ogdensburg, Sackett's Harbor, and Black Rock.

General Van Rensselaer conceived the plan of making a bold and sudden move into Canada, with a view of capturing Jamestown, and there establishing winter quarters. The affair of the capture of the two English brigs with fifty men had roused great enthusiasm, and the country was anxious for some success of arms to alleviate the depression occasioned by Hull's surrender. General Van Rensselaer confided the immediate command of the expedition to his relative, Colonel Solomon Van Rensselaer an officer of coolness and courage, who, with three hundred militia and three hundred regulars, under Colonel Chrystie, on October 13th began crossing the river.

AFFAIR AT JAMESTOWN.

The troops were on the river bank ready to embark an hour before daylight, but from some mismanagement there was not a sufficient number of boats to transport the whole, and they were compelled to cross in detachments. Colonel Chrystie's boat was swept down the river by the current, and he was wounded. On a second attempt he succeeded in landing. With about a hundred men Colonel Van Rensselaer led them up the bank, and halted to await the arrival of the remainder. It was now daylight, and the little command was in full view of the enemy, who opened a deadly fire. Every commissioned officer was either killed or wounded. Finding that the river bank afforded but little protection, Colonel Van Rensselaer determined to storm the Queenstown heights. He had now received four wounds, and was compelled to relinquish the command to Captains Peter Ogilvie, Jr., and John Ellis Wool. In a very short time the fort was taken and the heights occupied by the Americans. The enemy took refuge in a stone house, from which they opened a destructive fire and made two unsuccessful attempts to recapture the lost ground. General Brock rallied his men and led them on, but while moving at the head of the Forty-ninth Grenadiers he fell mortally wounded. General Van Rensselaer recrossed the river and assumed command, but hastening back to urge forward re-enforcements, the command fell to General Decius Wadsworth, who, however, did not assume to control the movements. Two light batteries from the Canada shore played on the boats attempting to cross, and there was no artillery with which the Americans could resist.

Colonel Scott had volunteered his services for the

expedition, but they were declined, for the reason that arrangements had been made for detachments under Colonel John R. Fenwick and Lieutenant-Colonel James Robert Mullaney to sustain the assaulting columns. Permission was, however, given to Colonel Scott to march his regiment to Lewiston and act as circumstances might require.

He arrived there at 4 A. M. on the 13th. Finding no boats to transport his command, he placed his guns on the American shore, under the direction of Captains Towson and Barker. Seeing that a small portion of the troops had crossed over, and knowing the peril of Van Rensselaer's little force, he took one piece of artillery into a boat, and, accompanied by his adjutant, Lieutenant Isaac Roach, Jr., he crossedt to the Canada shore. Wadsworth at once relinquished the command of the troops to him, and he soon animated every one with courage and resolution.

Six feet five inches in height, clad in a new uniform, he became a conspicuous mark for the enemy. The re-enforcements which had now crossed over increased the force to about six hundred, of which more than half were regulars. These were placed under Colonel Scott's directions in the most commanding positions, where they awaited further re-enforcements. About this time a body of five hundred Indians joined the British troops. The British with their Indian allies moved forward to the assault, but were speedily driven back. A second time they moved forward, but with the same result. They kept up a desultory firing, during which a body of Indians moved suddenly out and surprised an outpost of militia. Scott, who was at this moment engaged in unspiking a gun, rushed to the front, and, rallying his men, sent the dusky warriors rapidly in retreat. The British general Sheaffe, who held the command at Fort George, having heard the firing, at once put his troops in motion and marched for the scene of the conflict. Sheaffe's command consisted of eight hundred and fifty men. These, added to the garrison which the Americans were attacking, was a formidable force to be met by three hundred men. In the meantime the American troops had refused to cross the river and were in a state of mutiny. No entreaties, orders, or threats of Van Rensselaer could avail to move them. But the three hundred brave fellows, with only one piece of artillery, stood their ground. General Van Rensselaer, from the American shore, sent word to Wadsworth to retreat. Colonels John Chrystie and Scott, of the regulars, and Captains James Mead, Strahan, and Allen, of the militia, and Captains Ogilvei, Wool, Joseph Gilbert, Totten, and McChesney, took council of their desperate situation. Colonel Scott told them that their condition was desperate, but that the stain of Hull's surrender must be wiped out. "Let us die," he said, "arms in hand. Our country demands the sacrifice. The example will not be lost. The blood of the slain will make heroes of the living. Those who follow will avenge our fall and our country's wrongs. Who dare to stand?" he exclaimed. A loud ringing shout "All!" came from the whole line.

General Sheaffe did not move to immediate attack on his arrival. He marched his troops slowly the entire length of the American line, and then countermarched.

As resistance was entirely hopeless, the order was given to retire. The whole line broke in disorder to the river, but there were no boats there to transport them. Two flags of truce were sent to the enemy, but the officer who bore them did not return. Colonel Scott then fixed a white handkerchief on the end of his sword, and, accompanied by Captains Totten and Gibson, passed under the river bluff and started to ascend the heights. They were met by Indians, who fired on them and rushed with tomahawks to assault them. A British officer happily arrived and conducted them to the quarters of General Sheaffe, and Colonel Scott made formal surrender of the whole force. The number surrendered, except some skulking militia who were discovered later, was two hundred and ninety-three. The American loss in killed, wounded, and captured was near one thousand men.

General Van Rensselaer was so mortified at the conduct of the militia that he tendered his resignation. The British general Brock was next day buried under one of the bastions of Fort George, and Colonel Scott, then a prisoner, sent orders to have minute guns fired from Fort Niagara during the funeral ceremonies, which orders were carried out— an act of chivalry and courtesy which greatly impressed the British.

The American officers who had been captured were lodged in a small inn at the village of Newark and divested of their arms, and a strong guard was posted at the door. Two Indians, Captain Jacobs and Brant, sent word that they wished to see the tall American, meaning Colonel Scott. The alleged object of their visit was to see if Scott had not been wounded, as he had been fired at several times at close range. On entering the room, Jacobs seized Scott by the arm and attempted to turn him around. Scott seized the Indian and threw him against the wall. Both then drew their knives, and advancing on the prisoner said, "We kill you now!" The sentinel at the door was not in view, and Scott, making a spring, seized a sword, which he quickly drew from the scabbard, and, placing his back against the wall in the narrow hall, defied his assailants. At this critical moment Captain Coffin, nephew of General Sheaffe and his aid-de-camp, entered the room and caught Jacobs by the throat and presented a cocked pistol to his breast. Both savages now turned on him, and Scott closed in to defend the captain. At this moment the guard entered, and arrested the two Indians and conducted them out of the room.

The volunteer officers and men were paroled and sent home, while the regulars were embarked for Quebec. On the passage to Quebec a priest of a Caledonian settlement reproached Colonel Scott severely for being a traitor to George III. Respect for his profession brought out a mild reply. In 1827, General Scott being at Buffalo on board a Government steamer, the master of the vessel asked permission to bring into his cabin a bishop and two priests. The bishop was recognized as the same prelate who had acted so rudely. General Scott, however, heaped coals of fire on his head by treating him and his party with the greatest courtesy.

After a cartel of exchange had been agreed upon, Colonel Scott and the other regulars, prisoners, were embarked on a vessel for Boston. As they were about to sail, Colonel Scott's attention was attracted by an unusual noise on deck. Proceeding from the cabin to the scene of the disturbance, he found a party of British officers in the act of separating from the other prisoners such as by confusion or brogue they judged to be Irishmen. The object was to refuse to parole them, and send them to England to be tried for high treason. Twenty-three had been selected and set apart for this purpose.

Colonel Scott learned with indignation that this proceeding was under the direct orders of Sir George Prevost, the Governor General. He at once protested, and commanded the remaining men to be silent and answer no questions. This order was obeyed despite the threats of the British officers, and none others than the twenty-three were separated from their comrades. He then addressed the party selected, explaining the laws of allegiance, and assuring them that the United States Government would protect them by immediate retaliation, and, if necessary, by an order to give no quarter hereafter in battle. He was frequently interrupted by the British officers, but they failed to silence him. The Irishmen were put in irons, placed on board a frigate, and sent to England. After Colonel Scott landed in Boston he proceeded to Washington, and was duly exchanged. He at once addressed a letter to the Secretary of War as folows:

"SIR: I think it my duty to lay before the Department that on the arrival at Quebec of the American prisoners of war surrendered at Queenstown they were mustered and examined by British officers appointed to that duty, and every native-born of the United Kingdom of Great Britain and Ireland sequestered and sent on board a ship of war then in the harbor. The vessel in a few days thereafter sailed for England with these persons on board. Between fifteen and twenty persons were thus taken from us, natives of Ireland, several of whom were known by their platoon officers to be naturalized citizens of the United States, and others to have been long residents within the same. One in particular, whose name has escaped me, besides having complied with all the conditions of our naturalization laws, was represented by his officers to have left a wife and five children, all of them born within the State of New York.

"I distinctly understood, as well from the officers who came on board the prison ship for the above purposes as from others with whom I remonstrated on this subject, that it was the determination of the British Government, as expressed through Sir George Prevost, to punish every man whom it might subject to its power found in arms against the British king contrary to his native allegiance. I have the honor to be, sir,

"Your most obedient servant,
"WINFIELD SCOTT,
"*Lieutenant Colonel, Second U. S. Artillery.*"

This report was forwarded by the Secretary of War to both houses of Congress, and the immediate result was that Congress, on March 3, 1813, passed an act of retaliation. In May, 1813, at the battle of Fort George, a number of prisoners were captured. Colonel Scott, being then chief of staff, selected twenty-three to be confined and held as hostages. He was careful, however, to entirely exclude Irishmen from the number. Eventually the twenty-three men sent to England were released, and Scott took great interest in securing their arrearages of pay and patents for their land bounties.

The doctrine of perpetual allegiance had always been maintained by the British Government, and examples were numerous of the arrest or detention of prisoners claimed as British subjects. After this act of Colonel Scott no other prisoners were set apart by the British to be tried for treason.

These transactions gave rise to discussion of the question throughout the country and in both houses of Congress. President Madison, and Mr. Monroe as Secretary of State, took strong ground against the British claim. While subsequent treaties were silent on the question, the right is no longer asserted by Great Britain, and has been recognized by treaty. Colonel Scott then returned to Washington.

CHAPTER II.

Scott ordered to Philadelphia—Appointed adjutant general with the rank of colonel—Becomes chief of staff to General Dearborn—Death of General Pike—Leads the advance on Fort Niagara—Anecdote of Scott and a British colonel—Commands the expedition to Burlington Heights—March for Sackett's Harbor—Meets a force at Cornwall—Retreat of Wilkinson—Scott appointed brigadier general—Attack on and surrender of Fort Erie—Battle of Chippewa—Lundy's Lane and wounding of Scott—Retreat of the army to Black Rock—Fort Erie—Visits Europe.

FROM Washington Colonel Scott was ordered to Philadelphia to take command of another battalion of his regiment. In March, 1813, he was appointed adjutant general with the rank of colonel, and about the same time promoted to the colonelcy of his regiment. Notwithstanding his command of the regiment, he continued to perform staff duties. At this time General Dearborn was in command of the American forces at Fort Niagara, consisting of about five thousand men. In May, Colonel Scott, with his regiment, joined General Dearborn, and Scott became chief of staff. He first organized the service among all the staff departments, several of which were entirely new, and others disused in the United States since the Revolutionary War. On the British side of the Niagara was Fort George, situated on a peninsula and occupied by British troops. Just previous to Colonel Scott's arrival at Niagara an expedition was landed from the squadron of Commodore Chauncey, commanded by General Zebulon Montgomery Pike, for the capture of York, the capital of Upper Canada. The assault was successful, and the place was taken with a large number of prisoners and valuable stores. General Pike was killed by the explosion of a magazine. Animated by the success of General Pike's expedition, General Dearborn determined to make an assault on Fort George, having the co-operation of Commodore Chauncey and his naval force. Arrangements were made for an attack on May 20th. Colonel Scott asked permission to join the expedition in command of his own regiment, which was granted.

The fleet weighed anchor at three o'clock in the morning, and by four the troops were all aboard. The place of embarkation was three miles east of Fort Niagara, and was made in six divisions of boats. Colonel Scott led the advance guard, at his special request, composed of his own regiment and a smaller one under Lieutenant-Colonel George McFeely. He was followed by General Moses Porter having the field train, then the brigades of Generals John Parker Boyd, William Henry Winder, and John Chandler, with the reserve under the able Colonel Alexander Macomb.

Commodore Isaac Chauncey had directed the anchorage of his schooners close to the shore in order to protect the troops in landing, and to open fire at any point on the shore where the enemy were suspected to be. Lieutenant Oliver Hazard Perry joined Commodore Chauncey on the evening of the 25th, and volunteered his services in assisting in the debarkation of the troops. This service required the greatest coolness and skill, as the wind was blowing strong and the current running rapidly; the vessels were difficult to manage, especially as they were under almost constant fire of the British guns. Perry accompanied Scott through the surf, and rendered valuable service. He it was who as Commodore Perry soon after became known to the world as the hero of Lake Erie.

The landing was effected on the British shore at nine o'clock in the morning a short distance from the village of Newark, now known as Niagara. The line of battle was promptly formed under cover of a bank ranging from six to twelve feet in height. The line of the enemy was formed at the top of the bank, consisting of about fifteen hundred men. The first attempt to ascend was unsuccessful. Scott, in attempting to scale the bank, received a severe fall, but recovering himself and rallying his forces, he advanced up the bank and was met by the enemy's bayonets. The British fell back and reformed under cover of a ravine, but a vigorous assault of less than half an hour put them in a complete rout. These forces were assisted by Porter's artillery and Boyd with a portion of his command, who had landed soon after the advance forces. The enemy were pursued to the village, where the Americans were re-enforced by the command of Colonel James Miller. It was learned from some prisoners that the British garrison was about to abandon Fort George and preparing to blow up the works. Two companies were dispatched toward the fort, but on nearing it one of the magazines exploded, and a piece of timber striking Colonel Scott, threw him from his horse, resulting in a broken collar bone. Recovering himself, he caused the gate to be forced, entered the fort, and with his own hands pulled down the British flag. The fort had suffered great damage from the artillery fire directed against it from the opposite shore. The enemy were pursued for five miles, when an order from General Morgan Lewis recalled Scott when he was in the midst of the stragglers from the British forces. The American loss was seventeen killed and forty-five wounded, and that of the British ninety killed, one hundred and sixty wounded, and over one hundred prisoners.

It will be remembered that about a year before Colonel Scott was for a short time a prisoner at Queenstown. Dining one evening with General Sheaffe and several other British officers, one of them asked him if he had ever seen the falls of Niagara. He replied, "Yes, from the American side." To this the officer replied, "You must have the glory of a successful fight before you can view the cataract in all its grandeur." Scott replied, "If it be your purpose to insult me, sir, honor should have prompted you first to return my sword." General Sheaffe rebuked the officer, and the matter ended.

This same colonel was severely wounded and captured at Fort George. Colonel Scott showed him every attention and had his wants promptly supplied. On visiting him one day the British officer said to him: "I have long owed you an apology, sir. You have overwhelmed me with kindness. You now, sir, at your leisure, can view the falls in all their glory."

Within two days after the capture of Fort George a body of some nine hundred British troops under command of Sir George Prevost, Governor General of Canada, landed at Sackett's Harbor, New York, for the purpose of destroying the stores and a vessel there on the stocks. General Jacob Brown, who subsequently came to the command of the United States army, hastily gathered a body of militia, attacked and drove the enemy back to their vessels, and saved the stores. On June 6th, General Winder, with about eight hundred men, had been re-enforced at Stoney Creek by a small force under General Chandler. They were in pursuit of the British forces who had escaped from Fort George under command of General Vincent. He determined not to await the attack of the Americans, but to attack himself. He moved out at night and attacked the center of the American line, which he succeeded in breaking, and captured both Generals Winder and Chandler; but the enemy was at last driven back, and a council of war decided on a retreat. Coming close on this disaster, Colonel Charles G. Boerstler, with a command of six hundred men, had been sent forward to capture the Stone House, seventeen miles from Fort George. The British force was much larger than Boerstler's, and on June 24th he was completely surrounded and forced to surrender. For some three months the main body of the army had remained inactive. Colonel Scott during the happening of the occurrences just related had been engaged in foraging expeditions for the supply of the army. These expeditions also resulted in combats between the opposing forces, in all of which Scott was successful. In July, 1813, he resigned the office of adjutant general and was assigned to the command of twenty companies, or what was known as a double regiment.

Burlington Heights, on Lake Ontario, was supposed to be the depot of military stores for the British, and in September an expedition was fitted out under Scott's command to capture it; but no stores being found there, he marched toward York, now called Toronto, where a large quantity of stores were taken and the barracks and storehouses burned. General Wilkinson being now in command of the army, a campaign was inaugurated for the capture of Kingston and Montreal. Kingston was an important port, and Montreal the chief commercial town of Lower Canada.

Wilkinson was ordered to concentrate at Sackett's Harbor early in October. General Wade Hampton was ordered to join him from northern New York. Wilkinson embarked on October 2d, and Scott was left in command of Fort George with some eight hundred regulars and part of a regiment of militia under Colonel Joseph Gardner Swift. Under directions of Captain Totten, of the engineers, work was rapidly advanced in placing the fort in tenable condition; but the work was not completed before October 9th, when, to Scott's surprise, the enemy near him moved down toward Wilkinson. As authorized by his orders, Colonel Scott turned the command of the fort over to Brigadier-General McLure, of the New York militia. It was arranged that Scott was to join Wilkinson, and that vessels for his transportation should be sent up to the mouth of the Genesee River.

On his arrival there he received information that Commodore Chauncey, commanding the fleet, had been detained by the protest of General Wilkinson against his leaving him, even for a few days. Scott was then compelled to undertake the long march for Sackett's Harbor by way of Rochester, Canandaigua, and Utica. The march was accomplished under many difficulties and with much suffering, as it rained almost incessantly, and the roads were in the worst of conditions. On his arrival in advance of his troops, he was appointed to the command of a battalion under Colonel Macomb. Being in command of the advance of the army in the descent of the St. Lawrence, he was not present at the engagement at Chrysler's Farm on November 11th. At that time, in conjunction with Colonel Dennis, he was forcing a passage near Cornwall, under fire of a British force, which he routed, and captured many prisoners.

The day before the occurrence of the affair just mentioned he landed at Fort Matilda, commanding a narrow place on the river, where he gained possession of the fort. The expedition which was announced for the conquest of Canada was, on November 12th, abandoned by its leader and projector, General Wilkinson, who commanded a retreat. This occurred when Scott was fifteen miles in advance of Chrysler's Field, there being no body of British troops between him and Montreal, and the garrison at the latter place had only four hundred marines and two hundred sailors.

Wilkinson's defense for his failure was that General Hampton had refused to join him at St. Regis for fear of lack of provisions and forage.

After the events just related, Colonel Scott was engaged in preparing the new levies of troops for the field and arranging for supplies and transportation for the next campaign.

On March 9, 1814, he was appointed to the rank of brigadier general, and ordered to join General Jacob Brown, commanding general of the United States army, then moving toward the Niagara frontier. On the 24th General Brown marched to Sackett's Harbor, where Scott established a camp of instruction. On assembling of the army at Buffalo, Scott was assigned to the command of the Ninth, Eleventh, and Twenty-fifth Regiments of infantry, with a part of the Twenty-second Regiment and Captain Towson's company of artillery. In addition to this command there were at this time at Buffalo the commands of Generals Porter and Eleazer Wheelock Ripley. The whole force was placed in camp under General Scott's immediate direction. In the latter part of June General Brown returned to Buffalo, and on the morning of July 3d Scott's brigade with the artillery of Major Jacobs Hindman, crossed the river and landed below Fort Erie, while Ripley's brigade landed a short distance above. Fort Erie was invested, attacked, and soon surrendered, and on the morning of the 4th Scott's brigade moved in advance in the direction of Chippewa. He was engaged for a distance of sixteen miles in a running fight with the British forces under the Marquis of Tweedale. Toward night the Marquis of Tweedale crossed the Chippewa River and joined the main army under General Sir Phineas Riall. Scott then took position on a creek some two miles from Chippewa. On the east was the Niagara River and the road to Chippewa, while on the west was a heavy wood. Between the wood and the river were two streams—the Chippewa and Street's Creek. General Riall, the British commander, was posted behind the

Chippewa, flanked on one side with a blockhouse and a heavy battery on the other.

Both of these streams were bridged on the road to Chippewa, the one over Street's Creek being nearest to Scott, while that over the Chippewa was nearest to Riall. On the morning of the 5th General Brown had determined to make the attack, but the enemy, anticipating it, made the first forward movement, and there were a number of skirmishes. General Porter, whose command consisted of volunteers, militia, and friendly Indians, first engaged the British and drove them back through the woods. General Riall at this moment was seen advancing with the main body of his army, and the retreating troops rallied, attacking Porter furiously, and, despite his own coolness and gallantry, his troops gave way and fled. This was about four o'clock, and General Brown, being with Porter, saw the advance of the British force, and meeting General Scott, said to him, "The enemy is advancing." General Brown then moved to the rear and ordered the advance of Ripley's brigade. The British army was composed of the One Hundredth Regiment, under the Marquis of Tweedale, the First Royal Scots, under Lieutenant-Colonel Gordon, a portion of the Eighth or King's Regiment, a detachment of the Royal Artillery, a detachment of the Royal Nineteenth Light Dragoons, and some Canadian militia and Indians. These were supported by a heavy battery of nine guns. Scott crossed the bridge under fire of this battery, losing a number of men. After crossing, the commands of Majors Henry Leavenworth and John McNeil, Jr., formed line in front opposite the center and left of the enemy. Major Thomas Sidney Jesup moved to the left and advanced to attack the enemy's right. Towson's battery was on the right, on the Chippewa road. Seeing that the British lines outflanked him, Scott ordered the movement of Jesup to the left. The battle now opened, Jesup holding in check the right wing of the enemy, his position in the wood concealing him from view. General Scott had now advanced to within eighty paces of the enemy, and ordering the left flank of McNeil's battalion formed on the right so that it was oblique to the enemy's charge and flanking him on the right. Scott called to McNeil's command, which had no recruits in it: "The enemy say we are good at long shot, but can not stand the cold iron. I call upon the Eleventh to give the lie to that slander. Charge!" The charge was made at once, supported by a corresponding charge of Leavenworth and a flank fire from Towson's battery. The British broke, and fled in great confusion.

In the meantime Major Jesup, commanding on the left, ordered his men to advance, which they did, driving the enemy into his intrenchments across the Chippewa. The British forces engaged were about twenty-one hundred men, and that of the Americans nineteen hundred. The British lost in killed, one hundred and thirty-eight; wounded, three hundred and nineteen; and missing, forty-six. The American loss was sixty killed, two hundred and forty-eight wounded, and nineteen missing. General Brown in his official report says: "Brigadier General Scott is entitled to the highest praise our country can bestow; to him more than to any other man am I indebted for the victory of July 5th. His brigade covered itself with glory. Every officer and every man of the

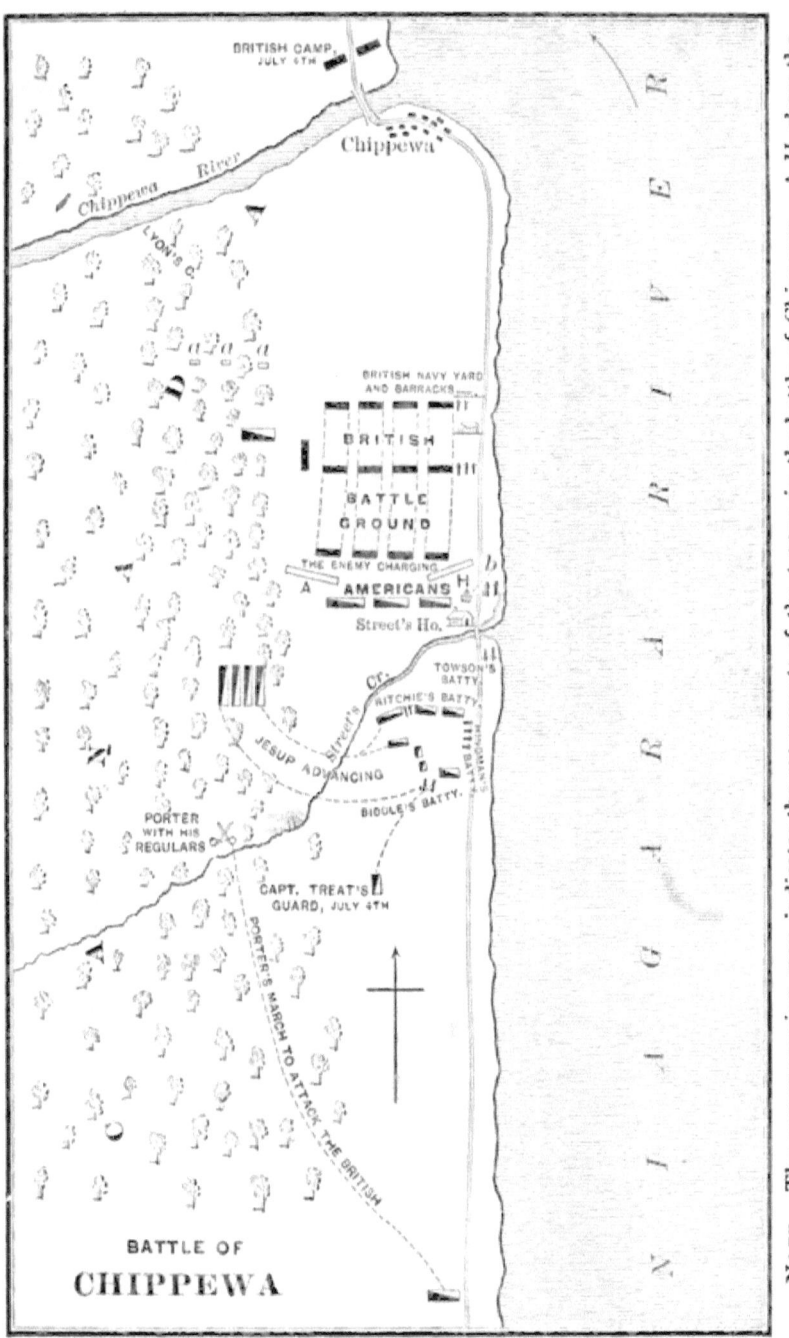

NOTE.—The accompanying map indicates the movements of the troops in the battle of Chippewa. A H show the position of Majors McNeil and Leavenworth when they made the final charge. *a, a, a,* the point to which General Porter drove the British and Indians. *b,* Street's barn.

Ninth, Twenty-second, Eleventh, and Twenty-fifth Regiments did his duty with a zeal and energy worthy of the American character." Two days after the battle of Chippewa General Scott forced a passage across the Chippewa, driving the enemy.

A fort called Messasauga was built after the campaign of 1813 by the British as a defense to Fort George, and being re-enforced by General Riall, he moved to Burlington Heights on Lake Ontario. It was General Brown's intention to capture these forts before beginning further or more extended operations. With this purpose, he ordered some heavy guns from Sackett's Harbor; but Commodore Chauncey being sick, and the enemy having a superior fleet on the lake, the attack on these forts was abandoned. General Brown then made a feint by moving up the Niagara and recrossing the Chippewa, with a view to draw the enemy down and to enable him to obtain supplies from Fort Schlosser. Failing in this, it was his purpose to send General Scott by the road from Queenstown and thus force Riall to battle.

On the afternoon of the 25th General Brown received a note from a militia officer who occupied some posts on the American side of the Niagara, that a thousand British troops had crossed from Queenstown to Lewiston, a few miles below the Chippewa. It was thought that the object of this movement was to capture the American magazines at Schlosser and cut off supplies from Buffalo. General Brown having determined to threaten the forts at the mouth of the Niagara, General Scott's command was put in motion for this purpose. It consisted of four battalions under Colonel Hugh Brady, and the commands of Majors Jesup, Leavenworth, and McNeil, Captain

Towson's artillery, and Captain Harris's detachment of cavalry, the whole force aggregating thirteen hundred men. After a march of two miles some mounted British officers were discovered on a reconnoitering expedition, their forces being a short distance off and hidden from view.

General Scott's orders were to march on the forts, as information had been received that Riall had divided his forces, sending a thousand of them across the river. He, however, determined to move forward and give battle. Dispatching Adjutant-General Jones to General Brown with information that the enemy was in his front, he moved on, and was astonished to see drawn up in line of battle on Lundy's Lane a larger force than he had fought at Chippewa; but he determined to give battle and rely upon re-enforcements being rapidly sent to him. Lieutenant Richard Douglass was now dispatched to inform General Brown of the situation. On the night of the 23d Lieutenant-General Sir Gordon Drummond had arrived at the mouth of the river with re-enforcements. This was not known to General Brown. Riall had marched down the road which Scott was to have taken on the 26th, coming by Queenstown, and had not sent any troops across the Niagara. His re-enforcements were coming up rapidly. The battle opened late in the afternoon. The British line, eighteen hundred strong, posted on a ridge in Lundy's Lane running at right angles with the river, was in front of Scott. The left of this line was on a road parallel to the river, with a space grown up with small timber, extending some two hundred yards. He ordered Major Jesup and Colonel Brady to take advantage of this and turn the enemy's left from the concealed position which the brushwood afforded. The other infantry forces had been placed in line with detachments of cavalry on both sides and held as reserves. The British, outflanking Scott on the left, made a movement to attack in flank and rear. This was repelled by Major McNeil with heavy loss. Jesup had succeeded in his movement, while Brady, Leavenworth, and Towson were engaged in the front. Jesup had captured General Riall and a number of other officers far in his front, and then resumed his line. At nine o'clock the British right was driven back from its assault on Scott's flank, and his left was turned and cut off. The center posted on the ridge held its place, supported by nine pieces of artillery. Another battalion of British troops was on its way as a re-enforcement, and but a short distance away, when General Brown arrived on the field, in advance of the reserve. He thus describes in his report what occurred from the time of his arrival:

"Apprehending that these corps were much exhausted, and knowing that they had suffered severely, I determined to interpose a new line with the advancing troops, and thus disengage General Scott and hold his brigade in reserve. Orders were accordingly given to General Ripley. The enemy's artillery at this moment occupied a hill which gave him great advantage and was the key to the whole position. It was supported by a line of infantry. To secure the victory it was necessary to carry this with artillery and seize the height.

"The duty was assigned to Colonel Miller. He advanced steadily and gallantly to his object, and carried the height and the cannon. General Ripley brought up the Twenty-third (which had faltered) to his support, and the enemy disappeared from before them. The enemy, rallying his forces, and, as is believed, having received re-enforcements, now attempted to drive us from our position and regain his artillery. Our line was unshaken and the enemy repulsed. Two other attempts having the same object had the same issue. General Scott was again engaged in repelling the former of these, and the last I saw of him on the field of battle he was near the head of his column and giving to its march a direction that would have placed him on the enemy's right. . . . Having been for some time wounded and being a good deal exhausted by loss of blood, it became my wish to devolve the command on General Scott and retire from the field; but on inquiry I had the misfortune to learn that he was disabled by wounds. I therefore kept my post, and had the satisfaction to see the enemy's last effort repulsed."

General Brown said to General Miller, when he saw that to win the battle the artillery on the ridge must be captured, "Sir, can you take that battery?" He replied, "I will try, sir," and at once moved forward, conducted by Scott, who was familiar with the ground, and with his gallant command drove the enemy from its stronghold and captured the guns.

General Scott, though severely wounded, was not disabled at the time mentioned in General Brown's report. Having two horses killed under him, he was at this time on foot, but was finally prostrated by his two wounds—one in the side, the other in the shoulder. The American loss was one hundred and seventy-one killed, five hundred and seventy-two wounded, and one hundred and seventeen prisoners; that of the British was eighty-four killed, five hundred and fifty-nine wounded, and two hundred and thirty-five prisoners.

Generals Brown and Scott both being disabled, General Ripley was sent to bring off the wounded and dead. The captured artillery, owing to want of horses and harness, was left on the field. The army now fell back to Chippewa and fortified the place.

It being learned that General Drummond was advancing on Chippewa with a large force, the place was evacuated and the army retreated to the ferry near Black Rock. A division was ordered to remain at Fort Erie and repair the fort, and Brigadier-General Gaines was, by General Brown's orders, placed in command of the army.

Very soon the British General Drummond appeared in front of Fort Erie and commenced a regular investment. Cannonading was begun on August 13th and continued at intervals, and on the 15th a heavy British column assaulted Towson's battery, which was stationed at the northwest angle of the fort. The assault was repelled by Captain Towson with the aid of Major Wood, commanding the Twenty-fifth Regiment. The western angle was then attacked, with a like result. The British eventually succeeded in obtaining possession of the exterior bastion of the old fort. Just at this time a number of cartridges in a building near by exploded, killing many of the British and expelling them from the fort. The losses in these affairs were: British—killed, fifty-seven; wounded, three hundred and nine; missing, five hundred and thirty-nine. American—killed, seventeen; wounded, fifty-six; missing, eleven.

General Brown resumed command on September 2d, and determined to attempt to relieve the siege by a sortie on the enemy's works. The investment had now lasted fifty days, and the British during that time had erected two batteries and were engaged on a third. The force was divided into three brigades, two of which were encamped out of range of the American cannon. At half past 2 P.M. on the 17th the American troops marched out and the action began. In less than half an hour the Americans had captured two of the batteries and two blockhouses. Very soon a third battery was abandoned, the cannon spiked and dismounted. General Drummond retired on the night of the 21st, and took post in his intrenchments behind the Chippewa. The British losses in this investment were, in killed, wounded, and prisoners, nearly a thousand, while the American loss was five hundred and eleven. Early in November the American army took up winter quarters in Buffalo, and this brought to a close the war on the Niagara.

The following statement of the losses on either side in this memorable campaign is interesting:

	British loss.	American loss.
Battle of Chippewa, July 5, 1814....	507	328
Battle of Niagara, July 25, 1814.....	878	860
Battle of Fort Erie, August 15, 1814.	905	84
Sortie from Fort Erie, Sept. 17, 1814.	800	511
Total........................	3,090	1,783

General Jacob Brown, the commander of this army, became General in Chief of the United States army March 10, 1821. He died September 24, 1828. General Brown was born in Bucks County, Pennsylvania, May 9, 1775. He was secretary to Alexander Hamilton, where he acquired military information and experience, and in 1809 was made a colonel of militia. In 1810 he was promoted brigadier general, and two years afterward was assigned to the command of the frontier from Oswego to Lake St. Francis. In July, 1813, he was appointed a brigadier general in the United States army and placed in command of the Army of Niagara with the rank of major general. His subsequent career is briefly mentioned in this work. He received the thanks of Congress, November 3, 1814, and a gold medal, now in possession of his son, General N. W. Brown, of Washington City.

General Eleazer W. Ripley became a brevet major general, and resigned in May, 1820. He was a member of the House of Representatives of the United States Congress (the Twenty-fourth) from Louisiana, and died March 2, 1839. Hugh Brady became a brigadier general by brevet. William McRee resigned as colonel in March, 1819; was afterward surveyor general of Missouri, and died in 1832. Thomas S. Jesup became quartermaster general of the army with rank of brevet major general. Henry Leavenworth died a brigadier general by brevet, July 21, 1834. John McNeil resigned as brigadier general by brevet; was afterward surveyor of customs at Boston. Jacob Hindman died a colonel, February 17, 1827. Roger Jones was adjutant general of the army, and brigadier general by brevet.

General Scott's wounds were so severe and painful that it was a long time before he was fit for duty. In September, 1814, Philadelphia and Baltimore were so threatened by the enemy that General Scott took nominal command for the defense of those cities. Everywhere on his route he received the highest evidences of the love and esteem of the people. At Princeton, N. J., he had a distinguished reception, and had conferred on him by the college the degree of Master of Arts. From Princeton he proceeded to Baltimore, and on October 16, 1814, assumed command of the Tenth Military District, with headquarters at Washington.

The treaty of peace was signed December 24, 1814, and ratified by the Senate, February 17, 1815. He was tendered the appointment of Secretary of War, but declined on the ground that he was too young. When his recommendations for colonel and brigadier general were presented to the President he expressed in both instances the fear that he was too young. It was in allusion to this that he gave this reason. He was then requested to act as Secretary until the arrival of William H. Crawford, at that period Minister to France, and who had been appointed Secretary of War. He declined this also, in deference to Generals Jacob Brown and Andrew Jackson. He was engaged for some time in reducing the army to a peace establishment, which being completed he was ordered to Europe for professional purposes. He was also intrusted with certain important and delicate diplomatic functions relating to the designs of Great Britain on the island of Cuba, and the revolutionary struggles between certain Spanish provinces in America.

CHAPTER III.

Is received and entertained by prominent civilians and military men in Europe—Marries Miss Mayo—Offspring—Thanks of Congress—Thanks of the Virginia Legislature voted, and also a sword—Controversy with General Andrew Jackson and correspondence—Prepares general regulations for the army and militia—Controversy with General Gaines and the War Department about rank—In command of the Eastern Division—War with the Sac and Fox Indians—Black Hawk—Cholera breaks out among the troops.

GENERAL SCOTT received great attention from prominent military men in Europe. He was also treated with much respect by men of letters and science. On his return home, in 1816, he was assigned to the command of the seaboard, and established his headquarters in the city of New York. On March 11, 1817, he was married to Miss Maria D. Mayo, of Richmond, Va., daughter of Colonel John Mayo. She was a lady of many accomplishments and a belle in Virginia society. The issue of this marriage who lived to maturity were Virginia, who died unmarried; Cornelia who was married to Colonel Henry L. Scott, General Scott's adjutant general for many years, and who, dying, left one son, Winfield Scott, now a resident of Richmond, Va.; Camilla, who married Gould Hoyt, of New York, and died leaving children; Ella, who married Carroll McTavish, and has several daughters. She is now (1893) a resident of

Baltimore. Mrs. Scott died June 10, 1862. Two sons and two daughters died before reaching maturity. Mrs. Scott's remains were buried by the side of her illustrious husband at West Point.

In November, 1813, Congress passed a joint resolution complimenting General Scott for his skill and gallantry in the battles of Chippewa and Niagara and for his uniform good conduct throughout the war, and directed the striking and presentation to him of a gold medal. This was presented to him in a speech of great feeling and high compliment at the Executive Mansion in the presence of the members of the Cabinet and many other distinguished persons. On July 4, 1831, General Scott watched the last moments and closed the eyes of President Monroe in New York city. In February, 1816, the Legislature of Virginia passed a resolution unanimously returning thanks to General Scott for his services to his country, and also voted him a sword. This was followed by like action by the Legislature of New York. In 1815 he was elected an honorary member of the Society of the Cincinnati.

In April, 1817, General Andrew Jackson issued from Nashville, Tenn., an order reciting that "the commanding general considers it due to the principles of subordination which might and must exist in an army to prohibit the obedience of any order emanating from the Department of War to officers of the division who have reported and been assigned to duty, unless coming through him as the proper organ of communication." At a dinner party in New York soon after the publication of this order Governor Clinton desired to know General Scott's opinion of it. He expressed views in opposition to General

Jackson, and added that its tendency was mutinous. An anonymous writer published the details of this conversation in a New York paper called the Columbian, and a copy of it reached General Jackson, who wrote General Scott as follows:

"HEADQUARTERS DIVISION OF THE SOUTH,
"NASHVILLE, *September 17, 1817.*

"SIR: With that candor due the character you have sustained as a soldier and a man of honor, and with the fairness of the latter, I address you. Inclosed is a copy of an anonymous letter postmarked New York, August 14, 1817, together with a publication taken from the Columbian, which accompanied the letter. I have not permitted myself for a moment to believe that the conduct ascribed to you is correct. Candor, however, induces me to lay them before you, that you may have it in your power to say how far they be incorrectly stated. If my order has been the subject of your animadversions, it is believed you will at once admit it, and the extent to which you may have gone.

"I am, sir, respectfully,
"Your most obedient servant,
"ANDREW JACKSON.
"*General* W. SCOTT, *U. S. Army.*"

General Scott replied to this letter denying the authorship of the article, and said: ". . . I gave it as my opinion that that paper was, as it respected the future, mutinous in its character and tendency, and as it respected the past, a reprimand of the commander in chief, the President of the United States; for although the latter be not expressly named, it is a principle well understood that the War Department, without at least his supposed sanction, can not give a valid command to an ensign. . . . Even if I belonged to your division I should not hesitate to repeat to you all that I have said at any time on this subject if a proper occasion offered; and what is more, I should expect your approbation, as in my humble judgment refutation is impossible."

General Jackson replied to this in a very angry manner, and intimating that General Scott might, if he chose, call him to the field. Scott replied, and declined to write the challenge, "as his ambition was not that of Erostratus," intimating that he ruined his only chance of acquiring distinction by killing a defender of his country.

For years afterward Scott heard reports that General Jackson had made threats of personal chastisement whenever they should meet. In 1823, soon after General Jackson took his seat in the United States Senate, Scott made frequent visits there, and was entitled to the floor. Wearied at last with this state of things, he addressed General Jackson as follows:

"WASHINGTON, *December 11, 1823.*

"SIR: One portion of the American community has long attributed to you the most distinguished magnanimity, and the other portion the greatest desperation in your resentments.

"Am I to conclude that both are in error? I allude to circumstances which have transpired between us and which need not here be repeated, and to the fact that I have now been six days in your immediate vicinity without having attracted your notice. As this is the first time in my life that I have been within a hundred miles of you, and as it is barely possible that you may be ignorant of my presence, I beg leave to state that I shall not leave the district before the morning of the 14th inst.

"I have the honor to be, sir,
"Your most obedient servant,
"WINFIFLD SCOTT.
"*The Hon.* GENERAL A. JACKSON, *Senator, etc.*"

The following answer was promptly returned:

"MRS. O'NEIL'S, *December 11, 1823.*
"SIR: Your letter of to-day has been received. Whether the world is correct or in error as regards my "magnanimity" is for the world to decide. I am satisfied of one fact: that when you shall know me better you will not be disposed to harbor the opinion that anything like desperation in resentment attaches to me.

"Your letter is ambiguous, but, concluding from occurrences heretofore that it was written with friendly views, I take the liberty of saying to you that whenever you shall feel disposed to meet me on friendly terms, that disposition will not be met by any other than a corresponding feeling on my part.

"I have the honor to be, sir,
"Your most obedient servant,
"ANDREW JACKSON.
"*General* W. SCOTT."

General Scott was gratified at the reply, and called at once on General Jackson, who received him kindly and graciously, and the next day he departed for the West. In mentioning these facts General Scott adds that "it is painful to reflect that so amicable a settlement only meant with one of the parties a postponement of revenge to a more convenient season."

This remark is in allusion to Scott's recall from the Indian War in 1836. General Jackson died the 8th of June, 1845, General Scott being then at West Point. He was president of the Board of Examiners, which was in session when the news was received. He at once arose, and, addressing the board of visitors and academic staff, said: " Ex-President Jackson died at the Hermitage on the 8th inst. The information is not official, but sufficiently authentic to prompt the step I am about to take. An event of much moment to the nation has occurred. A great man has fallen. General Jackson is dead—a great general, and a great patriot who had filled the highest political stations in the gift of his countrymen. He is dead. This is not the place, nor am I the individual, to pronounce a fit eulogy on the illustrious deceased. National honors will doubtless be prescribed by the President of the United States; but in the meantime, and in harmony with the feelings of all who hear me, and particularly with those of the authorities of this institution, I deem it proper to suspend the examination of the cadets for the day, and to await the orders of the Executive of the United States on the subject."

General Scott in his early training had studied the science of war, using the works of the greatest and best-known authors. He was in his early life a close student, and when he entered the army was better equipped in the knowledge of the standard authors on the science of war than most men in the army. In 1821 he prepared a work entitled General Regulations for the Army, or Military Institutes.

This was the first book published in the United States which could be accepted as a manual for both the regular troops of the army and the militia. He had formerly, in 1814–'15, been president of a board of army officers which compiled a system of infantry tactics, a copy of the system which he had used in the camp of instruction at Buffalo in 1814. This was revised by another board, of which he was president, and was published in 1825.

In 1826 a board of army and militia officers was convened by order of the Secretary of War, of which he was made president, for the purpose of reporting a plan for the organization and instruction of the militia of the United States, a system of tactics for the artillery, a system of cavalry tactics, and a system of infantry and rifle tactics. The reports on the plan for the organization and instruction of the militia and that on the system of infantry and rifle tactics were written wholly by General Scott, and adopted by the board. Under a resolution of Congress in 1835 there was published a new edition of infantry tactics prepared by him.

General Scott was one of the pioneers in what is known as the temperance reform, and preceded Dr. Lyman Beecher in his celebrated discourses on this subject. In December, 1821, General Scott published his "Scheme for restricting the use of ardent spirits in the United States." It was first published in the National Gazette. He did not take ground for total abstinence, but against the use ardent of spirits, brandy, rum, and whisky. He was also a member of the society formed in New York in 1821 "for the prevention of pauperism, vice, and immorality."

General Scott, in 1823, took great interest in having the sons of General Paez, of Colombia, South America, admitted as students at the military academy at West Point, which drew from General Paez letters of thanks to General Scott and President Monroe.

A very serious controversy arose in 1828 between General Scott and General Edmund Pendleton Gaines on a question of rank. General Macomb had been appointed by President Adams major general of the United States army. There was at that time but one major general, and Scott held the rank of brevet major general, with an older date than Macomb's appointment, and he addressed a memorial to Congress claiming his superiority in rank to Macomb. He argued that from the beginning of the Revolutionary War down to the time of his appointment brevet rank was uniformly held to give rank and command, except only in the body of a regiment, etc.; that there existed in law or in fact no higher title or grade in the army than that of major general, there being no such thing as a commander in chief, except the President. That he [Scott] held a commission as major general, July 25, 1814, of older date than that of either Generals Macomb or Gaines. Congress did not pass an act, however, sustaining his claim, and the result was a construction by the authorities that a brevet appointment did not confer additional rank.

General Scott, on this decision of Congress, tendered his resignation, which was not accepted. When he was informed that the President and others high in authority sustained the action of Congress, he addressed a letter to Mr. Eaton, the Secretary of War, as follows:

A QUESTION OF RANK.

"NEW YORK, *November 10, 1829.*

"SIR: I have seen the President's order of the 13th of August last, which gives a construction of the sixty-first and sixty-second articles of war relative to rank or command.

"Humbly protesting that this order deprives me of rights guaranteed by these articles, and the uniform practice of the army under them, from the commencement of the Government down to the year 1828, when the new construction was first adopted against me, in obedience to the universal advice of my friends, who deem it incumbent on me to sacrifice my own connections and feelings to what may, by an apt error, be considered the repeated decision of the civil authority of my country, I have brought myself to make that sacrifice, and therefore withdraw the tender of my resignation now on file in your department.

"I also ask leave to surrender the remainder of the furlough the department was kind enough to extend to me in April last, and to report myself for duty. WINFIELD SCOTT.

"*The Hon.* J. H. EATON, *Secretary of War.*"

To this the Secretary of War replied:

"WAR DEPARTMENT, *November 13, 1829.*

"SIR: Your letter of the 10th instant is received, and I take pleasure in saying to you that it affords the department much satisfaction to perceive the conclusion to which you have arrived as to your brevet rights. None will do you the injustice to suppose that the opinions declared by you upon this subject are not the result of reflections and convictions; but since the constituted authorities of the Government have, with the best feelings entertained, come to conclusions adverse to your own, no other opinion was cherished or was hoped for but that, on your return to the United States, you would adopt the course your letter indicates, and with good feelings resume those duties of which she has so long had the benefit. Agreeably to your request, the furlough heretofore granted you is revoked from and after the 20th instant. You will accordingly report to the commanding general, Alexander Macomb, for duty. J. H. EATON.

" *To Major-General* WINFIELD SCOTT."

General Scott, on reporting to General Macomb, was assigned to the command of the Eastern Department, while General Gaines was assigned to the Western. From the assignment of General Scott to the command of the Eastern Department, for a period of nearly three years, his duties were those of an ordinary department commander, with no incidents necessary to be ingrafted into his biography.

A treaty had been made by the United States Government in 1804 with the chiefs of the Sac Indians, in which their lands east of the Mississippi were ceded to the Government, but with the reservation that so long as they belonged to the Government of the United States the Indians should have the privilege of occupying and hunting on them. The Sacs and Foxes were contiguous and friendly tribes, and their principal village was on a peninsula between the Rock River and the Mississippi. Their principal chief was known as Black Hawk. The United States Government in its treaty acquiring the title to these Indian lands made a guarantee that the Indians should be free from intrusion from any white settlers.

Their lands were very fertile, and soon white men in large numbers began to encroach on them, and no adequate steps were taken by the Government to protect the Indians in their treaty rights. In 1829 the Government ordered a public sale of lands which included a part of the Sac village. It was purchased by an Indian trader. This greatly disturbed the Chief Black Hawk, but he was assured that if the lands purchased by this agent had not actually been sold to the Government that the sale would be canceled and the Indian occupants allowed to remain. Nothing more was done in the matter until in the spring of 1831, when the corn planted by a number of Indians was plowed up by white settlers, and many annoying trespasses made by the whites upon the Indian occupants. The Chief Black Hawk then announced to the white settlers in the village that they must remove. This resulted in a memorial from some of the white settlers, in May, 1831, to the Governor of Illinois, stating that the Indians were committing depredations on them. The Governor called out seven hundred militia to remove a band of the Sac Indians, and so notified General Gaines. General Gaines, on May 29th, replied to the Governor that he had ordered six companies of troops from Jefferson City to Rock Island, and four other companies from Prairie du Chien, to assist the Governor's militia in repelling the Indians. When the United States troops reached Fort Armstrong a conference was held with some of the Indian chiefs, but with no practical results. On receiving this information

General Gaines called on the Governor of Illinois for additional forces, and on June 25th Governor Reynolds and General Joseph Duncan arrived at Rock River with sixteen hundred mounted militia. The Indians from the Sac village, being informed of this movement, deserted their homes with their wives and children and crossed the Mississippi. The next morning General Gaines occupied the Sac village without opposition.

A treaty was then made (June 30th) by General Gaines and Governor Reynolds with the Sacs, by which the Indians agreed to take up their abode west of the Mississippi River. In April, 1832, Chief Black Hawk and his tribe recrossed the Mississippi, in violation of the treaty previously made, for the purpose of joining the Winnebagoes and making a crop of corn and beans.

General Henry Atkinson at this time was in command of Fort Armstrong. He notified Black Hawk that he must recross the river or be driven back. The Indians refused to obey the order. Black Hawk endeavored to enlist some of the Northwestern tribes to join him, but failing to gain their assent, resolved to recross the Mississippi. He was encamped with his tribe at a place which the Indians called Kish-wa-cokee.

Some of the Illinois mounted militia were at Dixon's Ferry, on Rock River, not far from the Indian encampment. Major Stillman, commanding some three hundred volunteers, moved from Dixon's Ferry to Sycamore Creek on a scouting expedition. Black Hawk, being apprised of their approach, sent three of his young Indians bearing a white flag to meet them. One of these young Indians was captured and killed. Another party of five Indians, following the flag-of-truce bearers to assist in pacific negotiations, were met by the whites and two of them killed. The Illinois militia moved on and crossed Sycamore Creek. Black Hawk, who was exasperated at the killing of his men whom he had sent under flag of truce, advanced with his warriors on May 14th, met the Illinois militia, engaged and defeated them, and forced them to recross the creek.

This success greatly encouraged the Indians, but created great alarm and excitement with the white people of Illinois. Many small battles took place after this between the whites and Indians, and the war was brought to a close by the delivery of Black Hawk to the Indian agent, General Street, August 27th, by two of his followers who betrayed him. This war created necessarily great excitement and alarm in Illinois. It was the general expectation that the Winnebagoes and Pottawattomies would sympathize with Black Hawk, and the result would be a general Indian war. At this juncture General Scott was ordered to proceed to Illinois and take command of the forces to bring the Indians into subjugation. In July, acting under this order, he left Buffalo with about one thousand troops, destined for Chicago. The general and his staff, with about two hundred and twenty men, embarked on the steamboat Sheldon Thompson, and on July 8th it was announced that several of the soldiers were attacked with Asiatic cholera. The vessel arrived at the village of Chicago on the 10th with eighty sick men on board, one officer and fifty-one soldiers having died during the passage.

The fate of the troops who were embarked in

other vessels was even worse than those on the Thompson. Of the one thousand men who left Buffalo only about four hundred survived. General Scott gave every attention to the sick, exposing himself without fear day and night in seeing to the wants of his men. Leaving Colonel Abram Eustis in command, he proceeded to join General Atkinson at Prairie du Chien, which he reached on the 3d of August. The engagement called the Battle of Bad Axe had been fought before his arrival. He was here again confronted with the plague of cholera, which had broken out in Atkinson's command at Rock Island, and he devoted himself to the care of the sick and the consolation of the dying.

In this connection an extract from the Richmond Enquirer of August 7, 1832, will be of interest:

"LOUISVILLE, *July 27, 1832.*—The following is the latest official intelligence from Chicago. We are indebted to a commercial friend for it.—*Advertiser.*

"'HEADQUARTERS NORTHWESTERN ARMY,
"'CHICAGO, *July 15, 1832.*

"'SIR: To prevent or to correct the exaggerations of rumor in respect to the existence of cholera at this place, I address myself to your Excellency. Four steamers were engaged at Buffalo to transport United States troops and supplies to Chicago.

"'In the headmost of these boats, the Sheldon Thompson, I, with my staff and four companies, a part of Colonel Eustis's command, arrived here on the 8th. All on board were in high health and spirits, but the next morning six cases of undoubted cholera presented themselves. The disease rapidly spread itself for the next three days. About one hundred and twenty persons have been affected.

"'Under a late act of Congress six companies of rangers are to be raised and marched to this place. General Dodge, of Michigan, is appointed major of the battalion, and I have seen the names of the captains, but I do not know where to address them. I am afraid that the report from this place in respect to cholera may seriously retard the raising of this force.

"'I wish, therefore, that your Excellency would give publicity to the measures I have adopted to prevent the spread of the disease, and of my determination not to allow any junction or communication between uninfected and infected troops.

"'The war is not at an end, and may not be brought to a close for some time. The rangers may reach the theatre of operations in time to give the final blow. As they approach this place I shall take care of their health and general wants.

"'I write in great haste, and may not have time to cause my letter to be copied. It will be put in some post office to be forthwith forwarded. I have the honor to be

"'Your Excellency's most obedient servant,

"'WINFIELD SCOTT.

"'*His Excellency*, GOVERNOR REYNOLDS.'"

From the Richmond Enquirer, October 12, 1832.

" In laying the following article before our readers, our own personal feelings, as well as a just sense of gratitude to a meritorious officer, prompts us to add that we have known Winfield Scott long and have known him intimately, and that the conduct here attributed to him is precisely such as we should have expected, from his ardent patriotism, his humane disposition, and his distinguished intelligence."

From the Illinois Galenian, September 12, 1832.

"GENERAL SCOTT.—Perhaps on no former occasion has a more arduous and responsible duty been confided to any officer of our Government than that with which this gentleman has been clothed, in prosecuting to final issue the savage war upon our borders. And we hesitate not to say that in our estimation a better selection could not have been made.

"It might suffice, in justification of this assertion, to instance the promptitude of his movements to the scene of action, the ease with which he overcame space, and the facility with which he surmounted all obstacles opposed to the accomplishment of his object.

"But he had an enemy to encounter far more terrible than Black Hawk and his adherents—an enemy that bid defiance to military prowess and baffled all the skill of the tactician.

"That loathsome epidemic, the direful scourge of the Eastern hemisphere, the cholera, invaded his camp. Here was a new foe that had never yet been conquered. Victim after victim fell under its ravages. The general might have retired to some healthy clime, where he would have been freed from this pestilence, but not while his officers and men were falling around him; humanity prompted him to remain and succor a distressed army. During our stay at Rock Island the cholera commenced its work of death; and seeing the general almost every day, we had frequent opportunities of witnessing his untiring perseverance in and constant personal attention to all those duties appertaining to his official station, the calls of humanity, and the best interests of the country.

"On the arrival of the companies from Chicago (among whom the cholera had been severe) they were stationed on an island in Rock River, several miles from the fort, and all communication prohibited by special order. Some of his aids, on their way to Rock Island, having violated this order (without knowing it was given), were immediately ordered back to Rock River, while the general was left alone to perform all their respective duties. When a soldier was attacked with cholera he was the first to render assistance by the application of friction to the extremities in order to attract the fluids from the large internal vessels to the surface of the body. At the bake-house we found him one day giving instructions how to make the most wholesome bread, and on the next day we beheld one of his bakers consigned to the tomb. And if we follow him on, we next find him instructing those employed in the culinary art, so cautious is he about everything that his men eat and drink. And in order to insure temperance among the soldiers, he issued an order requiring every man found drunk to dig a grave.

"In his orders he was bound to be severe, and in their enforcement he was equally rigid. His whole soul seemed to be devoted to the benefit of his army.

"On one occasion he observed that his own honor, the duty he owed his country and his fellow-men, required his personal attention at his post, and also the severity of his orders. And if, in attending to his duties, he should be so unfortunate as to lose his life, the army could get along as well without him, but he could not get along without an army. Thus, with Roman firmness and a disinterested devotion of life to his country, has he remained at his post of duty. Such conduct deserves the highest praise, and we feel confident that it will be awarded by a grateful and virtuous community."

The cholera having subsided by the middle of September, negotiations were opened with the various Indian tribes at Rock Island. General Scott and Governor Reynolds were the commissioners on the part of the United States to make treaties with the Sacs, Foxes, Winnebagoes, Sioux, and Menomonees. The leading man among the Indians was Ke-o-Kuck, a Sac chief, who was of commanding appearance, eloquent in speech, and a brave warrior. He was not, however, a hereditary chief, and for this reason his tribe deposed him; but on General Scott's request he was again replaced as chief. General Scott conducted the negotiations in the way of speech-making at the request of his associate, Governor Reynolds. The speeches of Scott and those of the Indian chiefs were taken down by Captain Richard Bache, of the army, and are to be found in the archives of the War Department at Washington.

The result of the treaties was the cession to the United States by the Sacs and Foxes of about six million acres of land, the greater part of which is now included in the State of Iowa; and the United States gave in consideration of this cession a reservation of nearly four hundred square miles, on the Iowa River, to Ke-o-Kuck and his band, and agreed to pay the Indians an annuity of twenty thousand dollars per annum for thirty years to pay the debts of the tribe, and to employ a blacksmith and a gunsmith for them. The treaty also provided for ample space for hunting, and planting-grounds for the Indians and their posterity. A similar treaty was made with the other Indians. General Scott, on his return to Washington, was complimented by General Cass, the Secretary of War, " upon the fortunate consummation of his arduous duties," and he expressed his entire approbation of the whole course of his proceedings during a series of difficulties requiring higher moral courage than the operations of an active campaign under ordinary circumstances.

CHAPTER IV.

Troubles in South Carolina growing out of the tariff acts apprehended, and General Scott sent South—Action of the nullifiers—Instructions in case of an outbreak—Action of the South Carolina Legislature.

On the conclusion of the treaties with the Indian tribes, mentioned in the preceding chapter, General Scott went to New York, where he arrived in October, 1832. A few days after his arrival he received an order to proceed to Washington.

The passage of the tariff act of 1828 had produced great excitement in several of the Southern States, but especially in South Carolina. By this act the duties on foreign goods imported into this country were raised much higher than by any previous tariff. It was passed for the protection of American manufactures, of which at that time none were in the South, but all, or nearly all, in the New England States.

The cotton planters of South Carolina opposed and resisted it on the ground that it was not only in violation of the Constitution of the United States, but injurious to their interests, and in the interest of other States as opposed to theirs. They argued, as it is now argued, that a tariff is a tax, and that this tariff discriminated in favor of certain portions of the country as against other portions, and that therefore it unquestionably violated the fundamental law of the land.

This tariff act was passed on May 15, 1828, and on the 12th of June following the citizens of Colleton District, South Carolina, met at the courthouse in Walterborough and adopted an address to the people. Among other things this address stated: "For it is not enough that imposts laid for protection of domestic manufactures are oppressive, and transfer in their operation millions of our property to Northern capitalists. If we have given our bond, let them take our blood. Those who resist these imposts must deem them unconstitutional, and the principle is abandoned by the payment of one cent— as much as ten millions." The address assumed "open resistance to the laws of the Union."

Governor Taylor was asked to convene the Legislature. He declined to take action on the request of the Colleton meeting, on the ground that "the time of great public excitement is not a time propitious for cool deliberation or wise determination."

George McDuffie, a member of the House of Representatives in Congress from South Carolina, and a man of high character and great ability, was the leading spirit in the opposition to this tariff and resistance to its enforcement. At a dinner in Columbia, S. C., he recommended that the State fix a tax on Northern manufactured goods, and proposed as a toast "Millions for defense, but not a cent for tribute." In the district of St. Helena, S. C., a public meeting was held at which this resolution was adopted:

"*Resolved*, That, differing from those of our fellow-citizens who look to home production, or more consumption of the fabrics of the tariff States as a relief from our present burdens, we perceive in these expedients rather an ill-judged wasting of the public energy and diversion of the public mind than an adequate remedy for the true evil, the usurping of Congress, which (since that body will never construe down its own powers) can be checked, in our opinion, only by the action of States opposed to such usurpation."

The reference to "expedients, rather an ill-judged wasting of the public energy," was to the action of certain meetings in South Carolina where it was resolved to wear only their own manufactures, and abstain wholly from those made north of the Potomac. The supporters of nullification defended themselves on constitutional grounds and on the Kentucky and Virginia resolutions of 1798. Congress revised the tariff in May, 1832, modifying some of the duties imposed by the act of 1828. In October, 1832, the Legislature of South Carolina passed an act providing for the calling of a convention of the people of the State.

The object of the convention was "to take into consideration the several acts of the Congress of the United States imposing duties on foreign imports, for the protection of domestic manufactures or for other unauthorized objects; to determine on the character thereof, and to devise the means of redress."

The convention authorized under this act assembled on November 19, 1832. An ordinance was passed to provide for arresting the operations of certain acts of Congress of the United States purporting to be taxes laying duties and imposts on the importation of foreign commodities. On its final passage the word "arresting" was stricken out and the word "nullifying" substituted in its place.

The substance of this ordinance was to interdict the action of the courts, and to require all officers to take an oath to obey the ordinance and the laws passed to give it effect. It also declared that the tariff acts of 1828 and 1832 were null, void, and not binding on the State, its officers or citizens. It further declared it to be unlawful for any of the constituted authorities of the State or of the United States to enforce the payment of the duties imposed by the act within the limits of the State of South Carolina. Other provisions were that no case of law or equity decided in South Carolina, in which was involved the question of the validity of the ordinance of the South Carolina convention, or any act of its Legislature to give it effect, should be appealed to the Supreme Court of the United States, or be regarded if appealed; and that, if the General Government should employ force to carry these acts into effect, or endeavor to coerce the State by closing its ports, South Carolina would consider the Union dissolved, and would proceed to organize a separate government. A union convention was called in South Carolina to endeavor to suppress the movement inaugurated by the ordinance of the recent convention.

The States of Alabama, Tennessee, and Georgia— the first through its Governor, Gayle, and the latter by resolutions of their Legislatures—took strong anti-nullification grounds. On December 10th President Andrew Jackson issued his famous proclamation exhorting all persons to obey the laws, and denouncing the South Carolina ordinance. He said in this proclamation: "I consider, then, the power to annul a law of the United States, assumed by one State, incompatible with the existence of the Union, contradicted expressly by the letter of the Constitution, unauthorized by its spirit, inconsistent with every principle on which it was founded, and destructive of the great object for which it was formed."

"This, then, is the position in which we stand. A small majority of the citizens of one State in the Union have elected delegates to a State convention. That convention has ordained that all the revenue laws of the United States must be repealed, or that they are no longer a member of the Union. The Governor of that State has recommended to the Legislature the raising of an army to carry the secession into effect, and that he may be empowered to give clearance to vessels in the name of the State. No act of violent opposition to the laws has yet been committed, but such a state of things is hourly apprehended; and it is the intent of this instrument to proclaim not only that the duty imposed on me by the Constitution—'to take care that the laws be faithfully executed'—shall be performed to the extent of the powers already vested in me by law, or of such other as the wisdom of Congress shall devise and intrust to me for that purpose, but to warn the citizens of South Carolina, who have been deluded into an opposition to the laws, of the danger they will incur by obedience to the illegal and disorganizing ordinance of the convention; to exhort those who have refused to support it to persevere in their determination to uphold the Constitution and laws of their country, and to point out to all the perilous situation into which the good people of that State have been led; and that the course they are urged to pursue is one of ruin and disgrace to the very State whose rights they affect to support."

This proclamation, of which the foregoing are extracts, was signed on December 10, 1832. The ordinance adopted by the convention of South Carolina was passed November 24th; and the Legislature of South Carolina, which had formulated laws necessary to carry out the ordinance, adjourned on December 21st.

President Jackson, in anticipation of the troubles likely to arise, had, as early as October 29th, directed General Macomb to issue an order to Major Heileman, commanding the United States troops at Charleston, stating that "it is deemed necessary that the officers in the harbor of Charleston should be advised of the possibility of attempts being made to surprise, seize, and occupy the forts committed to them. You are therefore especially charged to use your utmost vigilance in counteracting such attempts. You will call personally on the commanders of Castle Pinckney and Fort Moultrie, and instruct them to be vigilant to prevent surprise in the night or day on the part of any set of people whatever who may approach the forts with a view to seize and occupy them. You will warn the said officers that such an event is apprehended, and that they will be held responsible for the defense, to the last extremity, of the forts and garrisons under their respective commands, against any assault, and also against intrigue and surprise.

"The attempt to surprise the forts and garrisons, it is expected, will be made by the militia, and it must be guarded against by constant vigilance, and repulsed at every hazard. These instructions you will be careful not to show to any persons other than the commanding officers of Castle Pinckney and Fort Moultrie."

Two companies of artillery were ordered to Fort Moultrie on November 7th, and on the 12th General Macomb directed Major Julius Frederick Heileman that a building called " The Citadel," in Charleston, and which was the property of the State of South Carolina, should, with its State arms, be delivered up if demanded by the State authorities. He was further instructed to act in this matter with the greatest courtesy; but should he be attacked, he must make a stubborn defense.

This was the state of affairs in South Carolina at the time stated. On November 18th, President Jackson, after a conference with General Scott, ordered him on a confidential or secret order to Charleston. The order was, of course, issued from the War Department by direction of the President, and the main points of it are as follows :

". . . The possibility of such a measure furnishes sufficient reason for guarding against it, and the President is therefore anxious that the situation and means of defense of these fortifications should be inspected by an officer of experience, who could also estimate and provide for any dangers to which they may be exposed. He has full confidence in your judgment and discretion, and it is his wish that you repair immediately to Charleston and examine everything connected with the fortifications. You are at liberty to take such measures either by strengthening these defenses or by re-enforcing these garrisons with troops drawn from any other posts, as you may think prudence and a just precaution require.

"Your duty will be one of great importance and of great delicacy. You will consult fully and freely with the collector of the port of Charleston, and you will take no step, except what relates to the immediate defense and security of the posts, without their order and concurrence. The execution of the laws will be enforced through the civil authority and by the method pointed out by the acts of Congress. Should, unfortunately, a crisis arise when the ordinary power in the hands of the civil officers shall not be sufficient for this purpose, the President shall determine the course to be taken and the measures adopted. Till, therefore, you are otherwise instructed, you will act in obedience to the legal requisitions of the proper civil officers of the United States.

"I will thank you to communicate to me freely and confidentially upon every topic upon which you may deem it important for the Government to receive information.

"Very respectfully, your obedient servant,

"LEWIS CASS."

General Scott, acting in obedience to these orders, arrived in Charleston November 28th, two days after the passage of the ordinance. He found, on his arrival and after conferring with many of the leading people, that the sentiment in regard to the action of the convention was divided, there seeming to be as many persons in opposition as those who favored it.

His arrival created no special notice, as he had been in the habit of visiting Charleston about this time of year in discharge of his duties as inspector. It should be added to what has been said in regard to his conference with President Jackson before leaving Washington, that the President announced to him in the most emphatic terms that "the Union must and shall be preserved." On asking General Scott for any suggestions he had to make, the general told the President that Fort Moultrie, Castle Pinckney, and the arsenal at Augusta should be strongly garrisoned. He also advised that a number of troops, sloops of war, and revenue cutters would be needed at Charleston to enforce the collection of duties on foreign importations. The President said to him: "Proceed at once and execute those views. You have my *carte blanche* in respect to troops; the vessels shall be there, and written instructions will follow you."

The President at this interview invited General Scott to remain and take supper with him. He declined, on the ground that he desired to call on his friend ex-President Adams before leaving. To this President Jackson replied, "That's right; never forget a friend."

On his journey he met with an accident and sprained his ankle. This turned out a fortunate thing, for it enabled him to delay so as to spend needed time in Charleston, Savannah, and Augusta without exciting any suspicion of the real object of his visit. Had it been known that he was there to make preparations for defense and to strengthen the garrisons, it would have excited the populace who sustained the action of the convention, and might have resulted in open hostilities. He visited Fort Moultrie and Castle Pinckney, and gave oral confidential orders to enlarge and strengthen both places. Orders were also sent for re-enforcements in single companies, which excited no alarm. These important matters being accomplished, he went to Savannah and posed as a sick man, for the reason that an early return to Fort Moultrie might have excited alarm. In the latter part of January he returned by sea to Fort Moultrie, but his presence there was unknown to all outside of the fort.

In the meantime the leaders of nullification had, at a large meeting, agreed that no attempt to execute the ordinance should be undertaken before the adjournment of Congress on March 3d following. The Legislature of South Carolina, at its meeting in December, had passed laws for the raising of troops and providing money for the purchase of arms and ammunition, and many organizations of volunteers had been formed wearing the palmetto cockade and buttons. A very decided and unexpected rebuff was given by the Court of Appeals of South Carolina, which decided, in the case of State *vs.* Hunt (2 Hills, S. C. Reports), that the ordinance which required the citizens of South Carolina to take a test oath of exclusive allegiance to the State was unconstitutional. It is a curious piece of history that the palmetto buttons worn by the volunteer nullifiers were manufactured in Connecticut.

There was in Charleston, as in other parts of the State, a very large number of Unionists. Both parties in Charleston held frequent meetings, and it was with great difficulty that riots or encounters between the two were prevented.

The officers of the army and navy at and near Charleston during these perilous times showed great prudence. Their first public display was the celebration of Washington's birthday; but the most intense nullifier could raise no objection to this. During these exciting times a fire broke out in the city of Charleston, and General Scott, being one of the first to observe it, called for volunteers and went to the scene, and, with the assistance of the naval volunteers and men of the army, succeeded in extinguishing the fire. This act of General Scott, seconded by army and navy men, had much to do with quieting the intense political excitement in Charleston.

In the latter part of January, 1833, the General Assembly of Virginia passed a resolution asking Congress to modify the tariff, and also to appoint a commissioner to South Carolina and endeavor to conciliate that State. The commissioner appointed was Benjamin Watkins Leigh. On his request, Mr. James Hamilton, president of the South Carolina convention, called it to assemble, when it rescinded the ordinance, the troops which had been called were disbanded, and the whole State and country were happily relieved of an impending internecine war. Congress had passed the compromise act, and the United States troops and vessels which had been sent to Charleston were withdrawn, and peace and quiet again dawned on the lately excited city.

Mr. Leigh, the Commissioner of Virginia to South Carolinia, says of General Scott's part of that historic period: . . . " General Scott had a large acquaintance with the people of Charleston; he was their friend; but his situation was such that many of the people—the great majority of them—looked upon him as a public enemy. . . . He thought, as I thought, that the first drop of blood shed in civil war—in civil war between the United States and one of the States—would prove an immedicable wound, which would end in a change of our institutions. He was resolved, if possible, to prevent a resort to arms, and nothing could have been more judicious than his conduct. Far from being prone to take offense, he kept his temper under the strictest guard, and was most careful to avoid giving occasion for offense; yet he held himself ready to act if it should become necessary, and he let it be known that he strictly understood the situation. He sought the society of the leading nullifiers, and was in their company as much as they would let him be, but he took care never to say a word to them on the subject of political differences; he treated them as friends. From the beginning to the end his conduct was as conciliatory as it was firm and sincere, evincing that he knew his duty and was resolved to perform it, and yet his principal object and purpose was peace. He was perfectly successful, when the least imprudence might have resulted in a serious collision."

CHAPTER V.

Events that led to the war in Florida—Treaty of Camp Moultrie and its stipulations—Complaints of Indians and whites—Treaty of Payne's Landing—Objections of the Indians to complying with the latter treaty—Councils and talks with the Seminoles—Assiola—Murder of mail carrier Dalton—Murder of Charley Amathla—Dade's massacre—Murder of General Thompson and others—General Clinch—Depredations by the Indians on the whites and by the latter on the Indians—Volunteers—Military departments of Gaines and Scott.

It is proper to give as brief a *résumé* as the subject will permit of the events that led to the outbreak of hostilities in Florida.

General Jackson, when Governor of Florida in 1821, urged upon the Government the necessity of adopting measures to send back to their own reservations the large number of Creek Indians who had left their nation and settled with other tribes in Florida. He argued that this was an encroachment by the Creeks, and that an increase of Indians in this territory would lead to unhappy results. Colonel Joseph M. White, the delegate from the territory of Florida, fully concurred with General Jackson in this view, and so informed the Secretary of War.

The Government, disregarding these wise suggestions, entered into a treaty with the Florida Indians, September 18, 1823, at Camp Moultrie, stipulating for their continued residence in the territory for twenty years. They were by this treaty established in the heart of the country, and their claims to the lands acknowledged and guaranteed. The treaty provided, among other things, that the Seminole Indians should relinquish all their claim to lands in Florida except a tract estimated to contain some five millions of acres, within the limits of which they agreed to abide.

The Government of the United States agreed to pay to the Indians two thousand dollars to aid them in removal to the new reservation, to furnish them with certain articles of husbandry and stock to the amount of six thousand dollars, to furnish them with corn, meat, and salt for one year, to pay them forty-five hundred dollars for their improvements on their surrendered lands, to allow them one thousand dollars per annum for a blacksmith and one thousand dollars per annum for a school fund, and these last two allowances to extend during the term of the treaty. Complaints were made by the whites, and counter complaints by the Indians, of depredations, but the preponderance of testimony is that the whites were the principal aggressors. These Indians were slaveholders, having a number of negroes held in slavery by the same tenure that slaves were held by the whites in Florida. The whites commenced and carried on a systematic and continued robbery of the slaves and cattle belonging to the Indians, sending them to Mobile for sale. A protest was made by the inhabitants of ten of the Seminole towns, complaining in substance that the white people had carried all their cattle off; that the white men first commenced to steal from them; that within three years six Indians had been killed by the whites, admitting that the Indians had taken satisfaction, but were not even on that score by three.

Complaints from whites of Indian depredations and counter complaints from the Indians became so frequent that the President determined to endeavor to make a new treaty, abrogating that of Camp Moultrie. For this purpose Colonel James Gadsden, of Florida, was appointed a commissioner to carry out this purpose. The Indians, by invitation, assembled at Payne's Landing, on the Ocklawaha River, on May 8, 1832. The points agreed upon were that the Seminole Indians relinquish their claim to the tract of land reserved for them by the second article of the Camp Moultrie treaty, containing four million thirty-two thousand six hundred and forty acres, and to remove west of the Mississippi River and there become a constituent part of the Creeks.

The United States engaged to pay the Seminoles fifteen thousand four hundred dollars as a consideration for the improvements on the lands which they abandoned, and a further sum of two hundred dollars each to two negroes, Abraham and Cudjoe, each Indian to be furnished with a blanket and homespun frock, and a sufficient quantity of corn, meat, and salt for one year's support after arriving in the new reservation. Two blacksmiths, at one thousand dollars a year, were agreed to be furnished for a period of ten years, and an annuity of three thousand dollars for fifteen years to be paid after their arrival in the West; which sum, together with the four thousand dollars stipulated for in the Camp Moultrie treaty, making seven thousand dollars per annum, was to be paid to the Creek nation with their annuities.

In order to relieve the Seminoles from vexatious demands on them for their slaves and other property, the United States stipulated to have the matter investigated, and to liquidate such as were satisfactory, provided the amount did not exceed seven thousand dollars. This treaty was executed on May 9, 1832, and signed by Holata Amathla and fourteen other chiefs. Seven of the chiefs were deputed to visit and explore the new country, accompanied by their interpreter and by Major John Fagan, formerly Indian agent in Florida. The delegation reported their approval of the country, and the ratification on the part of the Indians was made by seven of the chiefs at Fort Gibson, La.

This ratification by the seven chiefs was in excess of their authority, as they were only authorized to examine the country and report the result of their mission to a general council of the nation, which was to be convened on their return.

Colonel Gadsden, the commissioner on the part of the United States, addressed a letter to the Secretary of War, in which he said: " There is a condition prefixed to the agreement without assenting to which the Florida Indians most positively refused to negotiate for their removal west of the Mississippi. Even with the condition annexed, there was a reluctance, which with some difficulty was overcome, on the part of the Indians to bind themselves by any stipulations before a knowledge of the facts and circumstances would enable them to judge of the advantages or disadvantages of the disposition the Government of the United States wished to make of them. They were finally induced, however, to assent to the agreement. . . .

"The payment for property alleged to have been plundered was the subject most pressed by the Indians, and in yielding to their wishes on this head a limitation has been fixed in a sum which I think, however, will probably cover all demands which can be satisfactorily proved. Many of the claims are for negroes said to have been enticed away from their owners during the protracted Indian disturbances, of which Florida has been for years the theater. The Indians allege that the depredations were mutual, that they have suffered in the same degree, and that most of the property claimed was taken as reprisal for property of equal value lost by them. They could not, therefore, yield to the justice of restitution solely on their part, and probably there was no better mode of terminating the difficulty than by that provided for in the treaty now concluded. The final ratification of the treaty will depend upon the opinion of the seven chiefs selected to explore the country west of the Mississippi River. If that corresponds to the description given, or is equal to the expectations formed of it, there will be no difficulty on the part of the Seminoles. If the Creeks, however, raise any objections, this will be a sufficient pretext on the part of some of the Seminole deputation to oppose the execution of the whole arrangement for removal."

On March 8, 1835, the Hon. John H. Eaton addressed a letter to Lewis Cass, Secretary of War, raising the question whether the treaty of Payne's Landing was valid, it not having been ratified until 1834. To this the Secretary replied that the question had been referred to the Attorney General, and that he had decided that the obligation of the treaty was not affected by the delay, but that the Indians might be required to move in the years 1835-'37.

The Indian agent called a meeting of the Indians, who assembled in council on October 23, 1834. The agent stated that he had convened them by order of the President, who said that he had complied with all the promises made to them, and that they must prepare to move by the beginning of cold weather. He further stated that he had a proposition to them from the Creeks, and exhibited a map of the country allotted to them west of the Mississippi.

The proposition from the Creeks was that the Seminoles, instead of settling in the country allotted to them, in a separate body, settle promiscuously among the Creeks. The agent stated in regard to this last proposition: "It is left, as it should be, entirely optional with you, and no persons but yourselves have any right to say you shall or shall not accede to the proposition." Other questions were submitted, such as the disposition of their cattle, whether they preferred to march by land or go by water, and the manner in which they desired the annuity paid them. The Indians then retired for a private council, and on their return Holata Amathla said: "My brothers, we have now heard the talk that our father at Washington has sent us. He says that we made a treaty at Payne's Landing, and we have no excuse now for not doing what we promised; we must be honest. Let us go, my brothers, and talk it over, and don't let us act like fools."

At four o'clock in the afternoon of the same day the Indians met in private council and were addressed by Assiola, in which he opposed emigrating from Florida to the Creek country, denouncing the

Creeks as bad Indians. He also denounced the agent for advising them to remove "from the lands which we live on—our homes and the graves of our fathers." He announced that when the Great Spirit told him to go he would go. But he said the Great Spirit had told him not to go. He also threatened the white people with his rifle, for he still had that, and some powder and lead. He also said that if any of the Indians wanted to go West they would not be permitted to do so. Assiola was followed by Holata Amathla, who strongly urged his brothers to abide by the treaty of Payne's Landing, and advised them to "act honest and do as our great father at Washington tells us." Jumper, the sense-keeper, also urged a compliance with the last-named treaty, because if they did not comply the white men would make them. Chief Arpincki proposed that Holata Amathla be selected to represent to the agent the objections of the nation to removal. This was declined by Holata Amathla, and Jumper was selected in his stead to speak the sentiments of the people on the next day.

On October 24, 1834, the Indians again met in council. The agent asked them if they were ready to reply to the proposals made to them. Holata Mico and Miconopy made short talks. When Jumper rose he complained that a treaty had been made or rather forced on the Indians at Payne's Landing before the twenty years provided in the Camp Moultrie treaty had expired. He was one of the chiefs who had gone to look at the new lands and liked them, but did not like the neighbors they would have, and spoke of these latter Pawnees as savages and horse thieves. He told the agent that his talk always seemed good, but that the Indians did not want to go West. Holata Amathla, who was also one of the chiefs who went West, objected to his people removing there for substantially the same reason as Jumper. Charley Amathla said that seven years of the time stipulated in the Camp Moultrie treaty remained unexpired. He did not say that he would not go, but did not think he would give an answer until the expiration of the seven years. He also complained that the distance to the West was so great that many would die on the way. In these talks the chiefs spoke well of the agent. The latter, in reply, said: "I have no answer to make to what you have said to me to-day. My talk to you yesterday must and will stand, and you must abide by it." He then repeated the question he had previously submitted, and told them to deliberate further, and let him know when they were ready to meet him. Another meeting was held on October 25, 1834. The agent told them he was ready to receive their answers. The speakers on the part of the Indians said their people still refused to comply with the treaty of Payne's Landing and leave their native country. They thought the agent was mad with them. General Thompson, the agent, told them he was not mad, but was their friend; that what they said was not an answer to his questions, and added, "Your father, the President, will compel you to go." He argued that the treaty of Payne's Landing had been duly signed. This was denied by Miconopy, when the general told him he lied, and that by the terms of the treaty the decision of the delegation sent out to view the country was binding on the Seminoles, and they were compelled under its provisions to move. He told them that the Payne's Landing treaty abrogated that made at Camp Moultrie. Replying to Charley Amathla's assertion that the last treaty had been forced upon them, he said: "You say that the white people forced you into the treaty of Payne's Landing. If you were so cowardly as to be forced by anybody to do what you ought not to do, you are unfit to be chiefs, and your people ought to hurl you from your stations." He explained to them the white people's Government; that the Indians living among white people might be charged with all kinds of offenses under the law, and would not be permitted to testify themselves; that the Cherokees, Creeks, Choctaws, and Chickasaws who live in the States were moving beyond the Mississippi River, because they could not live under the white people's laws, and the Seminoles were a small handful compared to their number; that when the jurisdiction of the State government was extended over them the Indian laws and customs would have to be abolished; and told them it was this view of the subject that had induced the President to settle them beyond Florida; and told them further that the land to which they were to go should be theirs "while grass grows and water runs." It was for this reason the treaty had been made with them at Payne's Landing, and for the same reason they would be compelled to keep it and comply with their bargain. His speech was a long one, reiterating, elaborating, and emphasizing the determination of the Government to make them move, whether they desired to or not. During this speech the agent was interrupted by Assiola, who urged Miconopy to be firm, and to assure the agent that he did not care whether any more annuity was paid or not. The agent closed by hoping that mature reflection would make them act like honest men, and not compel him to report them to their father, the President, " as faithless to your engagements." The Indians then, through Assiola and Miconopy, announced positively and emphatically that their answer had been made, and that they did not intend to move. The agent told them that he was satisfied now that they were willfully and entirely dishonest in regard to their engagements with the President, and regretted that he had to so report them. He told them the talk he had given them must and should stand, and directed them to retire and prepare their stocks to receive their annuity on the following day.

It will be remembered that by the treaty of Payne's Landing it was stipulated that seven chiefs should be sent to examine the lands to which it was proposed to remove the Seminoles. They were to report its general aspect and fertility to the nation, but were not invested with power to ratify the treaty. That was the province of the nation in general council. Jumper, as stated in these pages, was one of the chiefs selected for the purpose of examining and reporting upon the new country. General Thompson, the agent, had told the chiefs in council that "no person has a right to say to you, You shall go, or that you shall accede to the proposition made to you by the Creeks; but it is left, as it should be, entirely optional with you." This is in singular contrast to the words heretofore quoted from the agent, and altogether different from his assurance to one of the chiefs: "The President, backed by the Secretary of War" (the Indian Bureau was then under the jurisdiction of the War Department) "and the whole Congress, never should compel me to act so dishonorably as to violate the treaty [of Camp Moultrie] made with your people. If such a thing were required of me I would spurn the President's commission and retire to the bosom of my family." General Thompson reported to the authorities at Washington what had taken place, as just related, and stated that, in view of the circumstances, no doubt remained that the Indians intended to resist the execution of the treaty of Payne's Landing. After giving a full statement of the situation, he felt it his "imperious duty" to urge the necessity of a strong re-enforcement at Fort King, and the station of a strong force at Tampa Bay, as early as possible. "An imposing force, thus marshaled to coerce the refractory people, would have the effect to crush the hopes of the chiefs and those who had been tampering with them into a proper respect for the Government, afford protection to the neighboring white settlements, and supersede the necessity of Holata Amathla and his followers fleeing the country." At this time the force at the two posts mentioned was two hundred and thirty-five men. General Thompson, sustained by Governor William P. Duval, continued to urge upon the Government an increase of the military force. The latter, in a letter to the Secretary of War, informed that official that even with a respectable military force stationed at Fort Brooke and Tampa Bay the agent and superintendents would have much difficulty in carrying the treaty of Payne's Landing into effect. The necessity for additional military force was urged by Generals Clinch and Eaton and Lieutenant Joseph

W. Harris, the disbursing agent. These representations went unheeded. In the whole of Florida there were but two hundred and fifty men of the United States army, while more than three thousand were stationed at other convenient points totally inactive.

When the time came for the removal of the Big Swamp Indians they were so notified. But having been previously informed that they would be expected to go, they did nothing in the way of planting crops, and were destitute of food. Corn was distributed by the agents to the most needy. It was concluded to make another effort to secure their peaceful removal, and on April 22, 1835, several hundred of them assembled in council. After the council was opened General Thompson explained to them the treaty of Payne's Landing, and read a letter from President Jackson, in which he besought them as his children, to whom he had always acted honestly and kind, to comply with the treaty and go to the lands selected for them, telling them they must go; that they had sold all their land and did not have a piece "as big as a blanket to sit upon," and had no right to stay. The letter concluded: "If you listen to the voice of friendship and truth, you will go quietly and voluntarily; but should you listen to the bad birds that are always flying about you, and refuse to remove, I have then directed the commanding officer to remove you by force. This will be done. I pray the Great Spirit, therefore, to incline you to do what is right." After the letter had been read through and interpreted, Jumper rose and opposed the treaty, but deprecated force. Miconopy and others sustained Jumper's views *as to the treaty*, but were silent on the question of forcible resistance. General Clinch then addressed them, and told them the time of expostulation had passed, that persuasion had been exhausted, and wound up by telling them "it was the question now whether they would go of their own accord or go by force." On the next morning the chiefs and warriors sent word to the agent that they wanted to talk to him. On assembling, Miconopy was absent. Jumper, the spokesman, announced that he stood firm, but the veteran chief Fueta Susta Hajo (Black Dirt) spoke passionately and eloquently in favor of the execution of the treaty. After he had concluded, General Thompson placed on the table a paper, dated April 23, 1835, which pledged the Seminole tribe to voluntarily acknowledge the treaty at Payne's Landing on May 9, 1832, and the treaty concluded at Fort Gibson on March 28, 1833 (the one signed by the seven chiefs who had gone to visit the country to which the Seminoles were to remove), and freely submitting and assenting to said treaties in all their provisions. This paper received the signatures of eight principal chiefs, among them Fueta Susta Hajo and eight subchiefs. Five of the principal chiefs, Jumper among them, stood aloof and would not sign. Miconopy, who was absent, sent word by Jumper that he would not abide by the treaty. Upon this the agent said he would no longer regard Miconopy as a chief, and said his name should be stricken from the council of the nation. This action on the part of the agent was arbitrary and wholly unauthorized, and was severely censured by General Cass, Secretary of War.

On August 11th the mail carrier Dalton was met by a party of Micosukee Indians six miles from Fort Brooke and killed. The body was found a few days afterward, and General Clinch immediately sent a demand for the surrender of the murderers, but they eluded capture by seeking refuge in the "Old red sticks" in the neighborhood of Ouithlacoochee. This murder, it was claimed, was in retaliation for the killing of an Indian in the previous June.

On August 19, 1835, at the request of Holata Amathla and twenty-five others, a council of the Seminoles was convened. At the request of the other chiefs Holata Amathla opened the council, saying they had come to talk about matters of great interest. He referred to the treaty of Payne's Landing, the visit to the West of the seven chiefs, and the promises that had been made; stated that the Seminoles wanted their separate agent, and paid a high compliment to General Thompson, who, he said, had always told them the truth The speech was forwarded to Washington, but no notice was taken of it. This nonaction on the part of the authorities at Washington served to intensify the distrust and suspicions of the Indians as to the good faith of the Government, and caused many of those who had expressed a willingness to move to join the ranks of those who objected to doing so. Hostilities soon commenced. The Long Swamp and Big Swamp Indians commenced pillaging. Three of them were caught and subjected to exceedingly cruel treatment by the white settlers. Many outrages were perpetrated on both sides. The Indians were notified to bring in all their cattle, ponies, and hogs to be turned over to a United States agent and appraised, the owners to be paid on their arrival across the Mississippi. Six of the principal chiefs and some others surrendered their stock. The sale, however, was indefinitely postponed. The Big Swamp Indians resolved to retain possession of the country, and condemned to death all those Indians who should oppose their views. This caused many of the friendly Indians to take refuge in the United States forts. About four hundred and fifty fled to Fort Brooke, and on November 9th they encamped on the opposite side of Hillsboro River. The hostile Indians, fearing that the secrets of their councils had become known, made every effort to win over to their side those who were disposed to comply with the treaty. Assiola and about four hundred warriors went to the house of Charley Amathla and demanded that he pledge himself to oppose removal. He declined, saying he would sacrifice his life before he would violate the pledge he had given his great father. Assiola attempted to shoot Charley, but was prevented by Abraham, the interpreter. Assiola left, but soon returned with a small party to the house and murdered him in cold blood. A number of the murdered man's followers at once made their escape to Fort King, while others joined the hostile party. Charley Amathla was regarded as a brave, resolute, and upright man. He had saved the life of Assiola, and his murder was an act of horrible ingratitude. The Indians now abandoned their homes and took refuge in the impenetrable swamps.

At this time the entire military force in Florida amounted to four hundred and eighty-nine officers and men, and were distributed as follows: At St. Augustine, one company, fifty-three men; at Fort Brooke, on Hillsboro Bay, three companies, one hundred and fifty-three men; at Fort King, six companies, three hundred and fifty-three men. The Seminoles were located in the peninsula of Florida, a region of fens, swamps, and creeks almost inapproachable. They claimed that the Government had not carried out in good faith the treaties made with them. Their great leader and chief was Assiola, sometimes called Powell, and improperly spelled Osceola, whose father was a white man and his mother a woman of the Creek Indian tribe. Among most of the tribes of Southern Indians the children took rank from the mother. He was recognized among the Indians as a Creek. He did not inherit the title or place of a chief, but won it by his native ability, cruelty, and courage. In his early days he was insolent in his manners, and kept apart from the society of his people.

When General Alexander Ramsay Thompson was agent of the United States for these Indians, on one occasion Assiola appeared before him and announced that the lands claimed by the Government belonged to the Indians; that the Indians could take care of themselves, and did not need General Thompson's services. He was arrested and placed in confinement, and after being imprisoned some time expressed regret, signed the treaty, and was released. Subsequently he rendered valuable service in arresting criminals, and regained the confidence of the whites. This confidence, however, was of short duration.

War having been declared in the name of the Florida Indians, a detachment of volunteers with some regulars, under General Duncan L. Clinch, moved to the Ouithlacoochee, the Indian encampment. Three days before the event which will be described as occurring at Ouithlacoochee, Major Francis Langhorne Dade, with a small command, had moved from Fort Brooke to relieve the post of Fort King.

Major Dade and his command had marched sixty-five miles in five days, intrenching themselves each night in their encampment. On the sixth night they were attacked by Indians and negro allies, and out of one hundred and twelve all were slain except three. The officers killed were Major Francis Langhorne Dado, Captain George Washington Gardiner, Captain William Frazier, Lieutenants William E. Basinger, J. L. Keayes, Robert Richard Mudge, Richard Henderson, and Dr. John Slade Gatlin. Total killed, officers and men, one hundred and seven; escaped, three. A handsome monument has been erected to their memory at West Point. Returning to General Duncan L. Clinch's advance on Ouithlacoochee, here he was attacked by Assiola and his followers after he had crossed the river; but the general succeeded in repelling the attack and driving the Indians. While the battle resulting in the massacre of Major Dade and his command was being fought, the death of Thompson and others was effected within a few hundred yards of Fort King, on February 28th. All of the troops except Thomas W. Lendrum's company of the Third Artillery, about forty strong, had been withdrawn on the 26th, to re-enforce General Clinch at Lang Syne plantation, with a view to his striking a blow at the families of the Indians supposed to be concealed in the swamps and hammocks of the Ouithlacoochee River, with the hope of drawing the Indian warriors out and bringing on a general engagement. All those attached to the fort or agency were directed not to pass beyond the picketing. Thompson slept inside the defenses and passed the greater part of the day at the agency, about one hundred yards beyond the works. The sutler, Rogers, had moved his goods into the fort, but was in the habit of taking his meals at his residence, six hundred yards away in the skirt of a hammock to the southwest of the fort.

On the day of the massacre Lieutenant Constantine Smith, of the Second Artillery, had dined with General Thompson, and after dinner the two went out for a walk. They had proceeded about three hundred yards beyond the agency office when they were fired upon by a party of Indians who were concealed in the hammock on the border of which the sutler's house stood. The reports of the rifles, and the war-whoop repeated, were heard within a brief time, other volleys more remote were fired, when the smoke of the firing was seen at the fort. Captain Lendrum at once called out his men, who were at that time engaged in strengthening the pickets. He was not aware of the absence from the fort of General Thompson and Lieutenant Smith; he supposed the firing was a ruse to draw him out and cut him off from the fort. Very soon several whites and negroes came in and informed him that Mr. Rogers, his clerks, and themselves had been surprised at dinner, and the three former had fallen into the hands of the Indians. A small command was at once dispatched to succor and pursue, but the butchery had been as brief as it was complete, and a last war-whoop had been given as a signal for retreat. The bodies of General Thompson, Lieutenant Smith, and Mr. Kitzler were soon found and brought in; those of the others were not found until the following morning. General Thompson's body had fourteen bullets in it and a deep knife-wound in the left breast. Lieutenant Smith and Mr. Kitzler had each received two bullets in the head. The bodies of Rogers the sutler and Robert Suggs were shockingly mangled, the skulls of each being broken, and all save Suggs were scalped. The party was led by Assiola, and consisted of fifty or sixty Micosukees. Two other Indians were in the party attired as chiefs, but were not recognized. This information comes from an old negro woman who was in the house and who concealed herself so as to elude the Indians, and made her escape to the fort after the massacre.

Information of the butchery was at once dispatched to General Clinch. General Richard Keith Call, with Colonels Richard C. Parish and Leigh Read, having arrived on the 29th with about five hundred volunteers from the adjoining counties, who had previously been ordered to scour the country on the right and left flank, joined the United States troops, numbering about two hundred under General Clinch. Orders were issued for a forward movement at sunrise on December 29th. They arrived near the Ouithlacoochee on the 30th, and threw up breastworks around their encampment. On arriving at the river next morning it was found too deep to be forded. No Indians being in sight, one of the men swam the river and brought over a canoe. As only seven men could be taken over at a time, the work of crossing the troops was slow and tedious. General Clinch and Colonels Samuel Parkhill and Read crossed over, and, in conjunction with General Call, began the construction of rafts on which the baggage and stores could be crossed over. The regulars were all over by twelve o'clock, and Major Alexander C. W. Fanning marched them into an open field surrounded on all sides either by a thick swamp or hammock, and there formed them into line, awaiting the crossing of the volunteers. When about fifty of the volunteers had crossed, and the officers were engaged in superintending the construction of the rafts, an alarm was given that the Indians were upon them. General Call at once put his men in line, and the Indians opened fire, but the volunteers poured a heavy volley into the hammock, which silenced the fire of the Indians for a time; but they soon collected their forces and opened a galling fire on the regulars. General Clinch ordered a charge, which was gallantly led by Major Fanning, but the Indians maintained their ground. A second charge was more successful, driving the Indians some distance back. The chiefs made every effort to rally them, but without success.

During the battle General Call, Colonel John Warren, and Major James G. Cooper, with a number of volunteers, crossed the river at imminent peril, and the two latter immediately engaged and fought with the most determined bravery. General Call had formed the volunteers that last crossed into two parallel lines, placing one above and the other below the crossing place, for the purpose of protecting the troops on the other side and those who were recrossing with the dead and wounded. He therefore did not reach the field until the enemy were repulsed, though his services were eminently useful in directing the crossing. Clinch at this time was not advised of the disaster to Major Dade's command.

The term of service of the volunteers having expired, General Clinch marched them, on January 2d, to Fort Drane and disbanded them. In this last-named engagement the regulars and volunteers, numbering, all told, two hundred and twenty-seven men—under the able leadership of Clinch, Major Campbell Graham, Major Fanning, Colonel John Warren, General Richard K. Call, Cooper, and Lieutenant George Read—succeeded in defeating over seven hundred Indians who had chosen their ground and were protected by the swamps and hammocks. The volunteer officers, to whom great credit was due, were Major (afterward Brigadier General) Leigh Read, whose horse was shot under him, Colonel John Warren, Colonel Parkhill (of Richmond, Va.), Colonel William J. Mills, Major Cooper, Captain Martin Scott, and Captain William J. Bailey. The services of General Call and Majors Gamble and Wellford were of great value. General Clinch makes mention of Major J. S. Little his aid-de-camp, Captains Gustavus S. Drane, Charles Mellon, and Gates, Lieutenants George Henry Talcott, Erastus A. Capron, John Graham, William Seaton Maitland, and Horace Brooks, of the United States army, and Colonel McIntosh, Lieutenants Youman, Stewart, Nathaniel W. Hunter, Cuthbert, and Adjutant Joseph A. Phillips, of the Florida volunteers, of the officers of the medical staff. Special mention was made of Drs. Richard Weightman, Hamilton, Philip G. Randolph, and Brandon. The returns of the killed and wounded were as follows:

REGULARS.

Killed, 2 artificers and 2 privates...................... 4
Wounded, 1 captain and 2 lieutenants.............. 3
Two sergeants and 4 corporals..................... 6
Private soldiers.......................... 43
                                                        52

VOLUNTEERS.

Wounded, Colonel Warren, Major Cooper, and Lieutenant Youman................... 3
Private soldiers.......... 4
                                                    7 59==63

Previous to and immediately after this engagement the Indians divided themselves into small parties for the purpose of devastating the country. They made their appearance simultaneously in the southern part of the peninsula as far north as Picolata and from the extreme east below St. Augustine to the west, carrying off everything that was useful to them and destroying the remainder. At New River, on the southeast side of the peninsula, they murdered the wife, children, and teacher in the family of Mr. Cooley, carrying off provisions and horses, and setting fire to the house on their departure.

The settlements in that neighborhood were abandoned, the inhabitants taking refuge near the lighthouse on Cape Florida; but they had been there only a short time when, the Indians making their appearance, they were compelled to seek shelter and protection elsewhere.

The ruthless destruction of property and of lives on the east side of the peninsula was heartrending. Their principal ravages, however, were on the east side from St. Augustine to the south. Major Benjamin A. Putnam, with a small detachment of men, marched into this country with a view to drive the Indians away. He was met by an overpowering number of the savages, and forced to retreat. In fact, no part of the State seemed to be free from these murderous savages.

General Clinch made requisitions on the Governors of Georgia, South Carolina, and Alabama to aid the Floridians in their unequal warfare with the savages. It was felt by the citizens of Florida that the Government at Washington showed great apathy, if not real indifference, to their condition. A meeting was called in Charleston, S. C., early in January, for the purpose of aiding the people of Florida with men and means, but General Eustis informed the meeting that General Clinch had sufficient force and supplies under his command to subdue any number of Indians and negroes that could be brought to oppose him. On January 12th, intelligence having been received from General Clinch asking for six hundred men, the committee conferred with General Eustis and requested him to send a company of United States troops with arms and ammunition for the defense of St. Augustine. This was granted, and the citizens of Charleston chartered a steamboat and placed on board one thousand bushels of corn, one hundred barrels of flour, thirty barrels of beef, twenty barrels of pork, and ten tierces of rice. On January 20th another meeting was called to raise volunteers for Florida. The banks of Charleston subscribed twenty-five thousand dollars as a loan to the Government. The committee dispatched a schooner, loaded with corn, rice, bread, beef, pork, and military and hospital stores, and sent a physician to attend the sick.

Four companies of volunteers were put in motion on the 27th for St. Augustine—viz., the Washington Light Infantry, Captain Ravenel; Washington Volunteers, Captain Finley; German Fusileers, Captain Timrod; and Hamburgh Volunteers, Captain Cunningham. These volunteer companies arrived at St. Augustine on January 30th, and were at once sent out to scour the country for hostile Indians; they were, however, relieved from duty on February 12th, on the arrival of the South Carolina militia and United States troops under Major Reynold Marvin Kirby. These troops were placed on the same duty as their predecessors, but there was no engagement with the hostile Indians until the latter part of March. An instance of the chivalric spirit of the South Carolina volunteers is worthy of mention. On requisition of the Governor for three companies to be furnished for Florida, Colonel Chesnut, of Camden, called out his regiment. After telling them what was wanted, he requested those who desired to volunteer in defense of their suffering neighbors to step forward. The whole regiment marched forward and tendered their services. At the same time four thousand dollars were contributed for their equipment.

On receipt of the intelligence of the Dade massacre in Savannah, a company of Georgia volunteers at once embarked for Picolata. A meeting of the Richmond Blues and Richmond Hussars, of Augusta, was called for the purpose of rendering aid. The city council appropriated the necessary funds to supply arms and ammunition. The ladies of Augusta volunteered to make the uniforms, and in less than a week these volunteers were on their way to Picolata. These companies were composed of the *élite* of the city. Supplies of all kinds were sent by Mayor Joseph Beard to Fort Drane and the posts on the St. John's, which were poorly equipped with ordnance and quartermaster's stores. He also sent a six-pounder cannon with necessary equipments of grape, canister, and round shot, ten thousand rounds of musket ball and buckshot cartridges, and a general supply of needful articles. Further supplies were drawn on their arrival at Picolata.

This action of Quartermaster Beard was most fortunate, as it was found that the military posts, by the neglect of the War Department or its subalterns, had been reduced to such an extremity that in case of attack they must necessarily have been shorn of the means of defense, and would have fallen into the hands of the enemy. Nothing but the timely arrival of supplies saved these posts from destruction.

There were no means of transportation at Picolata, and the quartermaster procured horses at Jacksonville for the purpose of forwarding one of the six-pounders to Fort Drane. Four of the horses on arrival were found unfit for service, but, fortunately, General John M. Hernandez was able to furnish ten chicken carts, and the quartermaster was authorized to make impressments for transportation. The Richmond Blues, one hundred and twelve strong, with the Camden and Glynn mounted volunteers, numbering twenty-seven, and the Darien Infantry of about thirty, under command of Captains Robertson, R. Floyd, and Thomas S. Bryant respectively, took up line of march as an escort to the two six-pounders, ordnance stores, twenty-five wagons and carts laden with provisions, and passed through the heart of the enemy's country, arriving on February 15th, without obstruction, at the garrison of Fort Drane.

Supplies under the same escort were at once forwarded to Fort King. Subsequently the following-named companies of Georgia volunteers arrived in Florida: The Hancock Blues, Captain A. S. Brown; State Fencibles, Captain J. A. Merriwether; Macon Volunteers, Captain Isaac Seymour; Morgan Guards, Captain N. G. Foster; Monroe Musketeers, Captain John Cureton; Washington Cavalry, Captain C. J. Malone; Baldwin Cavalry, Captain W. F. Scott. Major Ross, with several companies of mounted men from Georgia, arrived later, but owing to the advanced season, much to their disappointment, did not enter the field.

Going back to January 15th, General Edmund Pendleton Gaines, who was on a tour of inspection through the Western Department, first heard of the troubles in Florida, and at once called on the Governor of Louisiana and requested him to hold in readiness a body of volunteers for service in subduing the Seminole Indians.

He also wrote to the adjutant general at Washington, urging that no time be lost in succoring the troops in Florida, and saying, from his knowledge of the Seminole character, that at least four thousand men would be required to subdue them, protected and aided by a strong naval force.

At that time the United States was divided into two military departments by a line drawn from the southern part of Florida to the northwestern extremity of Lake Superior. The Eastern Department was under the command of General Winfield Scott, and the Western under that of General Gaines, and by reference to a map it will be seen that the line passed directly through the theater of hostilities in Florida. The meeting of these two distinguished generals was purely accidental. General Scott was in Washington when the news was received of General Clinch's engagement with the Seminoles. After dispatching his letter to the adjutant general, General Gaines proceeded to Pensacola for the purpose of getting the co-operation of the naval forces at that station. He found, however, that Commodores Dallas and Bolton and Captain Webb had received orders to direct their attention to the inlets of Florida, whence they had sailed. He received here the most alarming intelligence of the state of affairs in Florida. He proceeded to Mobile on January 18th, and there learned that Fort Brooke was invested by the Indians and the garrison in great danger of being cut off and slaughtered. He at once sent an express to General Clinch, supposed to be at Fort King, stating that he would arrive at Fort Brooke about February 8th with seven hundred men, and requested General Clinch to take the field and march southward and form a junction with him at Fort Brooke.

As the crisis demanded immediate action, and General Scott being present to receive the instructions of the Government in person, he was charged with the direction of the campaign without regard to department boundaries. General Gaines had left his headquarters at Memphis, Tenn., on a tour of inspection through his department, and it was very uncertain when or where the orders and instructions of the Government would reach him; and as the immediate services of an officer of high rank of mind and discreet judgment were required to maintain the neutrality of the United States during the war between the Texans and Mexicans, General Gaines was selected for that important duty. However, the official dispatches did not reach General Gaines until he had already taken the field in Florida and marched from Fort Brooke to Fort King, within ninety-five miles of where General Scott had established his headquarters.

In pursuance of this plan, Lieutenant-Colonel David E. Twiggs was ordered to receive into service the eight companies of volunteers requested of the Governor of Louisiana, adding them to the command of such regular troops as might be in the vicinity of

New Orleans, all to be held in readiness for a movement to Tampa Bay. The troops were mustered into service on February 3d. General Gaines having arrived in New Orleans on January 27th, chartered three steamers to convey the troops and stores. The Legislature of Louisiana had appropriated eighty-five thousand dollars for the equipment of her volunteers, and on February 4th the chartered steamers, with the Louisiana volunteers and one company of regulars, were under way, and on the same day another steamer, with Colonel Twiggs and Companies B, E, G, H, I, and K of the regulars, left New Orleans. The vessels arrived safely at Hillsboro Bay, four miles distant from the garrison, on February 8th, 9th, and 10th, and the troops were immediately disembarked and camped just outside of the fort.

The fort was a triangular work formed by pickets with blockhouses at the apex, the base resting on the bay and flanked on the west by Hillsboro River. It was found that there were at the fort about two hundred regular troops, composed of Companies A, B, C, and H of the Second Artillery, and Company A of the Fourth Infantry, with Majors Francis S. Belton, Richard Augustus Zantzinger, and John Mountford, Lieutenants John Breckenridge Grayson, Samuel McKenzie, John Charles Casey, Thomas C. Legate, Edwin Wright Morgan, Augustus Porter Allen, and Benjamin Alvord, and Surgeons Henry Lee Heiskell and Reynolds. Major Belton was the commanding officer of the post.

General Gaines, having received instructions at Pensacola from the Secretary of War to repair and take charge of the forces which were assembling on the Mexican frontier, announced the fact to Colonel Twiggs; but the troops, on hearing this, manifested great dissatisfaction, and insisted that as they had volunteered to go under the command of General Gaines, he in good faith should be their leader. Following is the text of the letter of the Secretary of War to General Gaines:

"WAR DEPARTMENT, WASHINGTON, *January 23, 1835.*

"SIR: I am instructed by the President to request that you will repair to some proper position near the western frontier of the State of Louisiana, and there assume the personal command of all the troops of the United States which are or may be employed in any part of the region adjoining the Mexican boundary.

"It is not the intention of this order to change at all the relations between yourself and the military departments under your command, to require your personal presence at a point where public considerations demand the exercise of great discretion and prudence. . . ."

The pressure not only from the troops in the field but from outside sources was so great that General Gaines felt it his duty to enter the field. Besides, that was thought a propitious time to begin active operations, as the day before the arrival of the Louisiana troops the friendly Indians had engaged the hostiles in a battle about four miles from Fort Brooke. Although at this date, as before mentioned, General Scott in Washington had been ordered to assume command in Florida, General Gaines was entirely ignorant of such order.

Orders were accordingly issued assigning officers to their respective duties. Captain Ethan A. Hitchcock, First Infantry, was announced Assistant Inspector General of the Department, and Lieutenant James Farley Izard, of the Dragoons, to be Acting Brigade Major. The artillery and infantry of the United States army, together with the Louisiana volunteer forces under Adjutant-General Persifor F. Smith, were to constitute "the light brigade." (Here is an instance of a staff officer being assigned to command troops.) The whole force to be under the command of Lieutenant-Colonel David E. Twiggs, Fourth Infantry.

The Louisiana volunteers were divided into two battalions, the first composed of the companies of Captains Burt, Lee, Williams, Rogers, and Thistle, under Lieutenant-Colonel Thomas Lawson, Surgeon. (Here is another case of a staff officer and surgeon ordered to the command of troops.) The second battalion was composed of the companies of Captains Samuel F. Marks, William H. Ker, Magee, Smith, Abadie, and Barr, under Major Marks, the regiment to be commanded by Colonel Persifor F. Smith. Orders for marching were issued on the 13th, the troops to be supplied with forty rounds of ammunition and ten days' rations, five of which were to be carried in haversacks. During the Florida campaign the only articles drawn by the private volunteer soldiers were bread or flour, pork or beef, while only a few drew salt, sugar, and coffee. Major Richard M. Sands, of the Fourth Infantry, and Captain Barr's company of volunteers, amounting in all to one hundred and sixty men, were detailed for the protection of the fort, under command of Major Sands.

The army marched in three columns, equidistant one hundred yards, with a strong advance and rear guard. The center column was composed of one company of volunteers as advance guard, under command of Brigade Major Izard. Seven companies of United States artillery and infantry, under command of Lieutenant-Colonel William Sewell Foster; the baggage train, led by Captain Samuel Shannon; six companies of Louisiana volunteers as rear guard, under command of Lieutenant-Colonel Lawson. Right column: Four companies of artillery acting as light infantry, under command of Major Belton. Left column: Four companies of Louisiana volunteers, under command of Major Marks. The entire command consisted of nine hundred and eighty effective men, exclusive of the detachment under Major Sands, which, added to the force, would make it eleven hundred and forty men.

The Quartermaster's Department at the post was in a very bad condition, destitute of nearly everything that was necessary for the comfort of the troops. There was great scarcity of ordnance stores, but, happily, an abundant supply of subsistence stores.

CHAPTER VI.

Review of the army by General Gaines—Arrival of General Gaines at Fort King—Lieutenant Izard mortally wounded—Correspondence between General Gaines and Clinch—General Scott ordered to command in Florida—Disadvantages under which he labored—Preparations for movements—Commencement of hostilities against the Indians.

GENERAL GAINES reviewed the army on February 13th, and, accompanied by seventy-seven friendly Indians, took up line of march toward the Alafia River, to which point he learned that the hostile Indians had gone. The march was made under many difficulties, the horses of the baggage train breaking down and necessitating the loss of valuable articles of camp equipage. Near dark they encamped six miles from Fort Brooke. The next day they arrived at Warren, on the Alafia River, eighteen miles from the fort, and received two days' rations, which General Gaines had ordered sent around from Fort Brooke by water. Discovering no traces of Indians, he directed the march toward the grounds where Major Dade and his party were massacred. The boats having arrived at Fort Brooke with the sick and disabled and all superfluous baggage, the army moved in the direction of a deserted Indian village, passing the ruins of many fine plantations, and struck the military road near the Hillsboro River.

On the 17th they arrived at the river and halted. On the 18th, after burning two deserted Indian villages near the Big Ouithlacoochee River, the friendly Indians accompanying the expedition requested permission to return to Fort Brooke. General Gaines assured them that there was no danger to be apprehended; that he only required them to act as scouts and guides, and that they were not expected to go into battle.

The Ouithlacoochee was forded on the 19th, and that night a breastwork was thrown up on the ground which had been occupied by the ill-fated party of Major Dade. At daybreak of the 20th they resumed their march, and buried on their way the remains of Major Dade and Captain Frazier and eight other officers, and ninety-eight noncommissioned officers and privates.

It now became a question of importance whether to continue the march to Fort King, which post was thought to be besieged by the enemy, or to return to Fort Brooke. To Fort Brooke it was sixty-five miles, and to Fort King forty miles north. A large number of the volunteers were destitute of provisions. It would require five days to reach Fort Brooke, and but two to reach Fort King.

It having been reported at Fort Brooke that Fort King was assailed by the Indians and in danger of being cut off, and this opinion being strengthened by the noncompliance of General Clinch with the request of General Gaines to co-operate with him, it became General Gaines's duty to ascertain the cause. A large number of General Gaines's troops were in a destitute condition, and the senior assistant quartermaster, Captain Shannon, had a letter from the

Quartermaster General at Washington, dated January 19th, which stated that large supplies of provisions had been ordered from New York to Fort King. With these facts before him, General Gaines determined to move to Fort King, where he could ascertain the position of the enemy and at the same time strengthen the garrison.

The army under General Gaines arrived at Fort King on February 22d. Finding the post poorly supplied with subsistence, he dispatched Lieutenant-Colonel Foster, with an escort of the Fourth Infantry, to proceed to Fort Drane, twenty-two miles distant, where General Clinch was stationed with four companies of artillery and one of infantry and two companies of volunteers, and endeavored to get a supply of provisions. The detachment returned on the 24th with seven days' supplies. Here for the first time General Gaines was informed that General Scott was in command in Florida, and that he was then at Picolata organizing forces and gathering supplies.

General Gaines then determined that he could not remain at Fort King, as supplies were being exhausted as fast as they came in, and that to remain there would necessarily embarrass the operations of General Scott. It was also evident that the enemy would not be found by retracing his march to Fort Brooke, but that by moving by the battle ground of General Clinch, even should he not succeed in meeting the enemy, the mere presence of a large force would perhaps tend to concentrate him, and thus give security to the frontier and enable the inhabitants to give attention to planting their crops. Besides, he would find supplies at Fort Brooke, and on his arrival the command of Colonel Lindsay would be strengthened.

The army, being provided with two days' rations, moved out on the 27th, and arriving at the river, a halt was called, the baggage train being under protection of the rear guard, while General Gaines, with the main column and artillery, moved forward for the purpose of making a reconnoissance preparatory to crossing. Finding the river too deep to ford at the point reached, General Gaines and Colonel Smith made an attempt to cross about two hundred and fifty yards higher up. Reaching a small island in the middle of the river, a sharp fire was opened upon them, accompanied by the Indian war-whoop.

The troops returned the fire, and the field piece under Lieutenant Grayson was brought into action, which quickly silenced the war-whoop. The engagement lasted about three quarters of an hour, during which one volunteer was killed and seven wounded. General Clinch's old breastwork was enlarged and occupied by the troops during the night.

On the morning of the 28th the line was again formed, and after a circuitous march the army arrived at the crossing place. James Farley Izard, a first lieutenant of dragoons, being on leave of absence, volunteered his services to General Gaines, was assigned to duty as brigade major, and was about forming the guard when the sharp crack of a rifle and the war-whoop gave notice of the presence of the enemy. His horse had received a bullet in his neck. When he dismounted he proceeded to the bank of the river, when a ball from the enemy entered his left eye. He said to the men, "Keep your positions and lie close." He died in a few days from the effect of the wound. A desultory fight was kept up from nine in the morning until one o'clock in the afternoon, when the enemy withdrew. The troops threw up breastworks, inside of which they encamped for the night. Captain William G. Sanders, commanding the friendly Indians, was severely wounded. Captain Armstrong, of the United States transport schooner Motto, was wounded, and a soldier of Captain Croghan Ker's company of Louisiana volunteers was killed. General Gaines sent an express to General Clinch asking his co-operation by crossing the river eight or ten miles above and coming down on the enemy's rear. He notified General Clinch that he would not move from his position until he heard from him, and requested to be furnished with needed subsistence. The dispatch arrived on the following morning, and General Clinch sent it forward to General Scott at Picolata.

On the 29th, orders were issued for one third of the command to remain on duty inside of the encampment, while another third was engaged in strengthening the defenses. A detachment of two hundred Louisiana volunteers under command of Captain Thistle, an expert marksman, was detailed for the erection of a blockhouse near the river, while others were engaged in preparing canoes and rafts. Everything was quiet until ten o'clock, when a fire was opened by the Indians on the working parties and on three sides of the camp. The Indians were concealed in the palmettoes, about two hundred yards distant. They set fire to the grass and palmettoes, but a sudden shift of the wind carried the fire in their direction. The firing lasted about two hours, when the Indians retired. Captain Thistle and party returned to camp without having sustained any loss. The firing was renewed by the Indians about four o'clock in the afternoon, but soon subsided. The loss in General Gaines's camp was one noncommissioned officer of artillery killed, and thirty-two officers, noncommissioned officers, and privates wounded. General Gaines received a painful wound in the mouth. Lieutenant James Duncan, Second Artillery, Mr. W. Potter, secretary to General Gaines, and Lieutenant Ephraim Smith, of the Louisiana volunteers, were wounded.

General Gaines now sent another dispatch by some friendly Indians to General Clinch asking him to march his forces direct to Camp Izard instead of crossing above. He also asked for some mounted men and one or two field pieces with a sufficient supply of ammunition. General Gaines regarded this as a most favorable opportunity to attack the Indians while they were concentrated, and he thought that with such re-enforcements as he asked, and a supply of provisions, he could end the war in ten days. He had notified General Clinch, on February 28th, that he would make no sortie nor would he move from his position until he heard from General Clinch. In his second letter to General Clinch he wrote: " Being fully satisfied that I am in the neighborhood of the principal body of Indians, and that they are now concentrated, I must suggest to you the expediency of an immediate co-operation with the forces under your command. I have only to repeat my determination not to move from my position or make a sortie until I hear from you, as it would only tend to disperse the enemy, and we should then have difficulty in finding them."

If General Gaines had made an attack he would certainly have lost one or two hundred men. He had no transportation to convey the wounded, and was short of supplies, as his whole train consisted of one wagon and two carts. Had he made an attack and routed the enemy, he had no means of following them, and his victory would have been barren of results. The Indians made another attack on March 1st, and renewed it on the next day. These attacks were repeated daily until the 5th, when they sent forrward their interpreter, who wanted to know if Colonel Twiggs was in command, and saying they did not want to continue the war, but to shake hands and be friends. He was told to come at nine o'clock the next morning with a white flag. On Sunday morning, March 6th, Assiola and Colonel Hago, with others, appeared for a talk. Major Barron, Captain Marks, and others met them. They said they wanted to stop fighting; that they had taken up arms against the whites because they had been badly treated; that the whites had killed many of their men; that they would stop the war if the whites were withdrawn, and would not cross the river.

Major Barron replied that he would communicate what they said to General Gaines. Jumper asked if Colonel Twiggs was in camp. He was answered in the affirmative, but was told that General Gaines was in command. General Gaines directed Captain Hitchcock, of his staff, accompanied by Captain Marks, Dr. Harrall, and others, to confer with Jumper. On meeting Jumper he expressed a desire to see General Gaines, and said they would like to consult their governor, Miconopy, who was then some distance off. The Indians insisted on seeing General Gaines, and they were informed that he was ready to meet Miconopy, their governor. Nothing definite having been settled, they retired. At a subsequent meeting the Seminoles agreed to give up their arms and cease hostilities, and meet the commissioners again for a general treaty.

In the meantime General Gaines was re-enforced by Georgia troops, under command of Captains Edward B. Robinson and Bones, the Florida mounted militia, under command of Captain McLemore, and some regulars, under Captains Charles Myron Thruston and Graham, the whole under the command of General Clinch. They also brought beef cattle and other much-needed supplies. The Indians appeared again with a white flag and asked to confer with General Gaines, but were told that they must bring their governor, Miconopy, with whom General Gaines would confer.

General Gaines now turned over the command of the army to General Clinch, and on Thursday, the 10th, the army moved in the direction of Fort Drane. General Gaines left for Tallahassee and Mobile, and was the recipient of great attention by the citizens of those places.

Such was the situation when, on January 20, 1836, General Scott was ordered to take command of the army in Florida, which had been increased to twelve hundred regulars, besides volunteers, by the time he arrived there. He left Washington the day after receiving his orders and arrived at Picolata, on the St. John's River, and on February 22d issued orders forming the army into three divisions. The troops on the west bank of the St. John's River were placed under command of General Clinch, and constituted the right wing of the army. Those on the east bank of the St. John's River, under Brigadier-General Abram Eustis, constituted the left wing, and those at Tampa Bay, under Colonel William Lindsay, constituted the center. General Scott had been authorized to ask for volunteers from the States of Georgia, Alabama, South Carolina, and the Territory of Florida. Among other instructions given the general was the following: In consequence of representations from Florida that measures would probably be taken to transmit the slaves captured by the Indians to the Havana, orders were given the navy to prevent such proceedings, and General Scott was directed "to allow no pacification with the Indians while a slave belonging to a white man remained in their possession." There were a great many negroes among the Indians. In the band that massacred Major Dade and his command there were sixty-three of them mounted in one company. The negroes and Indians of mixed African and Indian blood were the most cruel members of the tribe.

Re-enforcements of militia were soon added to the army. The great disadvantages under which Scott labored necessarily delayed his movements until a late period. He found the quartermaster's department very deficient, and had the greatest difficulty in transporting supplies to Fort Drane. His supplies of ordnance were very limited, and the greater part of those on hand were unfit for use. To penetrate a country like Florida, filled with swamps, morasses, and almost impenetrable hammocks, required much preparation and labor. There was no chain of posts or settlements through the country, and the army was compelled to carry a heavy load of provisions and ordnance. To increase the difficulties, heavy rains had fallen which made the roads almost impassable. General Scott arrived at Fort Drane on March 13, 1836, with a very small force. Believing the enemy to be concentrated at or near the forks of Ouithlacoochee River, he adopted the following plan of operations:

The Florida army to constitute three divisions, to be known as the right, center, and left wings; the center being composed of Alabama volunteers, three companies of Louisiana volunteers, and two companies of United States artillery, amounting to twelve hundred and fifty men, to be commanded by Colonel William Lindsay. To move from Fort Brooke and take position at or near Chicuchatty, on March 25th. Signal guns to be fired each day thereafter at 9 A. M. to announce position. The right wing, composed of a battalion of Augusta volunteers under Acting Major Robertson; a battalion of Georgia volunteers under Major Mark A. Cooper; Major John M. Douglass, Georgia Cavalry; eleven companies of Louisiana volunteers, under Colonel Persifor F. Smith; Florida Rangers, under Major McLemore; the regulars, under Colonel James Bankhead; and Captain Clifton Wharton's company of Dragoons —in all amounting to about two thousand men, to be commanded by General Clinch. This wing to move from Fort Drane and be in position near Camp Izard, on the Ouithlacoochee River, between March 26th and 28th. Signal guns to be fired at 11 A. M. The left wing, composed of the South Carolina volunteers, under Colonel Abbott H. Brisbane; mounted volunteers, under Colonels Goodwyn and Butler— amounting to about fourteen hundred men—to be commanded by General Abram Eustis. This wing to move from Volusia and take position at or near Pilaklakaha on March 27th. Signal guns to be fired at ten o'clock each day.

Each wing to be composed of three columns, a center protected by a strong van and rear guard. The baggage train to be placed in the rear of the main column. The center and left wings, on assuming their respective positions, will fire signal guns, which will be responded to by the right wing. The right wing will then move up the cove or great swamp of the Ouithlacoochee in a southeast direction and drive the Indians south, while the center will advance to the north and the left to the west, by which united movement the Indians will be surrounded and left no avenue of escape. The operations of the army will be supported by the naval forces under Commodore Alfred J. Dallas, protecting the western coast of the peninsula, to cut off retreat and supplies.

Colonel Lindsay, commanding the center wing, arrived at Fort Brooke with eight companies of Alabama volunteers on March 6th, where he found a battalion of Florida troops, commanded by Major Read, and on the 10th was joined by one company of Louisiana volunteers, under command of Captain George H. Marks.

On the 12th he discovered fires to the southeast, and it was soon reported that a large body of Indians was encamped a few miles distant. Colonel Lindsay directed Major Leigh Read with his battalion to make a reconnoissance in the direction of the Indians. Major Read moved during the night, and coming upon the Indians at daylight, surprised them and put them to flight with a loss of three killed and six taken prisoners. He also secured a quantity of camp equipage and some beef cattle.

Colonel Lindsay, not hearing from headquarters, determined to proceed as far as Hillsboro River and erect a stockade so as to place his supplies nearer to the scene of operations. This object having been effected, he left Major Read in charge of the fort, which he had named Fort Alabama, and returned to Fort Brooke on the 21st. During his absence dispatches were received from General Scott announcing the plan of campaign, and requesting Colonel Lindsay to be in position at Chicuchatty on March 25th. Major Read having been relieved, the line of march was taken up. The column being fired on by the Indians and several soldiers killed and wounded, Colonel Lindsay ordered a charge, which was executed by Captains Benham and Blount, commanding Alabama volunteers, and the Indians were driven from their covert into a pine woods.

On March 28th, three days after the time mentioned in the orders, this command was in position at Camp Broadnax, near Chicuchatty, in pursuance of General Scott's orders. The country over which they had marched was hilly, and in many places there were dense forests which retarded their movements, though the late period at which Colonel Lindsay received his orders would have prevented his arrival at the time specified in them. No censure can be attributed to General Scott for the delay, as it was impossible under the circumstances for him to have matured his plans earlier.

General Eustis, commanding the left wing, arrived at St. Augustine on February 15th, and at once established a chain of posts at intervals of from ten to twenty miles, extending along the Atlantic coast as far south as the Mosquito Inlet, in order to drive off the bands of depredators and to give protection to the plantations. Colonel Goodwyn's mounted South Carolina volunteers having arrived on March 9th, the several detachments of the left wing, with the exception of Colonel Pierce M. Butler's battalion and two companies of artillery under Major Reynold M. Kirby, were put in motion for Volusia, where they arrived on March 21st after encountering great difficulties, being compelled to cut the road nearly the whole distance. On the 22d they began crossing the St. John's River. When the vanguard, consisting of two companies under Captains Adams and T. S. Tripp, had reached the opposite shore they were attacked by about fifty Indians who were concealed in a hammock. Being re-enforced by George Henry and Hibler's companies, they charged the enemy and drove him. Two companies of mounted men were crossed above with a view of cutting off the retreat of the Indians, but they were too late. The loss in this battle was three killed and nine wounded. On the 24th, Lieutenant Ripley A. Arnold, with twenty-seven mounted men, was sent in quest of Colonel Butler and his command, who had not joined the main command, he having marched in the direction of New Smyrna. This detachment fell in with a party of twelve or fifteen Indians who gave battle. Two of the Indians were killed, and Lieutenant Arnold, having his horse shot, ordered a retreat, for which he was severely censured. The whole force of General Eustis's command being now concentrated on the west side of the St. John's River, opposite to Volusia, orders were issued to distribute thirteen days' rations, and the line of march to be taken up for Pilaklakaha, leaving the sick and wounded with two companies of Colonel Brisbane's regiment at Volusia, under command of Major William Gates, United States army. The roads being bad, they were unable to march more than seven miles in two days. On the 29th they reached the Ocklawaha, and, constructing a bridge, crossed over after sundown and discovered fires on the margin of Lake Eustis, which they supposed to be signals of the Indians. Colonel Butler, with a small command, accompanied by General Joseph Shelton, who was serving as a private soldier, moved in the direction of the fires and discovered four Indians, who at once retreated. One of these Indians, Chief Yaha Hayo, was killed, while the others made their escape. On the 30th Colonel Goodwyn was sent forward to reconnoiter, and when near Pilaklakaha was attacked by Indians, having three men and several horses wounded. Colonel Robert H. Goodwyn was soon re-enforced by General Eustis, and a battle ensued lasting nearly an hour. The Indians were driven into the swamp. On March 31st an express was sent to Scott for information and for the purpose of obtaining forage. A signal gun was fired on the following morning after their arrival, but not answered.

The right wing having assembled at Fort Drane, General Scott ordered General Clinch to put his troops in motion on March 25th and take position on the Ouithlacoochee; but a heavy rain prevented the movement until the morning of March 26th. General Clinch sent forward two flatboats drawn on wagons to await the arrival of the troops at the river. The movement was begun by Major Douglass with his mounted Georgians. The order of march was in three columns: the center, with the baggage train, headed by General Clinch, the right consisting of the Louisiana volunteers, under command of Colonel Persifor F. Smith, joined the line at Camp Smith, and the left, commanded by Colonel Bankhert, joined by Lieutenant Colonel William S. Foster's battalion of United States troops at Camp Twiggs, General Scott and staff with an escort of dragoons taking position in the center. Colonel Gadsden was appointed quartermaster general for Florida, and acting inspector general. When nine miles from Fort Drane information reached the army that some volunteers left in charge of a broken-down team had been attacked by the Indians and one man killed. On March 28th the column reached the Ouithlacoochee and encamped near Fort Izard. The river bank was occupied by sharpshooters and two pieces of artillery to protect the crossing. Foster Blodget, of the Richmond Blues of Augusta, Ga., swam the river and attached a rope to a tree on the opposite shore and planted the flag of his command. The whole command was passed over, but the rear division was fired upon by the Indians, who were quickly repulsed by the six-pounders. On the morning of March 30th a party of Indians was encountered, charged upon, and routed, and the same party were next day met and driven into the swamp. The column proceeded on its march and arrived at Tampa Bay on April 5th. They here learned that Colonel Lindsay had preceded them one day, being obliged to return for necessary subsistence.

It will be remembered that the center, being under Colonel Lindsay, took position at Camp Broadnax, near Chicuchatty, on March 28th. They were fired on by the Indians, but succeeded in driving them off. As his supplies had run short and the original plan of the campaign had been defeated, Colonel Lindsay returned with his command to Fort Brooke, arriving there April 4th. When Colonel Lindsay reached Fort Alabama, near the Hillsboro River, he learned that the post had been attacked on the morning of March 27th by three or four hundred Indians, who surrounded the breastwork and continued the attack for two hours, when they were repulsed with a loss of fifteen. The garrison lost one man killed and two wounded. General Eustis, for the same reasons which moved Colonel Lindsay, marched on April 2d from Pilaklakaha and encamped about sixteen miles from Fort Brooke, reporting to General Scott.

The whole army being now concentrated at or near Fort Brooke, the plan for a new campaign was discussed. They had found but small parties of the Indians in the cove or swamp region, and it was thought that they had gone to the southern part of the Florida peninsula and concealed themselves in the Everglades.

General Scott ordered Colonel Smith, of the Louisiana volunteers, to proceed by water to Charlotte Harbor and move north, while Colonel Goodwyn, with the South Carolina mounted men, was ordered to the lake at the head of Pease's Creek for the purpose of driving the Indians down. Having destroyed a large unoccupied Indian village on the left bank of that stream, and finding no Indians, the command returned to Hillsboro River and joined the left wing.

The Louisiana troops left Fort Brooke on April

MOVEMENT TO FORT DRANE.

10th and arrived at Pease's Creek on the 17th. They moved forward at once, but the weather was oppressive and the men were broken down by previous marches; many of them being destitute of shoes and other clothing, it was found necessary to return to camp. Out of over seven hundred Louisiana troops who had volunteered in January and entered the field the beginning of the next month, but one hundred and thirty were now left fit for duty. With these, however, and a small detachment of marines from the United States vessels in that vicinity, Colonel Smith determined to proceed. He embarked with one half of his command in canoes, the others proceeding by land. Meeting no Indians, he returned to Fort Brooke on April 27th, when the Louisiana troops were ordered to New Orleans to be mustered out of service. Colonel Smith proceeded to St. Mark's and reported to General Scott.

The right wing having remained at Tampa Bay from April 5th to the 13th, General Scott issued orders to General Clinch to move toward Fort Drane, and, after relieving Major Cooper, to co-operate with Colonel Lindsay, who had left Fort Brooke about the same time, for the purpose of penetrating the cove in a different direction from that pursued by the right wing on its march to Tampa, and to penetrate the forks of the Ouithlacoochee.

While Colonel Lindsay was engaged in constructing a defensive work on the military road near Big Ouithlacoochee, General Clinch encamped near Fort Cooper and dispatched some cavalry under Captain Malone to relieve the garrison, with instructions that should he meet the enemy, he was to advise General Clinch at once. When about three miles distant from the main body the Indians opened fire and at once retreated. The hammock was penetrated and searched, but no Indians were found.

Major Cooper was attacked by a large body of Indians and besieged for thirteen days. His loss was one man killed and twenty wounded. The Indians not having been found in any large numbers, the two wings separated, the center returning to Fort Brooke and the right to Fort King, where they arrived April 25th.

After the arrival of Colonel Goodwyn's mounted regiment, the left wing, accompanied by General Scott, took up line of march on the 18th for Volusia. A small party of Indians was encountered, but they fled and secreted themselves in a hammock. General Eustis's command arrived at Volusia on the evening of the 25th, and on the 28th all the volunteers from South Carolina marched to St. Augustine and were mustered out. On the arrival of Colonel Lindsay at Fort Brooke he was directed by General Scott to relieve the garrison at Fort Alabama, and disband the Alabama volunteers, leaving only regulars there.

They were attacked by the Indians with a loss of four killed and nineteen wounded. General Scott, accompanied by Colonel Gadsden, Captain Augustus Canfield, and Lieutenant Johnson, with a detachment of seventeen men, embarked in a steamboat at Volusia for the purpose of penetrating by the St. John's River the south part of the peninsula and selecting a site nearer to the seat of war as a depot for supplies. They proceeded to the head of Lake Monroe, but the boat was unable to pass the bar and they were compelled to return.

In his report of April 30th General Scott says:

"To end this war, I am now persuaded that not less than three thousand troops are indispensable—two thousand four hundred infantry and six hundred horse, the country to be occupied and scoured requiring that number." He further recommended that two or three steamers with a light draught of water, and fifty or sixty barges capable of carrying from ten to fifteen men each, be employed, but did not ask for the control of the operations he recommended, saying it was an honor he would neither solicit nor decline.

CHAPTER VII.

Scott prefers complaint against General Jesup—Court of inquiry ordered by the President—Scott fully exonerated by the court—Complaints of citizens—Difficulties of the campaign—Speech in Congress of Hon. Richard Biddle—Scott declines an invitation to a dinner in New York city—Resolutions of the subscribers—Scott is ordered to take charge of and remove the Cherokee Indians—Orders issued to troops and address to the Indians—Origin of the Cherokee Indian troubles—Collision threatened between Maine and New Brunswick, and Scott sent there—Correspondence with Lieutenant-Governor Harvey—Seizure of Navy Island by Van Rensselaer—Governor Marcy.

GENERAL SCOTT had, a short time previous to the events just narrated, complained to the War Department of disobedience of orders on the part of General Jesup, who had written a letter to the Globe newspaper in Washington charging that Scott's conduct had been destructive of the best interests of the country. Mr. Francis P. Blair, the editor to whom the letter was addressed, showed it to President Jackson, who indorsed on it an order to the Secretary of War to recall General Scott to Washington, and that an inquiry be held as to his delay in prosecuting the Creek War and the failure of the Florida campaign. On Scott's arrival in Washington he asked for a court of inquiry, which was ordered on October 3d, composed of Major-General

Alexander Macomb and Brigadier-Generals Henry Atkinson and Hugh Brady, with Colonel Cooper, General Macomb's aid-de-camp, as judge advocate. The court assembled at Frederick, Md., and was delayed some time by the absence of witnesses. General Scott addressed the court in his own defense.

The finding was unanimous that the plan of the Seminole campaign was well devised, and prosecuted with energy, steadiness, and ability; and as to the Creek campaign, the court decided that the plan of the campaign as adopted by General Scott was well calculated to lead to successful results, and that it was prosecuted by him, as far as practicable, with zeal and ability until he was recalled from the command. This was not only a full vindication, but a compliment to him expressed in the broadest sense.

He now addressed a letter to Secretary of War Joel R. Poinsett, asking the immediate direction of affairs in Florida, as this was a part of the geographical division to which he had been assigned, and a large number of the troops of his command had been ordered there; and that he was senior in rank to General Jesup, then commanding there. The members of Congress from his native State made a unanimous appeal to the Secretary of War seconding his application, but the application was denied.

Some citizens of Florida made complaints of the nonsuccess of the army, and severely censured General Scott. In fact, complaints of this nature were made against every officer who commanded in Florida, except General Zachary Taylor. It has been seen that the court of inquiry fully vindicated General Scott's course in the management of the war in Florida. The campaign, however, vindicated itself.

Considering the scarcity of all the means at hand, it is remarkable how much was accomplished with so little loss of life.

When General Scott undertook this campaign Florida was a *terra incognita*. The greater part of it had scarcely been visited by the whites, and very little was known of the settlements of the Seminoles. They were known by their approaches to the white settlements, and when the war broke out by their plunders and devastations. It was not known where their hiding places were, and this could only be determined by pursuing them. At the time of General Scott's assignment to the command all the information tended to locating them on the waters of the Ouithlacoochee and the St. John's Rivers; and accordingly against this portion of the country the movement of the army was directed.

It was not only the want of ordnance, clothing, and subsistence, but the geographical peculiarity of Florida—with its marshes, thickets, hammocks, everglades, and impenetrable swamps—that made this campaign almost fruitless, and which for years baffled all efforts of the Government to subdue this small but brave and desperate tribe of Indians.

In Congress General Scott's campaign in Florida was defended by some of the ablest men in the country. Richard Biddle, of Pennsylvania, in 1837, when the House of Representatives was engaged in a debate on appropriations for carrying on the war in Florida, said: " It would be recollected by all that after the war in Florida had assumed a formidable aspect Major-General Scott was called to the command. An officer of his rank and standing was not likely to seek a service in which, amid infinite toil and vexation, there would be no opportunity for the display of military talent on a scale at all commensurate with that in which his past fame had been acquired. Yet he entered on it with the alacrity, zeal, and devotion to duty by which he had ever been distinguished. . . .

"When the late General Brown, writing from the field of Chippewa, said that General Scott merited the highest praises which a grateful country could bestow, was there a single bosom throughout the wide republic that did not respond to the sentiment? I, for one at least, can never forget the thrill of enthusiasm, boy as I then was, which mingled with my own devout thankfulness to God that the cloud which seemed to have settled on our arms was at length dispelled. On that plain it was established that Americans could be trained to meet and to beat in the open field, without breastworks, the regulars of Britain. . . .

"Sir, the result of that day was due not merely to the gallantry of General Scott upon the field. It must in part be ascribed to the patient, anxious, and indefatigable drudgery, the consummate skill as a tactician, with which he labored night and day, at the camp near Buffalo, to prepare his brigade for the career on which it was about to enter. After a brief interval he again led that brigade to the glorious victory of Bridgewater. He bears now upon his body the wounds of that day. It had ever been the characteristic of this officer to seek the post of danger—not to have it thrust upon him. In the years preceding that to which I have specially referred—in 1812 and 1813—the eminent services he rendered were in the positions which properly belonged to others, but into which he was led by irrepressible ardor and jealousy of honor.

"Since the peace with Great Britain the talents of General Scott have ever been at the command of his country. His pen and his sword have alike been put in requisition to meet the varied exigencies of the service. When the difficulties with the Western Indians swelled into importance, General Scott was dispatched to the scene of hostility. There rose up before him then, in the ravages of a frightful pestilence, a form of danger infinitely more appalling than the perils of the field. How he bore himself in this emergency, how faithfully he became the nurse and the physician of those from whom terror and loathing had driven all other aid, can not be forgotten by a just and grateful country. . . .

"Mr. Chairman, I believe that a signal atonement to General Scott will one day be extorted from the justice of the House. We owe it to him; but we owe it still more to the country. What officer can feel secure in the face of that great example of triumphant injustice? Who can place before himself the anticipation of establishing higher claims upon the gratitude of the country than General Scott? Yet he was sacrificed. His past services went for nothing. Sir, you may raise new regiments and issue new commissions, but you can not without such atonement restore the high moral tone which befits the depositories of the national honor. I fondly wish that the highest and lowest in the country's service might be taught to regard this House as the jealous guardian of his rights, against caprice, or fanaticism, or outrage from whatever quarter. I would have him know that in running up the national flag at the very moment our daily labors commence, we do not go through an idle form. On whatever distant service he may be sent—whether urging his way amid tumbling icebergs toward the pole, or fainting in the unwholesome heat of Florida—I would enable him as he looks up to that flag to gather hope and strength. It should impart to him a proud feeling of confidence and security. He should know that the same emblem of majesty and justice floats over the council of the nation, and that in its untarnished luster we have all a common interest and a common sympathy. Then, sir, and not before, will you have an army or a navy worthy to sustain and to perpetuate the glory of former days."

Soon after the decision of the court of inquiry exonerating him from blame or censure General Scott was tendered a public dinner in New York from leading members of both political parties. He accepted the invitation, but it was subsequently postponed until about the middle of May, and before that time it was altogether declined, for reasons expressed in a note of which a copy follows:

"GENTLEMEN: Early last month I accepted the invitation to a public dinner which you and other friends did me the honor to tender me. In a few days the embarrassments of this great emporium became such that I begged the compliment might be indefinitely postponed. You, however, were so kind as to hold me to my engagement, and to appoint a day for the meeting, which is now near at hand. In the meantime the difficulties in the commercial world have gone on augmenting, and many of my friends, here and elsewhere, have been whelmed under the general calamity of the times. Feeling deeply for the losses and anxieties of all, no public honor could now be enjoyed by me. I must therefore, under the circumstances, positively but most respectfully withdraw my acceptance of your invitation.

"I have the honor to remain, gentlemen, with the greatest esteem, your friend and servant,

"WINFIELD SCOTT."

The subscribers to the dinner, on receipt of General Scott's letter, called a meeting, Cornelius W. Lawrence in the chair, and unanimously adopted the resolutions which follow:

"*Resolved*, That in the decision of General Scott to withdraw, for the reasons assigned, his acceptance of the public dinner designed to testify to him our high appreciation both of his private and public character, we find new evidence of his sympathy with all that regards the public welfare, and of his habitual oblivion of self where the feelings and interests of others are concerned.

"*Resolved*, That we rejoice with the joy of friends in the result, so honorable to General Scott, of the recent court of inquiry instituted to investigate his military conduct as commander in chief in Alabama and Florida, and that the President of the United States (Mr. Van Buren), in approving its proceedings, acted in gratifying unison with the general sentiments of the nation."

General Scott also received invitations from Richmond, Va., and Elizabeth, N. J., both of which places had been his former homes.

The Florida War was brought to a close by the defeat of the Indians by Colonel Zachary Taylor, in the decisive battle of Okechobee, for which he received the brevet of Brigadier General, and in 1838 was appointed to the chief command in Florida. Taylor was succeeded by Brigadier-General Armistead, and in 1842 General Worth succeeded to the command and made a treaty with Sam Jones and Billy Bowlegs, allowing them to remain and possess a large tract of land.

In the spring of 1836 General Scott was ordered to take charge of and superintend the removal of the Cherokee Indians to the reservation which had been set apart for them by treaty west of the Mississippi River. Great opposition to removal was expected from the Indians, and much fear felt by the inhabitants contiguous to their settlements. General Scott, however, by his kindness and generosity, won the confidence of the Indians, and was not compelled to resort to any act of violence. Twenty-four thousand five hundred and ninety-four were removed, two hundred and thirty-six having lost their lives on the steamboat Monmouth. Only seven hundred and forty-four remained east of the Mississippi River. The Cherokees occupied territory in the States of Georgia, North Carolina, Alabama, and Tennessee. Many of their leaders were well educated and were men of ability, and some of them were wealthy, owning fine farms and negro slaves. General Scott in his Memoirs says: "The North Carolinians and Tennesseeans were kindly disposed toward their red brethren. The Alabamians much less so. The great difficulty was with the Georgians (more than half the army), between whom and the Cherokees there had been feuds and wars for many generations. The reciprocal hatred of the two races was probably never surpassed. Almost every Georgian on leaving home, as well as after arrival at New Echota—the center of the most populous district of the Indian Territory—vowed never to return without having killed at least one Indian."

General Scott arrived at the Cherokee agency, a small village on the Hiawassee River in Tennessee, in the early part of May, 1838. He published and circulated two addresses—one to the troops and the other to the Indians—but had them circulated together.

Following is the address to the troops:

"HEADQUARTERS, EASTERN DIVISION,
"CHEROKEE AGENCY, *May 17, 1838.*

"Considering the number and temper of the mass to be removed, together with the extent and fastnesses of the country occupied, it will readily occur that simple indiscretions, acts of harshness, and cruelty on the part of our troops may lead, step by step, to delays, to impatience, and exasperation, and in the end to a general war and carnage—a result in the case of these particular Indians, utterly abhorrent to the generous sympathies of the whole American people. Every possible kindness compatible with the necessity of removal must therefore be shown by the troops; and if in the ranks a despicable individual should be found capable of inflicting a wanton injury or insult on any Cherokee man, woman, or child, it is hereby made the special duty of the nearest good officer or man instantly to interpose, and to seize and consign the guilty wretch to the severest penalty of the laws. The major general is fully persuaded that this injunction will not be neglected by the brave men under his command, who can not be otherwise than jealous of their own honor and that of their country.

"By early and persevering acts of kindness and humanity, it is impossible to doubt that the Indians will soon be induced to confide in the army, and, instead of fleeing to the mountains and forests, flock to us for food and clothing. If, however, through false apprehensions, individuals or a party here and there should seek to hide themselves, they must be pursued and invited to surrender, but not fired upon, unless they should make a stand to resist. Even in such cases mild remedies may sometimes better succeed than violence; and it can not be doubted, if we get possession of the women and children first, or first capture the men, that in either case the outstanding members of the same families will readily come in on the assurance of forgiveness and kind treatment.

"Every captured man, as well as those who surrender themselves, must be disarmed, with the assurance that their weapons will be carefully preserved and restored at or beyond the Mississippi. In either case the men will be guarded and escorted, except it may be where their women and children are safely secured as hostages; but in general, families in our possession will not be separated, unless it be to send men as runners to invite others to come in.

"It may happen that Indians will be found too sick, in the opinion of the nearest surgeon, to be removed to one of the depots indicated above. In every such case one or more of the family or the friends of the sick person will be left in attendance, with ample subsistence and remedies, and the remainder of the family removed by the troops. Infants, superannuated persons, lunatics, and women in helpless condition, will all, in the removal, require peculiar attention, which the brave and humane will seek to adapt to the necessities of the several cases."

Following is the address to the Indians:

"*Major-General Scott, of the United States Army, sends to the Cherokee people remaining in North Carolina, Georgia, Tennessee, and Alabama this*

" ADDRESS.

" CHEROKEES: The President of the United States has sent me with a powerful army to cause you, in obedience of the treaty of 1835, to join that part of your people who are already established in prosperity on the other side of the Mississippi. Unhappily, the two years which were allowed for the purpose you have suffered to pass away without following and without making any preparation to follow, and now, or by the time that this solemn address shall reach your distant settlements, the emigration must be commenced in haste, but, I hope, without disorder. I have no power by granting a further delay to correct the error that you have committed. The full moon of May is already on the wane, and before another shall have passed away every Cherokee man, woman, and child in those States must be in motion to join their brethren in the far West.

" My friends, this is no sudden determination on the part of the President, whom you and I must now obey. By the treaty the emigration was to have been completed on or before the 23d of this month, and the President has constantly kept you warned during the two years allowed, through all his officers and agents in this country, that the treaty would be enforced.

"I am come to carry out that determination. My troops already occupy many positions in the country that you are to abandon, and thousands and thousands are approaching from every quarter to render assistance and escape alike hopeless. All those troops, regular and militia, are your friends. Receive them, and confide in them as such. Obey them when they tell you that you can remain no longer in this country. Soldiers are as kind-hearted as brave, and the desire of every one of us is to execute our painful duty in mercy. We are commanded by the President to act toward you in that spirit, and such is also the wish of the whole people of America.

"Chiefs, headmen, and warriors, will you then by resistance compel us to resort to arms? God forbid! Or will you by flight seek to hide yourselves in mountains and forests, and thus oblige us to hunt you down? Remember, that in pursuit it may be impossible to avoid conflicts. The blood of the white man or the blood of the red man may be spilt, and if spilt, however accidentally, it may be impossible for the discreet and humane among you or among us to prevent a general war and carnage. Think of this, my Cherokee brethren! I am an old warrior, and have been present at many a scene of slaughter; but spare me, I beseech you, the horror of witnessing the destruction of the Cherokees.

"Do not, I invite you, even wait for the close approach of the troops; but make such preparations for emigration as you can, and hasten to this place, to Ross's Landing, or to Gunter's Landing, where you will be received in kindness by officers selected for the purpose. You will find food for all, and clothing for the destitute, at either of those places, and thence at your ease and in comfort be transported to your new homes according to the terms of the treaty.

"This is the address of a warrior to warriors. May his entreaties be kindly received, and may the God of both prosper the Americans and Cherokees, and preserve them long in peace and friendship with each other.   WINFIELD SCOTT."

There was some delay in bringing in the mountain Indians of North Carolina, but the Indians of Tennessee and Alabama were readily collected for emigration. General Scott remained with the Georgians, and followed up his printed addresses by suggestions which proved to be invaluable.

In a short time the Indians, excepting a few parties, were collected at the place of rendezvous. The camp selected was twelve miles in length, with a breadth of four miles. It was well shaded by large forest trees, and had a large number of springs furnishing an abundance of the best of water.

The sick were placed in hospitals, and attended by good physicians and furnished with everything necessary for their comfort. General Scott rode through the camps daily, and saw that every attention was given to the Indians which they required, and he made inquiries and gave special attention to the care of the sick and to the women and children. At length he placed the matter of the emigration of the Indians in the hands of the Cherokee authorities, having won the entire confidence and regard of the Indians, and he ordered all of the volunteers to their homes, except one company which he retained as a police force, and one regiment of regulars which it was thought necessary to retain to meet any unforeseen contingencies that might arise. Two other regular regiments were ordered off, one to Florida and the other to the Canada frontier. The company of volunteers retained was from Tennessee, and of it General Scott said: "The company of volunteers (Tennesseeans) were a body of respectable citizens, and under their judicious commander, Captain Robertson, of great value as a police force." The Cherokees were at this time receiving large sums of money from the Government in the way of damages and indemnities, and a number of gamblers and confidence men sought to enter their camps. They were, however, kept out by the vigilance of the Tennessee company.

In October the movement west began. General Scott accompanied them to the junction of the Ohio and Mississippi Rivers. General Scott gives credit for services and aid rendered him to his acting inspector general, Major Matthew Mountjoy Payne; Captain Robert Anderson, acting adjutant general (later the commander of Fort Sumter, and a brigadier general); Lieutenant Erastus Darwin Keyes, aid-de-camp, afterward major general, United States volunteers; Lieutenant Francis Taylor, commissary; Captains Page and Abner Reviere Hetzel, quartermasters; Lieutenant Henry L. Scott, Fourth Infantry, then aid-de-camp and inspector general; Major H. B. Shaw, aid-de-camp, Tennessee volunteers; Colonel William Lindsay, Second Artillery;

Colonel William S. Foster, Fourth Infantry; and Colonel Ichabod Bennett Crane, First Artillery. Generals Worth and Floyd rendered important service in this campaign, and their names should not be omitted.

It may be necessary, for a better understanding of the Cherokee Indian difficulties, to add something more to what has been written. The chief troubles which had arisen were in Georgia, and many complications arose between the Indians and the whites. In a case decided by the Supreme Court of the United States, the opinion being rendered by Chief-Justice John Marshall, the status of these Indians was thus defined: "Their relation is that of a nation claiming and receiving the protection of one more powerful; not that of individuals abandoning their national character and submitting as subjects to the laws of a master."

Regarding the acts of Congress to regulate trade with the Indians the Chief Justice said: "All these acts, and especially that of 1802, which is still in force, manifestly consider the several Indian nations as distinct political communities, having territorial boundaries, within which their authority is exclusive, and having a right to all the lands within those boundaries, which is not only acknowledged but guaranteed by the United States." By one of the treaties made by the United States Government with this tribe of Indians, it was enacted and agreed that "the United States solemnly guarantee to the Cherokee nation all their lands not hereby ceded," and, "that the Cherokee nation may be led to a greater degree of civilization, and to become herdsmen and cultivators, instead of remaining in a state of hunting, the United States will from time to time furnish

CAUSE OF THE TROUBLES IN GEORGIA. 137

gratuitously the said nation with useful instruments of husbandry." Acting under this treaty, a greater portion of the Cherokees had become both cultivators and herdsmen, and rivaled their white neighbors in both.

The trouble which arose in Georgia was from the fact that she claimed the right to extend her criminal jurisdiction over these Indians, and that the United States was bound to extinguish the Indian titles within her borders. This claim of Georgia, persistently pressed, caused the United States Government in 1802 to agree to purchase the Indian lands, and remove them to some other territory. The Indians resisted this action on the faith of treaties. Eventually a treaty was made with a portion of the Cherokees by which they were to relinquish their lands and accept lands across the Mississippi River. Many of the Indians resisted and never ratified this treaty, yet the Government insisted upon carrying out the treaty. General Scott received his orders on April 10, 1838, and first established his headquarters at a small village called Calhoun, on the Hiawassee River, in East Tennessee. Colonel Lindsay, an officer of merit and who enjoyed the full confidence of General Scott, was in immediate command of that territory, had established posts in many of the settlements, and had arranged to have the mountain passes well guarded.

Referring to these matters, the National Intelligencer of September 27, 1838, said: "The manner in which this gallant officer [Scott] has acquitted himself within the last year upon the Canada frontier, and lately among the Cherokees, has excited the universal admiration and gratitude of the whole nation. Owing to his great popularity in the North, his thorough knowledge of the laws of his own country, as well as of those which govern nations, united to his discretion, his great tact and experience, he has saved the country from a ruinous war with Great Britain. And by his masterly skill and energy among the Cherokees, united to his noble generosity and humanity, he has not only effected what everybody supposed could not be done without the most heartrending scenes of butchery and bloodshed, but he has effected it by obtaining the esteem and confidence of the poor Cherokees themselves. They look upon him as a benefactor and friend, and one who has saved them from entire destruction. All the Cherokees were collected for emigration without bloodshed or violence, and all would have been on their way to the West before the middle of July, had not humanity induced General Scott to stop the movement until the 1st of September. Three thousand had been sent off in the first half of June by the superintendent, before the general took upon himself the responsibility of stopping the emigration, from feelings which must do everlasting honor to his heart. An approval of his course had been sent on by the War Department, before his report giving information that he had stopped the emigration had reached the seat of Government. In the early part of January last the President had asked Congress for enlarged powers, to enable him to maintain our neutral obligations to England—that is, to tranquilize the Canadian frontiers. Before the bill passed Congress, General Scott had finished the work and effected all its objects. These, too, he effected by flying from one end of the frontier to the other in the dead of winter, and during the severest and coldest period of it. He returns to Washington, and is immediately ordered to the Cherokee nation, to take charge of the very difficult and hazardous task to his own fame of removing those savages from their native land. Some of his best friends regretted most sincerely that he had been ordered on this service, and, knowing the disposition of the world to cavil and complain without cause, had great apprehension that he would lose a portion of the popularity he had acquired by his distinguished success on the Canadian frontier. But behold the manner in which this last work has been performed! There is so much of noble generosity of character about Scott, independent of his skill and bravery as a soldier, that his life has really been one of romantic beauty and interest."

It was General Scott's intention to accompany the Indian emigration farther west, but receiving information that the Canadian insurgents were making renewed attempts on the Canadas, he was directed to proceed at once to that frontier.

Passing through the States of Kentucky and Ohio, accompanied by Captain Robert Anderson, he called upon their respective governors and arranged for the calling out of volunteers should they be needed, and also gave proper instructions to the United States marshals and district attorneys for such duties as they might be called upon to perform. He passed on rapidly to Cleveland, Sandusky, and Detroit, and met great assemblages of excited citizens, and, by his appeals and reasoning with them, prevailed upon them to desist from any acts in violation of the neutrality with Great Britain. Pending these important services, he learned of the trouble which had arisen between the State of Maine and the British colony or province of New Brunswick, and at once made haste for Washington. On his arrival at the capital, after reporting to the President, he was called before the committees on foreign affairs of both Houses of Congress, before whom he urged and succeeded in securing the passage of two bills—one authorizing the President to call out the militia for six months and to accept the service of fifty thousand volunteers, and the other to place to his credit ten millions of dollars. On taking leave of the President he said to him: "Mr. President, if you want war, I need only look on in silence. The Maine people will make it for you fast and hot enough. I know them. But if peace be your wish, I can give no assurance of success. The difficulties in its way will be formidable." The President replied, "Peace with honor"; and the general, who fully reciprocated the President's feeling, took his leave, accompanied by Captain Robert Anderson and Lieutenant E. D. Keyes, his aid-de-camp. He left with general instructions, but in certain events he was to act on his own judgment without restriction. Arriving in Boston, he met Governor Edward Everett, and arranged for calling out the militia and accepting volunteers if needed.

Governor Everett introduced him to his executive council with the following address: "General, I take great pleasure in introducing you to the members of the Executive Council of Massachusetts. I need not say that you are already known to them by reputation. They are familiar with your fame as it is recorded in some of the arduous and honorable fields of the country's struggles. We rejoice in meeting you on this occasion. Charged as you are with a most momentous mission by the President of the United

States, we are sure you are intrusted with a duty most grateful to your feelings—that of averting an appeal to arms. We place unlimited reliance on your spirit, energy, and discretion. Should you unhappily fail in your efforts, under the instructions of the President, to restore harmony, we know that you are equally prepared for a still more responsible duty. Should that unhappy event occur, I beg you to depend on the firm support of Massachusetts." He was then given a reception by the Legislature, and received on its behalf by Robert C. Winthrop.

From Boston he proceeded at once to Portland, where he found the people greatly excited, and demanding the immediate seizure and occupation of the disputed territory. At the capital, Augusta, where he next proceeded, he found the same excitement with the same demands. The Legislature was in session, and a large majority of its members were for war. The strip of disputed land was valuable chiefly for ship timber. Some British subjects had entered the territory and cut some of the timber, and the Governor of Maine sent an agent with a posse to drive them off. The British seized and imprisoned the agent, and much angry correspondence followed between the authorities of both sides.

General Scott soon determined that the only mode of settlement was to prohibit or have an agreement on both sides to leave the territory unoccupied by either party until the matters in dispute could be arranged between the governments of the United States and Great Britain, taking the matter out of the jurisdiction of the State of Maine and the province of New Brunswick. Previous to Scott's arrival in Maine the Legislature of that State had passed an act placing eight hundred thousand dollars at the disposal of the Governor and authorizing the calling out of eight thousand troops. Some of these troops had been organized and moved near the disputed territory, and others were held ready to move when ordered. British troops, both regulars and militia, had also been moved forward. Everything indicated a war. On February 27, 1839, President Van Buren had sent a message to Congress transmitting various documents received from the Governor of Maine, and a copy of a memorandum signed by the Secretary of State of the United States and the British Minister to the United States, which, it was hoped, would prevent a collision of arms. Mr. H. B. Fox, the British Minister, had acted without specific authority from his Government, and the memorandum therefore had only the force of a recommendation. All correspondence had for some time ceased between the governors of Maine and New Brunswick.

The Governor of New Brunswick, John Harvey, had been an adjutant general of one of the armies of Canada in the campaign of 1813, and was well known to General Scott. Scott, it will be remembered, was an adjutant general in this campaign, and he and Colonel Harvey had frequent correspondence, and it was so conducted as to create a feeling of respect on both sides. At one time in the campaign mentioned, when Scott was on a reconnoitering expedition, his party came upon Harvey, and a gun in the hands of a soldier near Scott was leveled on him. Scott caught the gun, and said, "Hold! he is our prisoner," but Colonel Harvey made a rapid turn and escaped.

On General Scott's arrival in Maine he had with

him a private letter from Sir John Harvey, the Colonel Harvey just mentioned, then Governor General of New Brunswick. It is proper to mention here, as additional reason for good feeling between General Scott and Sir John Harvey, that at one time in the War of 1813 an American soldier under Scott's command had come into possession of the uniform coat of a British staff officer, and in one of the pockets was found the miniature of a young lady. The portmanteau from which the coat and miniature were taken was marked "Lieutenant-Colonel Harvey." Scott purchased these articles from the soldier and sent them to Colonel Harvey. The picture was that of his young bride, then in England.

Governor Fairfield, of Maine, had on March 12th sent a message to the Legislature objecting to the terms of the memorandum, but recommending that, when fully satisfied that the Lieutenant Governor of New Brunswick had abandoned all idea of occupying the disputed territory with a military force, or of attempting the expulsion of citizens of Maine, he [the Governor] be authorized to withdraw the military force, leaving the land agent with a posse of armed or unarmed men, as the case might require, sufficient to drive out or arrest trespassers. The Legislature on March 20th passed resolutions in accordance with these recommendations. The message of the Governor of Maine and the resolutions of the Legislature required the lieutentant governor to make the advance.

General Scott, after the action of the Legislature above mentioned, sent a reply to Harvey's private letter, which he had held unanswered so long. This elicited a friendly reply, and other letters of the same character quickly followed on either side. A line of couriers was established between them to facilitate correspondence. Governor Harvey took the first step, and made the concessions which were necessary to appease the authorities of Maine, but the Governor did not feel authorized to withdraw the troops from the disputed territory unless authorized by the Legislature. General Scott mingled freely with members of the Legislature, urging pacific measures, and on March 20th resolutions were passed; and Scott having his memorandum with Sir John Harvey with all concessions to restore tranquillity, the Governor of Maine added his approval, and the question was transferred to the authorities of the United States and Great Britain, which resulted in a satisfactory settlement to both nations of this unhappy affair.

An uprising, confined chiefly to the French inhabitants of Upper Canada, occurred in 1837, in which they demanded a separation from the British Government, and they enlisted many sympathizers among citizens of the United States, especially among those living on the Canadian boundary. Organizations of sympathizers with the Canadians were secretly formed by American citizens to such an extent that the President of the United States issued a proclamation enjoining its citizens to observe neutrality. This did not quiet the excitement, but rather tended to increase it. Matters were brought to a crisis by the action of a certain Van Rensselaer, who had been dismissed from the Military Academy at West Point, and who styled himself "Colonel" Van Rensselaer. He organized a party of Americans reckless like himself, and took forcible possession of a small Brit-

THE AFFAIR OF THE CAROLINE. 145

ish island opposite to Fort Schlosser, on the American side, and known as Navy Island. This island was a short distance above the falls of Niagara. Young Van Rensselaer engaged a small steamboat called the Caroline to ferry parties from Navy Island, which he occupied, to Schlosser on the American shore.

The first night on which the Caroline began her voyages the British fitted out an expedition to capture her. Instead of making a descent on Navy Island within British territory, they boarded the steamer at Schlosser, on the American side, and thus violated our territory. The boat at the time of this invasion was filled with people, many of whom were there for idle curiosity, including a number of boys. In the *mêlée* of capture one American citizen was killed and several others wounded. They cut the boat from its moorings, set it on fire, and it drifted down the cataract. It was reported and generally believed that when the vessel went over the cataract it had a small number of wounded Americans on board.

The publication of this affair created the greatest excitement from one end of the country to the other. This occurred on December 29, 1837, but the news did not reach Washington until January 4th. On the evening of that day General Scott was to dine with President Van Buren and a number of other distinguished gentlemen. The entire party had arrived, but the President failed to appear. After a time he came in and spoke inaudibly to Henry Clay, one of the guests, and then said to General Scott: "Blood has been shed; you must go with all speed to the Niagara frontier. The Secretary of War is now engaged in making out your instructions." General Scott left at once, and passing through Albany, met William L. Marcy, the Governor of New York, who with his adjutant general (McDonald) accompanied him to the scene of the troubles. The United States troops at this time were all either in Florida or on the Western frontiers. General Scott, in passing through New York, had ordered some small detachments of army recruits to follow him. Governor Marcy was with him ready to answer his requisitions for militia, and he had the aid of the officers commanding on Lake Erie and the Detroit frontier and on the Niagara, Lake Ontario, and St. Lawrence. All United States marshals and other civil officers of the Government were ordered to support and aid him. He passed from one place to another, going where his services could be needed, exhorting the people to observe the neutrality proclamation of the President; and where he found them obstinate and determined, he notified them in terms which could not be mistaken that any attempt to violate this proclamation would be met by resistance from the Government, which would promptly overpower them.

Pending these troubles, a steamer called the Barcelona was taken from the harbor of Buffalo in January, 1838, and passed down the river, with a view to aid the insurgents on Navy Island. Scott, on learning of this, sent an agent who made terms to employ the Barcelona for the service of the Government. The vessel then proceeded back to Buffalo, where it was intended to use her on Lake Erie; but the Canadian authorities had determined to destroy her. As the vessel passed near Grand Island, within the jurisdiction of the United States, some armed British schooners had taken position, aided by land batteries, to open fire on her. This was on January 16th. General Scott and Governor Marcy stood on the river bank watching events. Batteries on the American side were put in preparation to return the fire of the British.

The day before the event just mentioned, Scott had written and dispatched a note "To the Commanding Officer of the Armed British Vessels in the Niagara":

"HEADQUARTERS, EASTERN DIVISION, U. S. ARMY,
"TWO MILES BELOW BLACK ROCK, *January 15, 1838.*

"SIR: With his Excellency, Governor Marcy, of New York, who has troops at hand, we are here to enforce the neutrality of the United States and to protect our own soil or waters from violation. The proper civil officers are also present to arrest, if practicable, the leaders of the expedition on foot against Upper Canada. Under these circumstances, it gives me pain to perceive the armed vessels mentioned, anchored in our waters, with the probable intention to fire upon that expedition moving in the same waters. Unless the expedition should first attack—in which case we shall interfere—we shall be obliged to consider a discharge of shot or shell from or into our waters, from the armed schooners of her Majesty, as an act seriously compromising the neutrality of the two nations. I hope, therefore, that no such unpleasant incident may occur.

"I have the honor to remain, etc.

"WINFIELD SCOTT."

The next morning, January 16th, the same information was given by General Scott to a British officer who called on him at his quarters. The Barcelona moved up the river, and Scott had his cannon pointed and his matches in readiness for firing. Scott stood on the highest point in full uniform and in view of the other shore. The vessel passed up unmolested, and doubtless by this act of Scott a war was averted.

In the meantime Van Rensselaer with his adherents had evacuated Navy Island and landed some miles below, where they were arrested by General Scott's orders. Thus ended a disturbance which might have resulted in war, and it can not be gainsaid that its peaceful settlement was due to the wisdom, firmness, and prudence of General Scott.

CHAPTER VIII.

Annexation of Texas—Causes that led to annexation—Message of the President—General Scott's letters regarding William Henry Harrison—Efforts to reduce General Scott's pay—Letter to T. P. Atkinson on the slavery question—Battle of Palo Alto, and of Resaca de la Palma, Monterey, and Buena Vista—"The hasty plate of soup"—Scott's opinion of General Taylor—Scott ordered to Mexico—Proposal to revive the grade of lieutenant general, and to appoint Thomas H. Benton—Scott reaches the Brazos Santiago—Confidential dispatch from Scott to Taylor—Co-operation of the navy—Letters to the Secretary of War as to places of rendezvous—Arrival and landing at Vera Cruz, and its investment, siege, and capture—Letter to foreign consuls—Terms of surrender—Orders of General Scott after the surrender.

THE Congress of the United States, on February 27, 1845, passed joint resolutions providing for the annexation of Texas, and they were approved by President Tyler on the 1st of March. A convention was called by President Jones, of Texas, to meet on the 4th of the succeeding July, to consider the matter of annexation to the United States. The convention ratified the proposal, and prepared a constitution for Texas as a State in the American Union. The question of annexation was submitted to a vote of the people of Texas and ratified by a large majority. On December 29th following, a joint resolution of the Congress of the United States was passed, which declared Texas admitted as a State into the Union.

It may be interesting to take a retrospective view of the causes, or rather the means, by which this important measure was brought about.

In the winter of 1842-'43 there appeared in a newspaper published at Baltimore a letter of Mr. Thomas W. Gilmer, a member of Congress from Virginia, urging the annexation of Texas. He argued among other things that the British Government had designs on Texas; that it proposed a political and military domination of the country, with a view to the abolition of slavery. At this time Texas and Mexico were at war. It was at once charged by the opponents of the scheme of annexation that Mr. Gilmer, who was known as the close political friend of Mr. John C. Calhoun, was simply acting as the mouthpiece of the latter. It will be remembered by those who are conversant with the proceedings of Congress that Mr. Calhoun, in the Senate in 1836, had offered some resolutions looking to the annexation of Texas. Mr. Webster, who was known as opposed to the measure, was the only member of President Harrison's Cabinet who remained with President Tyler. He resigned his portfolio as Secretary of State, and was succeeded by Mr. Hugh S. Legaré, of South Carolina, who, dying very soon after his appointment, was succeeded by Mr. Abel P. Upshur, of Virginia. Both of the latter named were known friends of the annexation scheme. There appeared not long after the publication of the Gilmer letter, in the Richmond Enquirer, a letter from General Andrew Jackson to Mr. Brown, in reply to a letter of Mr. Brown, in which he indorsed a copy of Mr. Gilmer's letter and asking General Jackson's views on the subject. General Jackson's reply was a thorough and hearty approval of the proposed immediate annexation of Texas. General Jackson's letter was dated from the Hermitage, his residence near Nashville, Tenn., March 12, 1843. The letter of General Jackson produced a profound effect throughout the country. Although out of office, old, and in the retirement of private life, he exercised more influence than any man living in the United States.

Mr. Calhoun succeeded Mr. Upshur as Secretary of State, and he was known as a friend of annexation. Mr. Van Buren, replying to a letter from Mr. William T. Hammett, a representative in Congress from Mississippi, announced his opposition to the immediate annexation of Texas, because it would produce a war with Mexico. He expressed himself in favor of the measure when it could be done peaceably and honorably. Mr. Clay announced his opposition to the measure. In December, 1843, the British Premier, Lord Aberdeen, in a dispatch to Sir Richard Packenham, British Minister at Washington, denied that Great Britain had any design on Texas, but announced (which was superfluous, and not germane to the charge which he felt called upon to deny) that "Great Britain desires and is constantly exerting herself to procure the general abolition of slavery thoughout the world." This provoked a correspondence between Mr. Calhoun and the British Minister. In his annual message to Congress at the commencement of the session of 1843–'44 the President expressed himself very strongly in regard to war being waged by Mexico against Texas. The proposed treaty for annexation was rejected by the Senate

June 8, 1844, by a vote of thirty-five to sixteen. Mr. Benton presented a plan for the peaceful acquisition of Texas, but the Senate refused to adopt it.

President Tyler in his last message again referred to the war between Mexico and Texas, and said: "I repeat now what I then said, that after eight years of feeble and ineffectual efforts to recover Texas, it was time that the war should have ceased."

When the convention of the Whig party met at Harrisburg, Pa., December 4, 1839, to nominate a candidate for the presidency, General Scott's name was presented. He had addressed a number of letters to members of the convention urging that, if there appeared any prospect of success, Mr. Clay should be selected, and if not, that the choice should fall on General William Henry Harrison. The total number of votes in the convention was two hundred and fifty-four. Of these, General Scott received the votes of New York, New Jersey, Connecticut, Vermont, and Michigan—in all, sixty-two. The States which had voted for General Scott gave their votes eventually to General Harrison, who received the nomination. General Scott said of General Harrison, "But the nomination and success of General Harrison," if his life had been spared some four years longer, would have been no detriment to the country. With excellent intentions and objects, and the good sense to appoint able counselors, the country would not have been retarded in its prosperity nor disgraced by corruption in high places. No one can, of course, be held responsible for sudden deaths among men. A single month in office ended President Harrison's life, when the plaint of Burke occurred to all, "What shadows we are, what shadows we pursue!"

In June, 1841, Major-General Macomb having died, General Scott was called to take up his residence in Washington as general in chief of the army. Among his first orders was one which put a stop to arbitrary and illegal punishments in the army.

An effort was made in the House of Representatives of the next Congress in 1844 to reduce his pay, but being resisted by Charles J. Ingersoll, of Philadelphia, and ex-President John Quincy Adams, it was voted down by a large majority. Mr. Adams, in the course of his remarks in opposition to the resolution, said that he "felt bound to declare that he did think it a very ill reward for the great and eminent services of General Scott during a period of thirty odd years, in which there were some as gallant exploits as our history could show, and in which he had not spared to shed his blood, as well as for more recent services of great importance in time of peace—services of great difficulty and great delicacy—now to turn him adrift at his advanced age. . . . That he could not for a moment harbor in his heart the thought that General Scott, if he had received from the Government thousands of dollars more than he had, would have received one dollar which he did not richly deserve at the hands of his country."

On February 9, 1843, he wrote from Washington to T. P. Atkinson, of Danville, Va., in reply to a letter from that gentleman, asking his opinions on the question of slavery. Mr. Atkinson was the son of an old friend of General Scott, and the letter was written to him as a probable candidate for the presidency. He took the position in this letter that Congress had no power under the Constitution to interfere with or legislate on the question of slavery within the States. He argued that it was the duty of Congress, however, to receive, refer, and report upon petitions which might be presented to it on the question of slavery, as on all other questions. He did not blame masters for not liberating their slaves, as he thought it would benefit neither the masters nor the slaves. He, however, held it to be the duty of slave owners to employ all means not incompatible with the safety of both master and slave to meliorate slavery even to extermination. He held that, with the consent of owners or payment of just compensation, Congress might legislate in the District of Columbia, although it would be dangerous to contiguous States.

He also, in March, 1845, in reply to a letter from J. C. Beckwith, corresponding secretary of a peace convention, wrote that he always maintained the moral right to wage a just and necessary war.

In March, 1845, as stated, Congress passed a joint resolution for the annexation of the republic of Texas, and in July of that year Brigadier-General Zachary Taylor, then commanding the first department of the United States army in the Southwest, was ordered to Texas. He embarked at New Orleans with fifteen hundred troops, and in August established his camp at Corpus Christi. Re-enforcements were dispatched to him rapidly, and in November his command amounted to about four thousand men.

On March 8, 1846, General Taylor, under orders from Washington, moved his army toward the Rio Grande, and on the 28th of that month encamped on that river opposite the Mexican city of Matamoros. He here erected a fort called Fort Brown, which commanded the city of Matamoros. The Mexican troops near Matamoros were at the same time busily engaged in fortifying the city. General Pedro de Ampudia, who commanded the Mexican forces at Matamoros, on April 12, 1846, addressed General Taylor a note requiring that within twenty-four hours he should retire from his position at Fort Brown and march beyond the Neuces, stating that the governments of Mexico and the United States were engaged in negotiations regarding the annexation of Texas, and that a failure or refusal of General Taylor to comply with this demand would be regarded by his Government as a declaration of war on the part of the United States. General Taylor replied in substance that he was there with his army under orders of his Government, that he declined to retire beyond the Neuces, and that he stood ready to repel any attack which might be made upon him. Soon after this correspondence General Mariano Arista was placed in the command formerly held by General Ampudia, and in May, with an army of six thousand men, he crossed the Rio Grande and attacked General Taylor at Palo Alto, and was signally defeated. General Arista retreated on the next day to Resaca de la Palma, where he was again defeated and his army routed, and he retired across the Rio Grande. General Taylor was now promoted to the rank of major general, and on May 18th took possession of Matamoros without opposition.

On September 9th he arrived at Monterey with about six thousand seven hundred men, chiefly volunteers. General Ampudia held the command here with ten thousand regular Mexican troops. General Taylor assaulted his position on September 19th, and after five days of almost continual fighting General Ampudia surrendered. General Taylor then transferred his headquarters to Monterey, but guarded the city of Saltillo with a strong force. He was about making an advance on San Luis Potosi, when a large portion of his force was ordered to join General Scott at Vera Cruz.

Concentrating his forces, some five thousand in number, he learned that General Antonio Lopez de Santa Anna was concentrating a force of twenty thousand men at San Luis Potosi, with a view to attack him. On February 21, 1847, he took position at a mountain pass called Buena Vista, a few miles from Saltillo, where, being attacked the next day by the Mexican army under General Santa Anna, he defeated them, and Santa Anna retreated to San Luis Potosi. This brief statement of the magnificent and almost unprecedented campaign of General Taylor is necessary to understand the part taken by General Scott in the war with Mexico.

General Scott was notified early in May, 1846, that he might be ordered to assume the command on the Mexican frontier. He expressed his disinclination to this duty, because it was, as he expressed it, "harsh and unusual for a senior, without re-enforcements, to supersede a meritorious junior, and that he doubted whether that was the right season, or the Rio Grande the right basis, for offensive operations against Mexico," and suggested a plan to conquer a peace, which he afterward planned and executed. Political reasons to some extent delayed action in sending General Scott to Mexico, and his views on the proper campaign in Mexico were not approved by President Polk. General Scott thought that unless his plan met the full approval and support of the Government, it might result disastrously, and expressed the sentiment, which became afterward a byword, that "soldiers had a far greater dread of a fire upon the rear than of the most formidable enemy in the front." The President declined to order him to the command.

Pending these affairs, the Secretary of War one day called at General Scott's office and found that he was absent. General Scott, on returning, learning that the secretary had called, wrote him a note in explanation of his absence, saying that "he had only stepped out for the moment to take a hasty plate of soup." This was also made a byword, and was used with a view to injure General Scott, or rather to ridicule him by his political opponents when he was a candidate of the Whig party for President in 1852. The successes of General Taylor had endeared him to the whole country, and his praises were in every one's mouth. Congress passed a resolution of thanks, with a promise to present him with a sword in recognition of his services. General Scott wrote to the Kentucky senators, to Hon. Jefferson Davis, and others in Congress, suggesting that instead of a sword the higher honor of a gold medal should be voted him, and this suggestion was adopted. General Scott made an indorsement on the resolution of Congress voting this medal, recommending that it be made in the highest style of art. About this time he was called upon by some Whig members of Congress to inquire if General Taylor was a Whig, and if he would not be a proper person for the Whigs to nominate as their candidate for the presidency.

General Scott spoke of him to these inquirers as

a man who had the true basis of a great character—pure, uncorrupted morals combined with indomitable courage. Kind-hearted, sincere, and hospitable in a plain way, he had no vice but prejudice, many friends, and no enemies. He also related an anecdote showing General Taylor's unscrupulous honesty and high sense of honor.

General Scott made repeated requests during the summer and autumn of 1846 to be ordered to Mexico. On November 23d he received the following order:

"WAR DEPARTMENT, WASHINGTON, *November 23, 1846.*

"SIR: The President several days since communicated in person to you his orders to repair to Mexico to take command of the forces there assembled, and particularly to organize and set on foot an expedition to operate on the Gulf coast, if, on arriving at the theater of action, you shall deem it to be practicable. It is not proposed to control your operations by definite and positive instructions, but you are left to prosecute them as your judgment, under a full view of all the circumstances, shall dictate. The work is before you, and the means provided or to be provided for accomplishing it are committed to you, in the full confidence that you will use them to the best advantage.

"The objects which it is desirable to obtain have been indicated, and it is hoped that you will have the requisite force to accomplish them. Of this you must be the judge when preparations are made and the time for action arrived. Very respectfully,

"Your obedient servant,

"W. L. MARCY, *Secretary of War.*

"*General* WINFIELD SCOTT."

General Scott was impressed with the belief that Mr. Marcy, the Secretary of War, and Hon. Robert J. Walker, of Mississippi, the Secretary of the Treasury, had the fullest confidence in his ability, and favored giving him the substantial direction of the war. He was also impressed with the kindness and confidence extended to him by President Polk, but on his arrival in New Orleans he was shown a letter from Alexander Barrow, then a Senator in Congress from Louisiana and a personal friend of General Scott, informing him that the President had asked that the grade of lieutenant general be established in the army, and that on the passage of such an act by Congress it was the intention of the President to confer this rank, and consequently the command of the army, upon Thomas H. Benton, then a Senator from Missouri. This was a great shock to General Scott, and he attributed it to political motives. He reasoned this way: "Scott is a Whig; therefore the Democracy is not bound to observe good faith with him. His successes may be turned to the prejudice of the Democratic party. We must, however, profit by his military experience, and if successful, by force of patronage and other helps, continue to crown Benton with the victory, and thus triumph both in the field and at the polls."

He reached the Brazos Santiago, near the mouth of the Rio Grande, in Christmas week, and proceeded from there to Camargo, where he expected to meet General Taylor, but, by some mismanagement or delay, his notification to General Taylor did not reach the latter.

A confidential dispatch from General Scott to General Taylor was opened, read, and freely discussed at headquarters at Monterey. A duplicate was sent forward, but the party in charge of it was killed at Villa Gran and the dispatch delivered to General Santa Anna. Taylor had made a movement toward Tampico, and hence did not receive the first dispatch delivered at Tampico. In the later dispatch General Scott had written him that he might have his choice of two armies—either remain as the commander of Northern Mexico, or accompany General Scott in command of a division toward the City of Mexico, with every assurance in either case of confidence and support.

General Scott anticipated the difficulty of timely concentration of forces off the Brazos large enough to give hope of success. He thought it necessary to have fifteen thousand troops, of which five thousand were to be regulars, and to have the co-operation of the navy. The time named for the concentration was the middle of January, so that the army might reach Vera Cruz by February 1st. He had requested the advice of General Taylor on these matters and all others in regard to the proposed campaign. He had intimated, in a letter of November 15th, that it would be necessary to withdraw a large number of troops from General Taylor, and thus reduce him to the defensive, while he thought it absolutely necessary for success that General Taylor should have a force sufficient to act offensively in the direction of San Luis Potosi. In addition to the volunteers and regulars at Tampico and those moving there, he desired that Worth's division of regulars, Duncan and Taylor's field batteries, a thousand mounted men, and all the volunteer infantry that could be spared be sent to General Taylor, only retaining a force sufficient to hold Monterey and protect his communications to Point Isabel. From New Orleans General Scott had written the Secretary of War that he approved of the rendezvous at Pensacola rather than at Brazos for the ordnance and ordnance stores. He also urged that volunteers be forwarded rapidly to Brazos. Subsequently he wrote the Secretary of War asking that ships with troops and supplies be ordered to Lobos Island. He addressed a letter to General George M. Brooke, commanding at New Orleans, giving detailed orders of what he required of him. He also wrote to Commodore Conner, and made suggestions about joint operations.

Failing to meet General Taylor, as he hoped and endeavored to do, with a view of a full and free conference, he felt compelled to issue orders detaching from the army of the Rio Grande such regular troops as were deemed necessary to lead the volunteers for the capture of Vera Cruz and the move on the capital, leaving General Taylor with a force sufficient to maintain himself at Monterey. He intended, had he seen General Taylor, to advise him to contract his line to the Rio Grande. General Taylor, supported by the authorities in Washington, favored the movement on the City of Mexico from Monterey and *via* San Luis Potosi, but General Scott had already formulated and determined on the movement which he made with such brilliant success. Orders were accordingly issued from Camargo, January 3, 1847, for the movement of troops from Monterey, and General Scott returned to Brazos Santiago. The embarkation for Vera Cruz was delayed by the non-arrival of the troops from Monterey and want of transportation. The Lobos Islands was selected as the place of rendezvous. This point is one hundred and twenty miles from Vera Cruz. When the greater part of the troops had arrived, they sailed past Vera Cruz and anchored, on March 7th, at Anton Lizardo, from which point it was determined to make the necessary reconnoissances.

General Scott was at this time ignorant of the movement of General Santa Anna toward Monterey, and expected, on landing or attempting to land, to be met by a formidable force of the enemy. On March 9th, the weather proving good, the fleet, consisting of some eighty vessels, including transports, moved up the coast with the naval steamers and five gunboats. General Scott was on board of the Massachusetts, and as she moved up, the troops from the decks of the vessels cheered him with great enthusiasm. The anchorage was made outside the range of the enemy's guns. General Scott had provided sixty-seven surf boats, and in these and some cutters fifty-five hundred men — the boats being steered by sailors furnished by Commodore David Conner—passed the Massachusetts and repeated their cheers to the commanding general. The whole force was landed at half past five in the afternoon, without the loss of a man or a boat and without serious opposition from the enemy. The remainder of the force was soon landed, amounting in all to something less than twelve thousand men.

The following appeared in the New Orleans Bulletin of March 27, 1847: "The landing of the American army at Vera Cruz has been accomplished in a manner that reflects the highest credit on all concerned; and the regularity, precision, and promptness with which it was effected has probably never been surpassed, if it has been equaled, in modern warfare. The removal of a large body of troops from numerous transports into boats in an open sea, their subsequent disembarkation on the sea beach, on an enemy's coast, through a surf, with all their arms and accouterments, without a single error or accident, requires great exertion, skill, and sound judgment.

"The French expedition against Algiers in 1830 was said to be the most complete armament in every respect that ever left Europe; it had been prepared with labor, attention, experience, and nothing had been omitted to insure success, and particularly in the means and facilities for landing the troops. This disembarkation took place in a wide bay, which was more favorable than an open beach directly on the ocean, and (as in the present instance) without any resistance on the part of the enemy; yet only nine thousand men were landed the first day, and from thirty to forty lives were lost by accidents or upsetting of boats; whereas on the present occasion twelve thousand men were landed in one day, without, so far as we have heard, the slightest accident or loss of life."

Both the city and the castle of San Juan de Ulloa were strongly garrisoned and well provisioned. It was General Santa Anna's opinion that the garrison at Vera Cruz and the castle could successfully resist a siege until the annual breaking out of the yellow fever, upon which he depended to cause the withdrawal of the American troops; hence he devoted himself to the collection of troops to advance on General Taylor. General Scott says: "The walls and forts of Vera Cruz in 1847 were in good condition. Subsequent to its capture by the French, under

Admiral Baudin and the Prince de Joinville, in 1838, the castle had been greatly extended, almost rebuilt, and its armament about doubled. Besides, the French were allowed to reconnoiter the city and castle and choose their positions of attack without the least resistance, the Mexicans deprecating the war with that nation, and hence ordered not to fire the first gun. Of that injunction the French were aware. When we approached, in 1847, the castle had the capacity to sink the entire American navy." Soon after the landing was effected, General Scott, accompanied by Colonel Joseph G. Totten and other officers of his staff, reconnoitered the land side of the city, the reconnoissance of the water front having been previously made.

The city was now completely invested, and all communication with the interior cut off. A complete blockade had been established by Commodore Conner. Several officers applied to General Scott for the privilege of leading storming parties. They were thanked, but no orders were given. In a meeting with his staff—Colonel Totten, chief engineer; Lieutenant-Colonel Ethan A. Hitchcock, acting inspector general; Captain Robert E. Lee, engineer; and Lieutenant Henry L. Scott, acting adjutant general—General Scott spoke as follows: "We, of course, gentlemen, must take the city and castle before the return of the *vomito*—if not by head-work, by the slow, scientific process of storming, and then escape by pushing the conquest into the healthy interior. I am strongly inclined to attempt the former, unless you can convince me that the other is preferable. Since our thorough reconnoissance, I think the suggestion practicable with a very moderate loss on our part.

The second method would no doubt be equally successful, but with the cost of an immense slaughter to both sides, including noncombatants, Mexican men, women, and children, because assaults must be made in the dark, and the assailants dare not lose time in taking and guarding prisoners without incurring the certainty of becoming captives themselves, till all the strongholds of the place are occupied. The horrors of such slaughter as that, with the usual terrible accompaniment, are most revolting. Besides these objections, it is necessary to take into account the probable loss of some two thousand, perhaps three thousand, of our best men in an assault, and I have received but half the number promised me. How, then, could we hope to penetrate in the interior? . . . For these reasons," I added, quoting literally, "although I know our countrymen will hardly acknowledge a victory unaccompanied by a long butcher's bill (report of dead and wounded), I am strongly inclined —policy concurring with humanity—to forego their loud applause and 'aves vehement' and take the city with the least possible loss of life. . . ."

General Scott's views were fully concurred in by Colonel Totten and others of his staff, and orders were issued for digging the trenches and the establishment of batteries. Very soon all outposts and sentries of the enemy were driven in. General Scott had warned the foreign consuls in the city of his proposed attack and had furnished them safe conducts out of the city, but they had not taken advantage of it. The marines of Commodore Conner's squadron, at his request, were now allowed to join the army, and, under command of Captain Alvin Edson, they were attached to the Third Artillery.

On the morning of the 10th the guns from the castle opened fire, but did very little damage. General Robert Patterson now joined Worth on his left, and extended the line of investment. Small parties of Mexicans were in sight in a valley, and a detachment under command of Colonel Cenovio approached the American camp and opened fire. The only damage done was the wounding of one soldier. General Gideon J. Pillow, with a part of his command and a six-pounder, opened fire on a large stone building occupied by the enemy and known as the magazine. They were soon driven off, and General Pillow advanced and attacked a small force in his front, driving them and occupying the magazine.

Colonels William T. Haskell's and Francis M. Wynkoop's regiments of Tennessee and Pennsylvania volunteers were moved on a small force on the road to Medelin, which retired, and two companies—one of artillery under command of Captain John R. Vinton, and one of infantry under command of Lieutenant A. P. Rogers—seized a point known as the limekiln, where it was proposed to plant a battery. General Twiggs moved on the 11th to extend the line of investment, which was now complete. General Scott then addressed a letter to the commanding officer of the city as follows:

"HEADQUARTERS OF THE ARMY OF THE UNITED STATES OF AMERICA, CAMP WASHINGTON, BEFORE VERA CRUZ,
"*March 22, 1847.*

"The undersigned, Major-General Scott, general in chief of the armies of the United States of America, in addition to the close blockade of the coast and port of Vera Cruz previously established by the squadrons under Commodore Conner, of the navy of said States, having more fully invested the said city with an overwhelming army, so as to render it impossible that it should receive from without succor or re-enforcements of any kind, and having caused to be established batteries competent to the speedy destruction of said city, he, the undersigned, deems it due to the courtesies of war in like cases, as well as to the rights of humanity, to summon his Excellency the governor or commander in chief of the city of Vera Cruz to surrender the same to the army of the United States of America, present before the place. The undersigned, anxious to spare the beautiful city of Vera Cruz from the imminent hazard of demolition, its gallant defenders from a useless effusion of blood, and its peaceful inhabitants—women and children inclusive—from the inevitable horrors of a triumphant assault, addresses this summons to the intelligence, the gallantry, the patriotism, no less than the humanity, of his Excellency the governor and commander in chief of Vera Cruz. The undersigned is not accurately informed whether both the city and the castle of San Juan de Ulloa be under the command of his Excellency, or whether each place has its own independent commander; but the undersigned, moved by the considerations adverted to above, may be willing to stipulate that if the city should by capitulation be garrisoned by a part of his troops no missile shall be fired from within the city or from its bastions or walls upon the castle, unless the castle should previously fire upon the city. The undersigned has the honor to tender his distinguished opponent, his Excellency the general and commander in chief of Vera Cruz, the assurance of the high respect and consideration of the undersigned, WINFIELD SCOTT."

To which he received the following reply:

"GOD AND LIBERTY!"
"VERA CRUZ, *March 22, 1847.*

"To MAJOR-GENERAL SCOTT: The undersigned, commanding general of the free and sovereign State of Vera Cruz, has informed himself of the contents of the note which Major-General Scott, general in chief of the forces of the United States, has addressed to him under date of to-day, demanding the surrender of this place and castle of San Juan de Ulloa, and in answer has to say that the above-named fortress as well as the city depends on his authority; and it being his principal duty, in order to prove worthy of the confidence placed in him by the Government of the nation, to defend both points at all cost, to which he counts upon necessary elements, and will make it good to the last, therefore his Excellency can commence his operations of war in a manner which he may consider most advantageous. The undersigned has the honor to return to the general in chief of the forces of the United States the demonstrations of esteem he may be pleased to honor him with. JUAN MORALES."

The city was garrisoned by a force of three thousand three hundred and sixty officers and men, and the castle had a force of one thousand and thirty, making a total of four thousand three hundred and ninety. It was certainly a brave determination of the Mexicans with this force to resist the formidable foe who had invested them and were ready to attack.

On March 22d, at 4.15 P. M., the mortar batteries opened fire, and from that time the firing was continued without ceasing until the 23d, when it was suspended for a few hours. The fire was returned from the batteries. Fire was also opened on the city from the vessels. Heavy guns having arrived, preparations were made for getting them ashore, but it was prevented by a heavy norther. The norther having subsided on the 23d, six heavy guns and a detachment from the navy were landed. On Commodore Matthew C. Perry's request a place in the trenches was assigned to the navy. On the 24th, Colonel Persifor F. Smith moved out to a small stream called the San Pedro and attacked and drove off a force of the enemy.

On the night of the 24th General Scott received a communication, signed by the British, French, Spanish, and Prussian consuls in Vera Cruz, asking time to permit the neutrals and women and children to withdraw from the city; to which he replied that up to the 23d the communication between the neutrals in Vera Cruz and the neutral ships of war lying off Sacrificios was left open to allow them an exit, and that he had given notice to the consuls. He therefore declined to grant the request unless it was made by the governor and commander in chief of Vera Cruz, accompanied with a proposition to surrender. On the 25th, the six heavy guns, the navy battery, and all the mortars opened fire. General Scott had determined that, if no proposition for surrender was made by the 26th, he would assault the works.

The command of the city having been turned over by General Morales to General Landero, the latter, on the 26th, addressed General Scott as follows:

"I have the honor of transmitting to your Excellency the exposition which has this moment been made to me by the señores consuls of England, France, Spain, and Prussia, in which they solicit that hostilities may be suspended while the innocent families in this place who are suffering the ravages of war be enabled to leave the city, which solicitude claims my support; and considering it in accordance with the rights of afflicted humanity, I have not hesitated to invite your Excellency to enter into an honorable accommodation with the garrison, in which case you will please name three commissioners who may meet at some intermediate point to treat with those of this place upon the terms of the accommodation. With this motive I renew to your Excellency my attentive consideration.

"God reward your Excellency, etc., etc., etc. (on account of the sickness of the commanding general).

"José Juan de Landero.

General Scott notified General Landero that he had appointed Brevet Major-General Worth, of the regular army, Major-General Pillow, of the volunteers, and Colonel Totten, chief of the engineer corps of the army, commissioners on his part to meet a like number to be appointed by General Landero. The latter announced the appointment on his part of Colonels Herrera, Gutierrez de Villa Nueva, and Lieutenant-Colonel Robles. The commissioners met at the Punta de Hornos, and on the 27th agreed upon terms.

The terms of capitulation were in substance that the Mexican troops should march out of the city with the honors of war, should stack their arms and

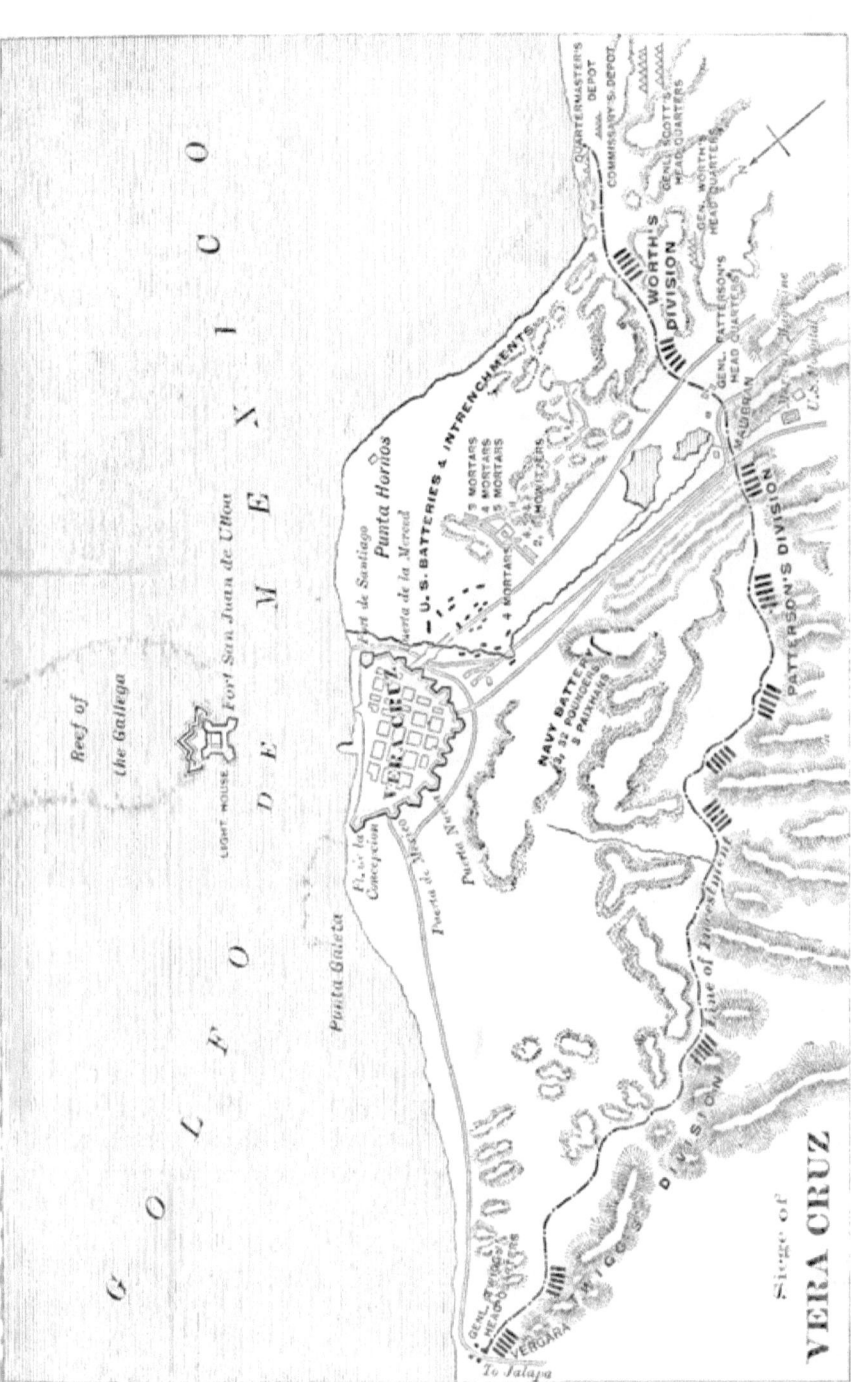

be paroled; that their colors, when lowered, should be saluted. Absolute protection was guaranteed to persons and property in the city. No private building was to be taken or used by the United States forces without previous arrangement and fair compensation. A Mexican historian says: "The sacrifice was consummated, but the soldiers of Vera Cruz received the honor due to their valor and misfortunes —the respect of the conqueror. Not even a look was given them by the enemy's soldiers which could be interpreted into an insult." Five thousand prisoners and four hundred guns were captured, and with a loss of only sixty-seven killed and wounded.

There is scarcely anything in history equal to this achievement of General Scott. Throughout the siege he shared all the dangers and hardships of his troops. He examined in person, aided by his very able staff officers, every detail of works of defense, and gave orders for the firing of the batteries.

One day during the siege General Scott was walking the trenches where a heavy fire of the enemy was directed. Seeing some of the soldiers standing up, General Scott ordered them not to expose themselves. "But, General," said one, "you are exposing yourself." "Oh!" said he, "generals nowadays can be made out of anybody, but men can not be had." The point of this reply is easy to understand. General Worth was appointed commandant and governor of Vera Cruz, with instructions to establish and enforce police regulations, but not to interfere with the functions of the civil magistrates in affairs between Mexicans.

He was authorized and instructed, after conferring with Commodore Perry, to establish a tariff of duties on articles imported, to be applied to the necessities of the sick and wounded of the army and navy and indigent inhabitants of the city of Vera Cruz; this to continue in force until instructions were received from Washington. General Worth, on assuming command, immediately issued an order to the alcalde as follows:

"Arms in possession of citizens to be given into the alcalde's possession and to be reported to headquarters. Drinking saloons to be closed, and not to be reopened hereafter except under special permission. Mexican laws as between Mexicans to be enforced, and justice administered by regular Mexican tribunals. Cases arising between American citizens of the army, or authorized followers of the same, will be investigated by military commissions."

To cover all cases arising by the military occupation of the country, General Scott had issued at Tampico his Martial-Law Order No. 40, and republished it at Vera Cruz. General Worth gave permission to the residents of the city to leave and enter the city freely between daylight and sunset. No duties were imposed on any of the necessaries of life.

On March 30th a combined military and naval expedition was organized to move to Alvarado, Commodore Perry in command of the naval contingent. The army detachment, under General John A. Quitman, consisted of the Georgia, Alabama, and South Carolina infantry, and a squadron of the Second Dragoons under command of Major Benjamin Lloyd Beall, and a section of the Third Artillery under Lieutenant Henry Bethel Judd.

The object of this expedition was to conciliate the inhabitants, and for the purchase of horses, mules, and cattle. Commodore Perry landed there on the 1st of April, followed by the arrival of General Quitman very soon afterward. Many citizens fled on the approach of the troops, and the town was surrendered to the American forces. Twenty-two cannon and some ammunition were captured, and five hundred horses secured by purchase. The troops returned to Vera Cruz, April 6th. A similar expedition for like purposes was undertaken by General Harvey, April 2d, for Antigua. A lieutenant and eight soldiers were captured, and some horses and cattle purchased. On April 3d, Brevet Colonel Henry Wilson, with the First United States Infantry and two companies of volunteers, was assigned to the command of Vera Cruz and the castle of San Juan de Ulloa.

Orders were now issued for an advance of the army on Jalapa, General David E. Twiggs, with the Second Division of regulars, to lead the movement on the 8th, two brigades of volunteers to follow. On the 9th Patterson's division moved, but, for want of transportation, Quitman's brigade, Colonel James H. Thomas, Tennessee mounted regiment, Worth's division, and the siege train were left at Vera Cruz. General Twiggs was notified by General Scott that he had information that General Santa Anna had arrived at Jalapa with six thousand troops, though he [General Scott] regarded the numbers as exaggerated. General Twiggs, on receipt of General Scott's notice, replied that the Mexicans would doubtless endeavor to hold the pass of Cerro Gordo between the National Bridge and Jalapa. Through Mexican sources he had information rating Santa Anna's force at from two thousand to thirteen thousand, and that he expected to arrive on the evening of the 11th at

Plan del Rio, the point where the Mexican advance was posted.

General Scott had received information that Generals Patterson and Twiggs had met a strong force of the enemy at Plan del Rio. Worth's division was ordered forward, and Quitman directed to follow in twenty-four hours. General Scott himself now moved out under a cavalry escort.

CHAPTER IX.

General Santa Anna arrives at Cerro Gordo—Engagement at Atalaya—General Orders No. 111—Reports from Jalapa—Report of engagement at Cerro Gordo—Occupation of Perote—Account of a Mexican historian—General Santa Anna's letter to General Arroya—Delay of the Government in sending re-enforcements—Danger of communications with Vera Cruz—Troops intended for Scott ordered to General Taylor—Colonel Childs appointed governor of Jalapa—Occupation of Puebla—Arrival of re-enforcements—Number of Scott's force.

GENERAL SANTA ANNA had arrived at Cerro Gordo on April 9th. General Scott, on his arrival, ordered (on the morning of the 11th) reconnoissances to be made on the Mexican left by Captain Robert E. Lee, which were resumed on the 16th. These reconnoissances determined the order of attack, which was to make a demonstration with the commands of Generals Pillow and Shields on the Mexican right, and press the mass of the army on their right. This movement being successful, the enemy's communications would be cut off. In the meantime the Mexicans were busily engaged in greatly strengthening their positions.

General Scott had not intended to attack the enemy in the absence of Worth's division, which had not yet arrived. A movement of Lieutenant Franklin Gardner, re-enforced later by the mounted rifles under Major Edwin Vose Sumner and a battalion of the

First Artillery under Lieutenant-Colonel Childs, to occupy a position near the base of the Atalaya, provoked a sharp conflict. General Santa Anna, being at the front, ordered re-enforcements. Colonel Thomas Childs withdrew, having advanced under a misapprehension. The American loss was ninety-seven, killed and wounded. General Scott returned to Plan del Rio and issued the following order:

"HEADQUARTERS OF THE ARMY,
"PLAN DEL RIO, *April 17, 1847.*
"GENERAL ORDERS NO. 111.

"The enemy's whole line of intrenchments and batteries will be attacked in front, and at the same time turned, early in the day to-morrow, probably before ten o'clock A. M. The second (Twiggs's) division of regulars is already advanced within easy turning distance toward the enemy's line. That division has instructions to move forward before daylight tomorrow and take up position across the national road, in the enemy's rear, so as to cut off a retreat toward Jalapa. It may be re-enforced to-day, if unexpectedly attacked in force, by regiments—one or two—taken from Shields's brigade of volunteers. If not, the two volunteer regiments will march for that purpose at daylight to-morrow morning under Brigadier-General Shields, who will report to Brigadier-General Twiggs in getting up with him, or to the general in chief if he be in advance. The remaining regiments of that volunteer brigade will receive instructions in the course of this day. The first division of regulars (Worth's) will follow the movement against the enemy's left at sunrise tomorrow morning. As already arranged, Brigadier-General Pillow's brigade will march at six o'clock to-morrow morning along the route he has carefully reconnoitered, and stand ready, as soon as he hears the report of arms on our right, or sooner, if circumstances should favor him, to pierce the enemy's line of batteries at such point—the nearer the river the better—as he may select. Once in the rear of that line, he will turn to the right or left, or both, and attack the batteries in reverse; or, if abandoned, he will pursue the enemy with vigor until further orders. Wall's field battery and cavalry will be held in reserve on the national road, a little out of view and range of the enemy's batteries. They will take up that position at nine o'clock in the morning. The enemy's batteries being carried or abandoned, all our divisions and corps will pursue with vigor. This pursuit may be continued many miles toward Jalapa until stopped by darkness or fortified positions; consequently the body of the army will not return to this encampment, but be followed to-morrow afternoon, or early the next morning, by the baggage trains of the several corps. For this purpose the feeble men of each corps will be left to guard its camp and effects, and to load up the latter in the wagons of the corps. A commander of the present encampment will be designated in the course of this day.

"As soon as it shall be known that the enemy's works have been carried, or that the general pursuit has been commenced, one wagon for each regiment and battery and one for the cavalry will follow the movement, to receive, under the direction of medical officers, the wounded and disabled, who will be brought back to this place for treatment in general hospital. The surgeon general will organize this important service, and designate that hospital, as well as the medical officers to be left at it.

"Every man who marches out to attack or pursue the enemy will take the usual allowance of ammunition and subsistence for at least two days.

"By command of Major-General Scott.
"H. L. SCOTT, *Acting Adjutant General.*"

The engineer train and troops under Lieutenant George Brinton McClellan having arrived, additional batteries were placed in position. General Santa Anna, believing that the Americans would attack his right, made his dispositions accordingly. Following are General Scott's reports of the battle made to the Secretary of War:

"HEADQUARTERS OF THE ARMY, PLAN DEL RIO,
"FIFTY MILES FROM VERA CRUZ, *April 19, 1847.*

"SIR: The plan of the attack, sketched in General Orders No. 111 herewith, was finely executed by this gallant army before two o'clock P. M. yesterday. We are quite embarrassed with the results of victory—prisoners of war, heavy ordnance, field batteries, small arms, and accouterments. About three thousand men laid down their arms, with the usual proportion of field and company officers, besides five generals, several of them of great distinction—Pinson Jarrero, La Vega, Noryuga, and Obando. A sixth general, Vasque, was killed in defending the battery (tower) in the rear of the line of defense, the capture of which gave us those glorious results.

"Our loss, though comparatively small in number, has been serious. Brigadier-General Shields, a commander of activity, zeal, and talent, is, I fear, if not dead, mortally wounded. He is some five miles

CERRO GORDO.

from me at this moment. The field of operations covers many miles, broken by mountains and deep chasms, and I have not a report as yet from any division or brigade. Twiggs's division, followed by Shields's (now Colonel Baker's) brigade, are now near Jalapa, and Worth's division is *en route* thither, all pursuing with good results, as I learn, that part of the Mexican army—perhaps six or seven thousand men—that fled before our right had carried the tower, and gained the Jalapa road. Pillow's brigade alone is near me at this depot of wounded, sick, and prisoners, and I have time only to give from him the names of First-Lieutenant F. B. Nelson and Second-Lieutenant C. G. Gill, both of the Second Tennessee Foot (Haskell's regiment), among the killed, and in the brigade one hundred and six of all ranks killed or wounded. Among the latter the gallant brigadier general himself has a smart wound in his arm, but not disabled; and Major R. Farqueson, Second Tennessee, H. F. Murray, second lieutenant, G. T. Southerland, first lieutenant, W. P. Hale, adjutant, all of the same regiment, severely, and First-Lieutenant W. Yearwood mortally wounded. And I know, from personal observation on the ground, that First-Lieutenant Ewell, of the Rifles, if not now dead, was mortally wounded in entering, sword in hand, the intrenchments around the captured tower. Second-Lieutenant Derby, Topographical Engineers, I saw also at the same place, severely wounded, and Captain Patten, Second United States Infantry, lost his right hand. Major Sumner, Second United States Dragoons, was slightly wounded the day before, and Captain Johnson, Typographical Engineers (now lieutenant colonel of infantry), was very severely wounded in reconnoitering some days earlier. I must not omit to add that Captain Mason and Second-Lieutenant Davis, both of the Rifles, were among the very severely wounded in storming the same tower. I estimate our total loss in killed and wounded may be about two hundred and fifty, and that of the enemy three hundred and fifty. In the pursuit toward Jalapa (twenty-five miles hence) I learn we have added much to the enemy's loss in prisoners, killed, and wounded. In fact, I suppose this retreating army to be nearly disorganized, and hence my haste to follow in an hour or two to profit by events. In this hurried and imperfect report I must not omit to say that Brigadier-General Twiggs, in passing the mountain range beyond Cerro Gordo crowned with the tower, detached from his division, as I suggested the day before, a strong force to carry that height which commanded the Jalapa road at the foot, and could not fail, if carried, to cut off the whole or any part of the enemy's forces from a retreat in any direction. A portion of the First Artillery under the often-distinguished Brevet-Colonel Childs, the Third Infantry under Captain Alexander, the Seventh Infantry under Lieutenant-Colonel Plympton, and the Rifles under Major Loring, all under the temporary command of Colonel Harvey, Second Dragoons, during the confinement to his bed of Brevet Brigadier-General P. F. Smith, composed that detachment. The style of execution, which I had the pleasure to witness, was most brilliant and decisive. The brigade ascended the long and difficult slope of Cerro Gordo, without shelter and under the tremendous fire of artillery and musketry, with the utmost steadiness, reached the breastworks, drove the enemy from them, planted the colors of the First Artillery, Third and Seventh Infantry, the enemy's flag still flying, and after some minutes of sharp firing finished the conquest with the bayonet. It is a most pleasing duty to say that the highest praise is due to Harvey, Childs, Plympton, Loring, Alexander, their gallant officers and men, for this brilliant service, independent of the great results which soon followed.

"Worth's division of regulars coming up at this time, he detached Brevet Lieutenant-Colonel C. F. Smith with his light battalion to support the assault, but not in time. The general, reaching the tower a few minutes before me and observing a white flag displayed from the nearest portion of the enemy's lines toward the batteries below, sent out Colonels Harvey and Childs to hold a parley. The surrender followed in an hour or two.

"Major-General Patterson left a sick-bed to share in the dangers and fatigues of the day, and after the surrender went forward to command the advanced forces toward Jalapa. Brigadier-General Pillow and his brigade twice assaulted with great daring the enemy's lines of batteries on our left; and, though without success, they contributed much to distract and dismay their immediate opponents.

"President Santa Anna, with Generals Canalizo and Ampudia, and some six or eight thousand men, escaped toward Jalapa just before Cerro Gordo was carried and before Twiggs's division could reach the national road above. I have determined to parole the prisoners—officers and men—as I have not the means of feeding them here beyond to-day, and can not afford to detach a heavy body of horse and foot, with wagons, to accompany them to Vera Cruz. Our baggage train, though increasing, is not yet half large enough to give an assured progress to this army. Besides, a greater number of prisoners would probably escape from the escort in the long and deep sandy road, with subsistence, ten to one, than we shall find again out of the same body of men in ranks opposed to us. Not one of the Vera Cruz prisoners is believed to have been in the lines at Cerro Gordo. Some six of the officers highest in rank refused to give their paroles, except to go to Vera Cruz, and hence, perhaps, to the United States.

"The small arms and their accouterments being of no value to our army here or at home, I have ordered them to be destroyed, for we have not the means of transporting them. I am also somewhat embarrassed with the many pieces of artillery—all bronze—which we have captured. It would take a brigade and half the mules of this army to transport them fifty miles. A field battery I shall take for service for the army, but the heavy metal must be collected and left here for the present. We have our own siege train and the proper carriages with us.

"Being occupied with the prisoners and all the details of a forward movement, besides looking to the supplies which are to follow from Vera Cruz, I have time to add no more, intending to be at Jalapa early to-morrow. We shall not probably meet with serious opposition this side of Perote, certainly not unless delayed by the want of the means of transportation.

"I have the honor to remain, sir, with high respect, your most obedient servant,

"WINFIELD SCOTT.

CERRO GORDO.

" P. S.—I invite attention to the accompanying letters to President Santa Anna, taken in his carriage yesterday; also to his proclamation issued on hearing that we had captured Vera Cruz, etc., in which he says: 'If the enemy advance one step more, the national independence will be buried in the abyss of the past.' We have taken that step.

" W. S.

" I make a second postscript, to say that there is some hope, I am happy to learn, that General Shields may survive his wounds. One of the principal motives for paroling the prisoners of war is to diminish the resistance of other garrisons in our march.

" HEADQUARTERS OF THE ARMY, JALAPA, *April 23*, 1847.

" SIR: In forwarding the reports of commanders which detail the operations of their several corps against the Mexican lines at Cerro Gordo, I shall present, in continuation of my former report, but an outline of the affair; and while adopting heartily their commendations of the ardor and efficiency of individuals, I shall mention by name only those who figure prominently, or, from position, could not be included in those subreports. The field sketch herewith indicates the position of the two armies. The *tierra caliente*, or low level, terminates at Plan del Rio, the site of the American camp, from which the road ascends immediately in a long circle among the lofty hills, whose commanding points had all been fortified and garrisoned by the enemy. His right, intrenched, rested on a precipice overhanging an impassable ravine that forms the bed of the stream; and his intrenchments extended continuously to the road, in which was placed a formidable battery. On the other side the lofty and difficult heights of Cerro Gordo commanded the approaches in all directions. The main body of the Mexican army was encamped on level ground, with a battery of five pieces, half a mile in rear of that height toward Jalapa. Resolving, if possible, to turn the enemy's left and attack in rear while menacing or engaging his front, I caused daily reconnoissances to be pushed, with the view of finding a route for a force to debouch on the Jalapa road and cut off retreat. The reconnoissance, begun by Lieutenant Beauregard, was continued by Captain Lee, engineers, and a road made along difficult slopes and over chasms out of the enemy's view; though reached by his fire when discovered, until, arriving at the Mexican lines, further reconnoissance became impossible without action. The desired point of debouchure, the Jalapa road, was not therefore reached, though believed to be within easy distance; and to gain that point it now became necessary to carry the heights of Cerro Gordo. The disposition in my plan of battle—General Orders No. 111, heretofore inclosed—were accordingly made. Twiggs's division, re-enforced by Shields's brigade of volunteers, was thrown into position on the 17th, and was of necessity drawn into action in taking up the ground for its bivouac, and the opposing height for our heavy battery. It will be seen that many of our officers and men were killed or wounded in this sharp combat, handsomely commenced by a company of the Seventh Infantry under Brevet First-Lieutenant Gardner, who is highly praised by all his commanders for signal services. Colonel Harvey, coming up with the Rifle Regiment and First Artillery (also parts of his brigade), brushed away the enemy and occupied the height, on which, in the night, was placed a battery of one twenty-four pounder and two twenty-four-pound howitzers, under the supervision of Captain Lee, engineers, and Lieutenant Hagner, ordnance. These guns opened next morning, and were served with effect by Captain Steptoe and Lieutenant Brown, Third Artillery, Lieutenant Hagner (ordnance), and Lieutenant Seymore, First Artillery. The same night, with extreme toil and difficulty, under the superintendence of Lieutenant Tower, engineer, and Lieutenant Laidley, ordnance, an eight-inch howitzer was put in position across the river and opposite to the enemy's right battery. A detachment of four companies under Major Burnham, New York, volunteers, performed this creditable service, which enabled Lieutenant Ripley, Second Artillery, in charge of the piece, to open a timely fire in that quarter.

"Early on the 18th the columns moved to the general attack, and our success was speedy and decisive. Pillow's brigade assaulting the right of the intrenchments, although compelled to retire, had the effect I have heretofore stated. Twiggs's division, storming the strong and vital point of Cerro Gordo, pierced the center, gained command of all the intrenchments, and cut them off from support. As our infantry (Colonel Riley's brigade) pushed on against the main body of the enemy, the guns of their own fort were rapidly turned to play on that force (under the immediate command of General Santa Anna), who fled in confusion. Shields's brigade, bravely assaulting the left, carried the rear battery (five guns) on the Jalapa road and aided materially in completing the rout of the enemy. The part taken by the remainder of our forces held in reserve to support and pursue has already been noticed. The moment the fate of the day was decided, the cavalry and Taylor's and Wall's field batteries were pushed on toward Jalapa in advance of the pursuing columns of infantry. Twiggs's division and the brigade of Shields (now under Colonel Baker) and Major-General Patterson were sent to take command of them. In the hot pursuit many Mexicans were captured or slain before our men and horses were exhausted by the heat and distance.

"The rout proved to have been complete, the retreating army, except a small body of cavalry, being dispersed and utterly disorganized. The immediate consequences have been our possession of this important city, the abandonment of the works and artillery at La Hoya, the next formidable pass between Vera Cruz and the capital, and the prompt occupation by Worth's division of the fortress of Perote (second only to San Juan de Ulloa), with its extensive armament of sixty-six guns and mortars and its large supply of material. To General Worth's report, annexed, I refer for details.

"I have heretofore endeavored to do justice to the skill and courage with which the heights of Cerro Gordo were attacked, naming the regiments most distinguished, and their commanders, under the lead of Colonel Harney. Lieutenant G. W. Smith led the engineer company as part of the storming force, and is noticed with distinction. The reports of this assault make favorable mention of many in which I can well concur, having witnessed the daring advance and perfect steadiness of the whole. Besides those already named, Lieutenant Brooks, Third Infantry, Lieutenant Macdonald, Second Dragoons, Lieutenant Vandorn, Seventh Infantry (all acting staff officers), Captain Magruder, First Artillery, and Lieutenant Gardner, Seventh Infantry, seem to have won special praise. Colonel Riley's brigade and Talcott's rocket and howitzer battery were engaged in and about the heights and bore an active part. The brigade so gallantly led by General Shields, and after his fall by Colonel Baker, deserves high commendation for its fine behavior and success. Colonels Foreman, Burnett, and Major Harris commanded the regiments. Lieutenant Hammond, Third Artillery, and Lieutenant Davis, Illinois volunteers, constituted the brigade staff. These operations, hid from my view by intervening hills, were not fully known when my first report was hastily written. Brigadier-General Twiggs, who was in immediate command of all advanced forces, has earned high credit by his judgment, skill, and energy. The conduct of Colonels Campbell, Haskell, and Wynkoop, commanding the regiments of Pillow's brigade, is reported in terms of strong approbation by Major-General Patterson. I recommend for a commission Quartermaster-Sergeant Henry, of the Seventh Infantry (already known to the army for intrepidity on former occasions), who hauled down the national standard of the Mexican fort. In expressing my indebtedness for able assistance—to Lieutenant-Colonel Hitchcock, acting inspector general; to Majors Smith and Turnbull, and respective chiefs of engineers and topographical engineers; to their assistant lieutenants, Lieutenants Mason, Beauregard, Stevens, Tower, G. W. Smith, McClellan, engineers, and Lieutenants Derby and Hardcastle, topographical engineers; to Captain Allen, chief quartermaster, and Lieutenant Blair, chief commissary, and to Lieutenants Hagner and Laidley, ordnance, all actively employed—I am compelled to make special mention of the services of Captain R. E. Lee, engineers. This officer greatly distinguished himself at the siege of Vera Cruz, was again indefatigable during these operations, in reconnoissance as daring as laborious, and of the utmost value. Nor was he less conspicuous in planting batteries and in conducting columns to their stations under the heavy fire of the enemy. My personal staff—Lieutenants Scott, Williams, and Lay, and Major Van Buren, who volunteered for the occasion—gave me zealous and efficient assistance. Our whole force present in action and in reserve was eight thousand five hundred. The enemy is estimated at twelve thousand or more. About three thousand prisoners, four or five thousand stands of arms, and forty-three pieces of artillery are taken. By the accompanying return I regret to find our loss more severe than at first supposed, amounting in the two days to thirty-three officers and three hundred and ninety-eight men—in all, four hundred and thirty-one, of whom sixty-three were killed. The enemy's loss is computed to be from one thousand to one thousand two hundred. I am happy in communicating strong hopes of the recovery of the gallant General Shields, who is so much improved as to have been brought to this place.

"Appended to this report are the following papers:

"(A) General return by name of killed and wounded.

"(B) Copies of report of Lieutenant-Colonel Hitchcock, acting inspector general (of prisoners taken), and accompanying papers.

"(C) Report of Brigadier-General Twiggs, and subreports.

"(D) Report of Major-General Patterson and report of brigade commanders.

"(E) Copy of report of Brigadier-General Worth announcing the occupation by his division of the castle and town of Perote without opposition, with an inventory of ordnance there found.

"I have the honor to remain, sir, with high respect, your most obedient servant,

"WINFIELD SCOTT.

A Mexican historian gives the following account of the close of the battle: "General Santa Anna, accompanied by some of his adjutants, was passing along the road to the left of the battery, when the enemy's column, now out of the woods, appeared on his line of retreat and fired upon him, forcing him back. The carriage in which he had left Jalapa was riddled with shot, the mules killed and taken by the enemy, as well as a wagon containing sixteen thousand dollars received the day before for the pay of the soldiers. Every tie of command and obedience now being broken among our troops, safety alone being the object, and all being involved in a frightful whirl, they rushed desperately to the narrow pass of the defile that descended to the Plan del Rio, where the general in chief had preceded, with the chiefs and officers accompanying him. Horrid indeed was the descent by that narrow and rocky path, where thousands rushed, disputing the passage, with desperation, and leaving a track of blood upon the road. All classes being confounded, military distinction and respect were lost; and badges of rank became marks of sarcasm that were only meted out according to their grade and humiliation. The enemy, now masters of our camp, turned their guns upon the fugitives, thus augmenting the terror of the multitude that crowded through the defile and pressed forward every instant by a new impulse, which increased the confusion and disgrace of the ill-fated day."

General Scott reports the strength of his army at Cerro Gordo at eight thousand five hundred, the killed and wounded four hundred and thirty-one, of which thirty-three were officers and three hundred and ninety-eight enlisted men. His estimate of the Mexican force was twelve thousand. The prisoners captured were about three thousand, and the killed and wounded between one thousand and twelve hundred. Forty-three cannon and three thousand five hundred small arms were captured. On the morning of the 22d the army moved to and occupied the town and castle of Perote without resistance.

General Santa Anna now retired to Orizaba, where he was met by many distinguished citizens. He addressed a letter to the *ad interim* President, General Arroya, as follows:

"ORIZABA, *April 22, 1847.*

"MY ESTEEMED FRIEND: The dispatch which I have forwarded to the Minister of War will already have informed you of the events which occurred on the 18th inst. The enemy made an extraordinary effort to force the pass, and, exasperated by the repulse he had experienced the day before, and because he knew his ruin was inevitable unless he succeeded, attacked me with his entire army, which was not less than twelve thousand men. He put everything on the hazard of the die, and the cast was favorable to him. I do not regard the cause of the nation as hopeless, if it will defend its honor and independence as circumstances may require. I presume you have taken all proper measures for the public safety, and first of all for that of the capital. I shall be able to aid it very soon if it will defend itself. At present I have with me five hundred men and four guns, and there is no doubt but I shall collect in a few days a force equal to that I rallied at Cerro Gordo. I only require that you send me some money through the medium of bills of exchange, as I find it impossible to raise a dollar. We must, my friend, not give up ourselves as lost, and, before God, you shall see that I will make no treaty with the enemy which will dishonor us or put us in worse condition. Write to me when convenient, and reckon always on the poor services of your most affectionate friend, who wishes you every happiness. A. L. DE SANTA ANNA."

The prisoners were all paroled, and the sick and wounded sent to Jalapa, where they were comfortably provided for.

General Scott was impatient at the delay of the Government in sending him re-enforcements. He feared that his communications with Vera Cruz might be cut off. The time of enlistment of the twelve months' volunteers would soon expire, and he desired to discharge them in time to leave the coast before the prevalence of the yellow fever.

He received information on April 27th that some one to two thousand recruits of the ten regiments recently provided for by Congress had been ordered to Brazos, and that every effort would be made to re-enforce General Taylor. The Secretary of War had ordered troops originally designed for General Scott to the relief of General Taylor, without notice to General Scott.

On May 4, 1847, he issued an order to the volunteer troops whose term of enlistment was about to expire, complimenting them for their services, but announcing his intention to discharge them. He then addressed the Secretary of War, saying: "To part with so large and so respectable a portion of the army in the middle of a country which, though broken in its power, is not yet disposed to sue for peace; to provide for the return home of seven regiments from this interior position at a time when I find it difficult to provide transportation and supplies for the operating forces which remain, and all this without any prospect of succor or re-enforcements in perhaps the next seven months, beyond some three hundred army recruits, presents novelties utterly unknown to an invading army before. With the addition of ten or twelve thousand new levies in April and May, asked for, and until very recently expected, or even with the addition of two or three thousand new troops destined for this army, but suddenly, by the orders of the War Department, directed to the Rio Grande frontier, I might, notwithstanding the unavoidable discharge of the old volunteers—seven regiments and two independent companies—advance with confidence upon the enemy's capital. I shall nevertheless advance, but whether beyond Puebla will depend upon intervening information and reflection."

The army, having received supplies of medicines, ammunition, clothing, salt, etc., made preparations to move. Colonel Childs was appointed governor of

OCCUPATION OF PUEBLA.

Jalapa, and a sufficient garrison left with him. General Twiggs was ordered to march to Perote. General Worth had occupied Perote on April 22d. The army then occupied Puebla, where during their prolonged stay the troops were daily drilled, but were given permission to visit the ancient city of Cholula and the adjacent country. This city in the time of Cortez had a population of one hundred and fifty thousand, but was now a hamlet containing a small population and the ruins of its ancient glory. General Scott relates that while in this region, " coming up with a brigade marching at ease, all intoxicated with the fine air and scenery, he was, as usual, received with hearty and protracted cheers. The group of officers who surrounded him differed widely in the objects of their admiration, some preferring this or that snow-capped mountain, others the city, and several the pyramid of Cholula that was now opening upon the view. An appeal from all was made to the general in chief. He promptly and emphatically replied, 'I differ from you all. My greatest delight is in this fine body of troops, without whom we can never sleep in the halls of the Montezumas, or in our own homes.' "

The first re-enforcements to arrive were eight hundred men, under Lieutenant-Colonel James Simmons McIntosh, escorting a train. They were delayed by an attack of the enemy near Jalapa, but, being joined by Brigadier-General George Cadwallader with a portion of his brigade and a field battery, the enemy was soon driven. Major-General Gideon J. Pillow arrived next with a thousand men, and on August 6th Brigadier-General Franklin Pierce joined with two thousand five hundred men.

General Scott felt compelled, on account of his reduced numbers, to order the garrison, under Colonel Childs at Jalapa, to join him. His force now was (including late re-enforcements) about fourteen thousand men, including two thousand five hundred sick in hospitals, and six hundred convalescents too feeble for duty. These convalescents and the same number of effective troops were left as a garrison under Colonel Childs, who was appointed commandant of the city of Puebla. This necessitated the almost total abandonment of the protection of his lines to his base at Vera Cruz, and communications to his Government. As Scott expressed it, "we had to throw away the scabbard and to advance with the naked blade in hand."

CHAPTER X.

Movement toward the City of Mexico—The Duke of Wellington's comments—Movements of Santa Anna—A commission meets General Worth to treat for terms—Worth enters Puebla—Civil administration of the city not interfered with—Scott arrives at Puebla—Scott's address to the Mexicans after the battle of Cerro Gordo—Contreras—Reconnoissance of the *pedregal*—Defeat of the Mexicans at Contreras—Battle of Churubusco—Arrival of Nicholas P. Trist, commissioner—General Scott meets a deputation proposing an armistice—He addresses a communication to the head of the Mexican Government—Appointment of a commission to meet Mr. Trist—Major Lally—Meeting of Mr. Trist with the Mexican commissioners—Failure to agree—Armistice violated by the Mexicans and notice from General Scott—Santa Anna's insolent note—The latter calls a meeting of his principal officers—Molino del Rey—Chapultepec—Losses on both sides.

THE army began its movement from Puebla toward the City of Mexico on August 6, 1847. Twiggs's division was in the advance, General William Selby Harney's cavalry leading and the siege train bringing up the rear. The other three divisions followed successively on the 8th, 9th, and 10th. No division was at any time more than seven or eight miles from support. It was expected that the army of Santa Anna would be met at Rio Frio, and hence General Scott's great caution in his movement to keep his divisions in supporting distance.

The Duke of Wellington was so interested in this

march of the army from Vera Cruz to the Mexican capital that he caused its movements to be marked on a map daily, as information was received. Admiring its triumphs up to the basin of Mexico, he now said: "Scott is lost. He has been carried away by successes. He can't take the city, and he can't fall back upon his base."

General Santa Anna, finding himself without money and with but a small following of troops at Orizaba, marched by way of Aculcingo and Amasoque to Puebla. In the meantime he was using all efforts to gather re-enforcements for his army. There was but one day's interval between the troops of General Worth and the Mexican brigades of Leonard Perez and the cavalry under General Alcorta, the whole of which was commanded by General Santa Anna when he passed Amasoque. Finding that he could not successfully defend Puebla, the Mexican general withdrew to San Martin and Amasoque. Soon afterward he moved on the road toward the City of Mexico.

Two or three miles from Puebla a commission met General Worth to treat for terms. A halt of a few hours was made, when the march was resumed, and the American forces without opposition marched into the Grand Plaza between the palace of the Governor and the cathedral.

A Mexican historian thus describes the first appearance and occupation of Puebla by the American troops: "The singular appearance of some of the soldiers, their trains, their artillery, their large horses, all attracted the curiosity of the multitude, and at the corners and squares an immense crowd surrounded the new conquerors. The latter—extremely fatigued, confiding in the mutual guarantees stipulated by the Ayuntamientimo and General Worth, or perhaps despising a people who easily permitted the occupation of their territory—stacked arms in the plaza while waiting for quarters, while some wandered into neighboring streets to drink pulque and embrace the leperos, with whom they seemed old acquaintances. [The leperos were the vagabonds of the city and country.] There is no doubt that more than ten thousand persons occupied the plazas and corners. One cry, one effort, the spirit of one determined man would have sufficed; and if once this multitude had pressed in on the enemy, they would have inevitably perished. Nothing was done. General Worth took quarters in the Governor's palace, east of the Grand Plaza, and upon its flagstaff hoisted the Stars and Stripes."

General Worth took possession of Puebla on May 15th, and, acting under orders of General Scott, he issued orders which gave assurance to the inhabitants that they would not be disturbed either in person or property, and that they could continue without molestation their ordinary business. The markets were kept open, and no officer or soldier was permitted to take anything without paying the regular market price.

The civil administration of the city was not interfered with. The police of the city was continued under the regulations of the city government. The churches, of which there were a large number, were opened, and continued their usual functions, and the attendance was largely augmented by the American officers and men. In fact, the city, except for the presence of the United States troops, was in all other respects governed and conducted as before its occupation.

General Scott left Jalapa on May 23d for Puebla. He arrived there on the 28th, and was met and escorted into the city by a number of officers. Along the streets of the city through which he passed the balconies were filled with Mexican ladies and the avenues crowded with men. The populace cheered him heartily and escorted him to the palace. The soldiers, volunteers and regulars, gave him the heartiest welcome, showing that he had the respect and confidence of the army, and the demonstrations of the Mexicans evidenced that they regarded him as a humane and Christian conqueror.

In this connection it is well to produce the address of General Scott to the Mexican people after the battle of Cerro Gordo :

"MEXICANS! The late events of the war and the measures adopted in consequence by our Government make it my duty to address you, in order to lay before you truths of which you are ignorant, because they have been criminally concealed from you. I do not ask you to believe me simply on my word—though he who has not been found false has a claim to be believed—but to judge for yourselves of these truths from facts within the view and scrutiny of you all. Whatever may have been the origin of this war, which the United States was forced to undertake by insurmountable causes, we regard it as an evil. War is ever such to both belligerents, and the reason and justice of the case, if not known on both sides, are in dispute and claimed by each. You have proof of this truth as well as we, for in Mexico, as in the United States, there have existed and do exist two

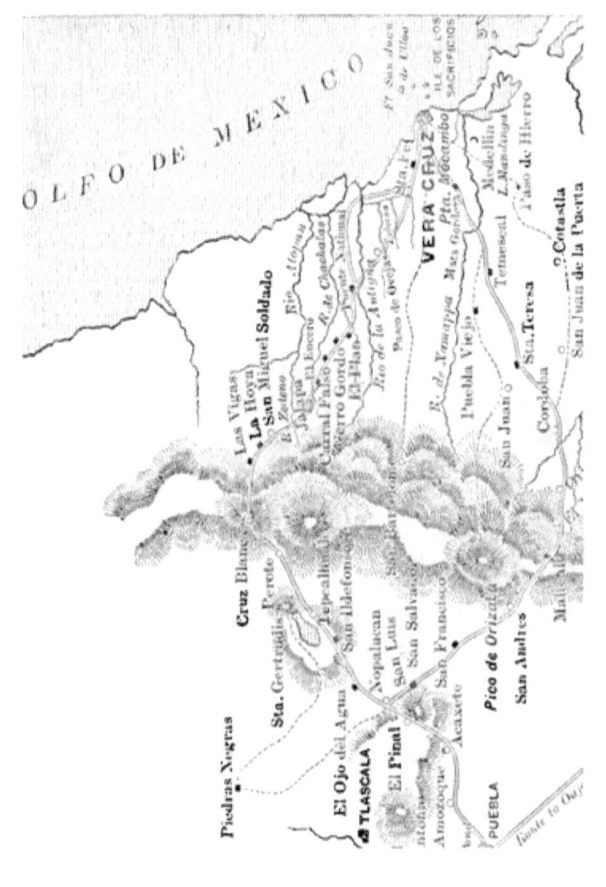

opposite parties, one desiring peace and the other war. Governments have, however, sacred duties to perform from which they can not swerve; and these duties frequently impose, from national considerations, a silence and reserve that displeases at all times the majority of those who, from views purely personal or private, are formed in opposition, to which Governments can pay little attention, expecting the nation to repose in them the confidence due to a magistracy of its own selection—considerations of high policy and of continental American interests precipitated even in spite of circumspection of the Cabinet at Washington. This Cabinet, ardently desiring to terminate all differences with Mexico, spared no effort compatible with honor and dignity. It cherished the most flattering hopes of attaining this end by frank explanations and reasonings addressed to the judgment and prudence of the virtuous and patriotic government of General Herrera. An unexpected misfortune dispelled these hopes and closed every avenue of an honorable adjustment. Your new Government disregarded your national interests, as well as those of continental America, and yielded, moreover, to foreign influences the most opposed to these interests, the most fatal to the future of Mexican liberty and of that republican system which the United States holds it a duty to preserve and protect. Duty, honor, and dignity placed us under the necessity of not losing a season of which the monarchical party was fast taking advantage. As not a moment was to be lost, we acted with a promptness and decision suited to the urgency of the case, in order to avoid a complication of interests which might render our relations more difficult and involved. Again, in the course of civil war, the Government of General Paredes was overthrown. We could not but look upon this as a fortunate event, believing that any other administration representing Mexico would be less deluded, more patriotic, and more prudent, looking to the common good, weighing probabilities, strength, resources, and, above all, the general opinion as to the inevitable results of a national war. We were deceived, and perhaps you Mexicans were also deceived, in judging of the real intentions of General Santa Anna when you recalled and when your Government permitted him to return. Under this state of things the Mexican nation has seen the results lamented by all, and by us most sincerely, for we appreciate as is due the valor and noble decision of those unfortunate men who go to battle ill-conducted, worse cared for, and almost always enforced by violence, deceit, or perfidy. We are witnesses, and we shall not be taxed with partiality as a party interested when we lament with surprise that the heroic behavior of the garrison at Vera Cruz in its valiant defense has been aspersed by the general who has just been routed and put to shameful flight at Buena Vista by a force far inferior to his own. The same general rewarded the insurgents of the capital, promoters of civil war, and heaped outrage upon those who had just acquired for themselves singular distinction by a resistance beyond expectation and of admirable decision. Finally, the bloody events of Cerro Gordo have plainly shown the Mexican nation what it may reasonably expect if it is no longer blind to its real situation—a situation to which it has been brought by some of its generals whom it has most distinguished and in whom it has most confidence. The hardest heart would have been moved to grief in contemplating any battlefield in Mexico a moment after the last struggle. Those generals whom the nation has paid without service rendered for so many years, have, in the day of need, with some honorable exceptions, but served to injure her by their bad example or unskillfulness. The dead and wounded on those battlefields received no marks of military distinction, sharing alike the sad fate which has been the same from Palo Alto to Cerro Gordo; the dead remained unburied and the wounded abandoned to the clemency and charity of the victor. Soldiers who go to battle knowing they have such reward to look for deserve to be classed with the most heroic, for they are stimulated by no hope of glory, nor remembrance, nor a sigh, nor even a grave! Again, contemplate, honorable Mexicans, the lot of peaceful and industrious citizens in all classes of your country. The possessions of the Church menaced and presented as an allurement to revolution and anarchy; the fortunes of rich proprietors pointed out for plunder of armed ruffians; and merchants and the mechanic, the husbandman and the manufacturer, burdened with contributions, excises, monopolies, duties on consumption, surrounded by officers and collectors of these odious internal customs; the man of letters and the legislator, the freeman of knowledge who dares to speak, persecuted without trial by some faction or by the very rulers who abuse their power; and criminals unpunished are set at liberty, as were those of Peroté. What, then, Mexicans, is the liberty of which you boast? I do not believe that Mexicans at the present day want the courage to confess errors which do not dishonor them, or to adopt a system of true liberty—one of peace and union with their brethren and neighbors of the North. Neither can I believe the Mexicans ignorant of the infamy of the calumnies put forth by the press in order to excite hostility against us. No, public spirit can not be created or animated by falsehood. We have not profaned your temples, nor abused your women, nor seized your property, as they could have you believe. We say it with pride, and we confirm it by an appeal to your bishops and the curates of Tampico, Tuzpan, Matamoros, Monterey, Vera Cruz, and Jalapa; to all clergy, civil authorities, and inhabitants of all places we have occupied. We adore the same God, and a large portion of our army, as well as of the people of the United States, are Catholics, like yourselves. We punish crime wherever we find it, and reward merit and virtue. The army of the United States respects, and will ever respect, private property of every class, and the property of the Mexican Church. Woe to him who does not where we are! Mexicans, the past is beyond remedy, but the future may yet be controlled. I have repeatedly declared to you that the Government and the people of the United States desire peace, desire your sincere friendship. Abandon, then, state prejudices; cease to be the sport of private ambition, and conduct yourselves like a great American nation. Abandon at once these old colonial habits, and learn to be truly free, truly republican. You may then soon attain prosperity and happiness, of which you possess all the elements; *but remember that you are Americans*, and that your happiness is not to come from Europe. I desire, in conclusion, to say to you with equal frankness that, were it necessary, an army of one hundred thousand Americans would soon be among you, and that the United States, if forced to terminate by arms their differences with you, would not do it in an uncertain or precarious, or, still less, in a dishonorable manner. It would be an insult to the intelligent people of their country to doubt their knowledge of your power. The system of forming guerrilla parties to annoy us will, I assure you, produce only evil to this country and none to our army, which knows how to protect itself and how to proceed against such cutthroats; and if, so far from calming resentments and passion, you try to irritate, you will but force upon us the hard necessity of retaliation. In that event, you can not blame us for the consequences which will fall upon yourselves. I shall march with this army upon Puebla and Mexico. I do not conceal this from you. From those capitals I may again address you. We desire peace, friendship, and union; it is for you to choose whether you prefer continued hostilities. In either case, be assured, I will keep my word. WINFIELD SCOTT."

Worth's division, now preceded by Harney's cavalry, moved from San Augustin on the main road toward the City of Mexico. These were followed by the other divisions of the army. On this route was situated the *pedregal*, which is a field of volcanic rock of very uneven surface. It is between the roads leading to the capital from San Augustin and Padierna. A reconnoissance of the *pedregal* was made by Lieutenants Robert E. Lee and Pierre G. T. Beauregard, who reported that there was a passage for wagons of only a mile, and the remainder might be crossed by infantry, carefully picking the way. The enemy were in position beyond the *pedregal* with considerable artillery.

General Scott, on the night of the 18th, ordered a movement in the direction of Padierna. Worth was ordered to cover San Antonio, Quitman to hold San Augustin, and Pillow to march over the *pedregal*, while Twiggs was to cover and support Pillow's movement. On the morning of this movement the Mexican General Blanco was ordered to construct batteries, and General Mejia to take position on the Pelon Cuauhtitlan to command the expected movements of the American army. General Santa Anna wrote from San Antonio through the Minister of War to General Valencia, at San Angel: "The general in chief directs me to say to your Excellency that the enemy having now [August 18th, 3 P. M.] taken up a position on our left in front of San Antonio with a part of his forces, it is clear that to-morrow at the latest he will undertake the attack of this fortification, although it appears there is a movement going on at the same time on our right. His Excellency therefore directs you at daylight to-morrow morning to fall back with your forces to Coyoacan, and send forward your artillery to the fort and the *tête-de-pont* at Churubusco."

General Valencia declined to obey this order, giving his reason as follows: "I should like much to be able to obey this order, but, in view of present circumstances, my conscience as a military man and my patriotism will not permit me. I believe the national cause will be lost if I should abandon these positions and the road leading from San Augustin through Padierna to these points. To me it is as clear as the light of day that the enemy will undertake his attack, if not to-morrow, the day after, and that he desires to make two attacks at the same time, the one true and the other false, and that, should he find at the commencement of his movements one of the points of attack abandoned, as this, for instance, he will pass by this route with all his forces, and thus be enabled to assail our flank and turn our rear; or, if he prefer it, he may pass on without obstruction to the City of Mexico."

General Valencia, however, ordered a thorough reconnoissance by General Mendoza, an engineer officer, who reported "that Padierna was absolutely indefensible, and that it was believed best to retire for reasons expressed in his note." General Valencia ordered Colonel Barreiro to Zacatepetl to watch and report the movements of the enemy. He further ordered Colonel Mendoza to occupy with his regiment the edge of the *pedregal*, having in his front a detachment of infantry under Captain Solos, and beyond him a detachment of cavalry To the left of Padierna was posted the corps of San Luis Potosi, to the right the brigade of Lieutenant-Colonel Cabrera, and on the ridge were the batteries and brigade of General Mejia. The supporting line were three battalions. The reserve at Anzaldo, a mixed company of infantry and cavalry, was the command of General Solos, supported on the right by two regiments of infantry.

Pillow's and Twiggs's divisions were observed by Colonel Barreiro to be moving over the mountain of Zacatepetl and the *pedregal*. On an open ridge commanding the *pedregal* General Valencia had planted guns which commanded the *pedregal* in the direction of San Augustin. On the morning of August 19th General Santa Anna ordered two battalions to move from Churubusco to San Antonio, Pillow's division of the American army having moved out from San Augustin on the road to Padierna, which was to be covered by Twiggs's division. Twiggs moved, following Quitman, and passed beyond San Augustin. General Alvarez closed on his rear. A working party of five hundred men under engineer officers was detailed from Pillow's division to make the road to Padierna practicable for artillery. While work was progressing on this road General Scott notified General Pillow that Valencia was placing heavy guns in position, and ordered that the work be pushed forward as rapidly as possible. Before the road was finished half the distance Twiggs's division passed Pillow's command, and its advance was fired upon by the Mexicans. General Persifor F. Smith ordered the mounted rifle regiment under Major William Wing Loring, aided by a section of Magruder's battery, to drive in the Mexican pickets. Lieutenant George B. McClellan placed the artillery in position, but before it was ready for action it received a fire from the guns on the elevated ridge beyond Padierna. The remainder of Smith's brigade and the other section of Lieutenant John Bankhead Magruder's battery were ordered forward, and the Mexicans were driven back. General Bennet Riley's brigade was ordered to the right, and to pass over the *pedregal* and take possession in the enemy's rear. General Cadwallader's brigade was ordered to support Riley's movement. General Scott, perceiving that re-enforcements were approaching Valencia from the City

CAPTURE OF PADIERNA.

of Mexico, ordered a regiment of General Franklin Pierce's brigade to move forward and occupy San Geronimo, and General James Shields with two regiments (New York, and Palmetto, South Carolina) was ordered forward as a support. General Persifor F. Smith now moved to the front across the *pedregal*, having left detachments as supports to the artillery of Magruder and Callender, which were ordered to open fire on the beginning of General Smith's movement. This movement of General Persifor F. Smith was led and conducted by Lieutenant Gustavus W. Smith. When this force reached the village or town of San Geronimo a large force of the enemy came in sight. Pierce's brigade was at once ordered to the front, and was met by a heavy fire. General Pierce having been disabled, Colonel Robert Ransom, of the Ninth Infantry, was in command of the forces, which were conducted by Lieutenant Isaac Ingles Stevens, and moved to the right and front of Magruder's battery. Ransom, uniting with the detachment left by General Smith, took possession of Padierna, driving the Mexican General Mendoza. Riley's command was the first to pass the *pedregal*, when it occupied the road on the opposite side with Captain Simon Henry Drum's company of the Fourth Artillery. A detachment of Mexican lancers escorting a train was encountered and captured.

Riley's command continued its advance, when a company of Mexican lancers was met and repulsed by Captain Silas Casey's company. A mounted force, under the Mexican General Frontera, consisting of two regiments, was met and repulsed by the Second Infantry under Captain Charles T. Morris and the

Seventh Infantry under Lieutenant-Colonel Joseph Plympton. General Frontera was killed while leading a charge. Riley now withdrew to San Geronimo, which he found occupied by Cadwallader's and Smith's brigades, and a regiment of Pierce's brigade under command of Colonel George Washington Morgan. When General Valencia's advanced forces were driven in by Twiggs's division on the *pedregal*, Valencia announced (August 19th, 2 P. M.) to General Santa Anna at San Antonio that the enemy were approaching Padierna, the artillery had opened fire, and the battle had begun. General Santa Anna at once, on receipt of this information, sent an officer to Coyoacan with orders to General Perez to move at once to Padierna, and himself with two regiments and five pieces of artillery proceeded to join him. He arrived at Coyoacan just at the time when the command of Perez was moving, and he ordered it to move rapidly.

On the evening of August 19th General P. F. Smith was in San Geronimo with three brigades of infantry, but without cavalry or artillery. His communications with the main army were cut off except through the *pedregal*. He determined to attack, however, the next morning at daylight, carry the enemy's works, and establish his communications with the main army. His disposition of troops was as follows for the night: Cadwallader's command in the outer edge of the village of San Geronimo, Riley's brigade parallel to it, the Rifles on the right, and the Third Infantry in the churchyard. In the night Captain R. E. Lee arrived, bearing a letter from General Scott asking to be informed of affairs beyond the *pedregal*. The information sought for was given, and Captain Lee was requested to inform General Scott of General Smith's intention to attack Valencia next morning, and asking that a diversion be made on Valencia's front. General Shields arrived at midnight, and was left to hold the village and cut off the enemy's retreat. In the meantime Colonel Ransom abandoned Padierna, which was soon afterward occupied by General Valencia's forces, but not without stout resistance by the small detachment left there.

At nightfall General Santa Anna fell back to San Angel, but failed to give notice of the movement to General Valencia. Mexican history states that at 9 P. M. Ramero and Del Rio arrived at Valencia's headquarters and delivered an order from Santa Anna to Valencia to retire. General Solos, however, who was present, denies this, saying that the order was qualified by one to spike the guns, destroy the ammunition, and saving only what could be safely transported. General Valencia declined to obey the order. At 2.30 P. M. of August 20th Smith's troops moved to reach Valencia's rear. Riley's brigade and Cadwallader's followed this movement. General Shields with the New York regiment of Colonel Ward B. Burnett and the South Carolina regiment under Colonel Pierce M. Butler remained at the village, to intercept and cut off the enemy's retreat and to prevent re-enforcements from reaching the Mexicans.

The night was intensely dark, and the streets of the village were very narrow, cut into gullies and very muddy. A heavy rain was pouring down, and the march was made under difficulties and necessarily slow. General Smith's position was on an eminence about one thousand yards from the enemy's works, from which point he made the attack. Riley moved up the ravine to a slope leading to a high point of the ridge and attacked the enemy some eight hundred yards distant. Cadwallader followed Riley, and the Mounted Rifles and Engineer Company moved to a position in rear of the force confronting Riley. The Third Infantry and First Artillery were held in reserve. The attack was made as ordered by General Smith, and the enemy fled, pursued by Riley, the Mounted Rifles, and Engineers.

The Third Infantry and First Artillery, held in reserve, were attacked by a force of cavalry, which was driven off, and Valencia was completely routed. General Shields, who held the village, seized the main road and cut off retreat in that direction. The enemy fled in the greatest confusion. The battle of Contreras was one of the most brilliant victories of the war. It opened the road to the City of Mexico. Seven hundred of the enemy were killed, eight hundred and thirteen prisoners were captured, including eighty-eight officers, of whom four were generals; many standards, twenty-two pieces of brass cannon, a large number of stands of small arms, seven hundred pack mules, many horses, and large quantities of ordnance stores were added to the outfit of the American army.

General Scott had planned to open up the way for the march of his army to the City of Mexico by the way of Padierna. Knowing or believing that a stubborn defense would be made by the Mexicans, he had ordered General Worth to march from San Antonio on the morning of August 20th, with Garland's brigade, by way of San Augustin to Padierna, to be fol-

CHURUBUSCO.

lowed by General Quitman, who was ordered to leave a cavalry force to hold San Antonio. But General Persifor F. Smith had won the battle before these troops arrived.

A sufficient guard having been left with the prisoners, General Persifor F. Smith was ordered with his brigade, the Mounted Rifles and Engineers, in pursuit of the fleeing enemy. They were attacked at San Angel, but the attacking party were soon driven off. General Pillow joined these forces at San Angel, and General Scott came up with them at Coyoacan, where he had ordered the army to halt.

From this point in the direction of the capital, Churubusco was one mile; two miles to the southeast was San Antonio. Churubusco is about six miles south of the City of Mexico, on a river of the same name, and on the road from San Angel and San Antonio from San Augustin. General Scott on his arrival ordered Captain Lee, with Captain Phil Kearney's company of the First Dragoons and a company of the Mounted Rifles, to make a reconnoissance. In the meantime Pillow and Cadwallader were to attack San Antonio in the rear, General Worth assailing it in front. A reconnoissance having been made of the convent of San Pablo, in the town of Churubusco, a brigade from Twiggs's division, a part of Smith's brigade, Riley's brigade, and Taylor's battery were ordered to attack. After the defeat of General Valencia at Contreras, General Worth returned with Garland's brigade in front of San Antonio. His orders were to attack as soon as Pillow and Twiggs, moving from Contreras, approached in the rear. Worth ordered Clarke's brigade to move over the *pedregal* and turn the right flank of the fortifications at San Antonio and cut the enemy's line of communication. Henry Francis Clarke's brigade was attacked on its march, but dispersed the attacking force, and soon encountered the rear of the Mexicans from San Antonio and engaged them. Pillow with Cadwallader's brigade, joined Worth in pursuit of the fleeing Mexican troops and both attacked the *tête-de-pont* in their front. Riley's brigade having been ordered forward, General Scott ordered Pierce's brigade to move by the road leading north from Coyoacan across the Churubusco River by a bridge, turn to the right, and seize the causeway in the rear of the *tête-de-pont*. General Scott, learning that General Shields, in the rear of the Mexican lines, was in danger of being cut off and captured, ordered Major E. V. Sumner with the Mounted Rifles under Major W. W. Loring, and the Second Dragoons under Captain Henry Hastings Sibley, to his support. The attack of the Americans being persistently pressed on all sides, the Mexicans gave way and made a precipitous retreat, pursued by the victorious Americans.

There remained yet to be captured the convent of San Pablo. This building, having very thick walls, was impervious to the attack of field pieces. It was defended by a well-constructed bastion, with flooded ditches, and guns placed in the embrasure. The attack was made by the First Artillery, followed by the Third Infantry. During the attack the enemy made several sallies from the convent, which were repulsed. The troops in the convent consisted of the Independencia and Bravo battalions, about six hundred and fifty each, with the necessary cannoneers for six guns, and in the *tête-de-pont* cannoneers for five guns, the San Patricio companies, and the battalion of Tlapa. Along the Rio Churubusco, on the north side, was the brigade of General Perez, some twenty-five hundred strong. The Mexicans made a brave and gallant defense, but were compelled to succumb. The battles of Contreras and Churubusco were fought on the same day, and were really one battle. In both actions the American loss was one hundred and thirty-nine killed and nine hundred and twenty-six wounded. The Mexican loss was near four thousand killed and wounded, with the loss of three hundred prisoners, thirty-seven cannon, and a large number of small arms with ammunition.

General Scott could easily have occupied the Mexican capital on the same day, but meanwhile Mr. Nicholas P. Trist had arrived from Washington with instructions from the President to endeavor to make a treaty of peace, and both he and General Scott thought it best to await the turn of events looking to that end. On the next morning, August 27, 1847, General Scott set out on the San Antonio road, and was met near Churubusco by a deputation bearing a white flag from the Mexican Government, proposing an armistice of thirty hours for burying the dead and collecting the wounded, which he at once rejected. The deputation accompanying the flag consisted of Señores Basadre, Mora y Villamil and Aranjos, who had been sent by Pacheco, Minister of Foreign Affairs. General Santa Anna expressed great dissatisfaction at the action of the Minister, on which he resigned. General Scott addressed a communication to the head of the Mexican Government and general in chief, in which he said that too much blood had already been spilled, and suggested that it was time the differences between the two republics should be settled. He mentioned (what was known to the Mexican authorities) that a commissioner on the part of the United States, clothed with full power to that end, was with his army. He expressed his willingness on reasonable terms to agree to a short armistice. While he proposed to wait until the next morning for a reply, he announced his intention " in the meantime to seize and occupy such positions outside of the capital as I may deem necessary to the shelter and comfort of this army."

The Mexican authorities, through Alcorta, Secretary of War and of the Navy, named two brigadier generals of the Mexican army, Mora y Villamil and Benito Quijano, to act as commissioners.

General Scott appointed as commissioners Major General John A. Quitman, Brigadier-General Franklin Pierce, and Brevet Brigadier-General Persifor F. Smith. The convention concluded its work on the 24th of August. It was agreed that hostilities should cease at once within thirty leagues of the Mexican capital. No work of a military character was to be done, and any re-enforcements or munitions of war except that now on its way to either army was to be stopped at a distance of twenty-eight leagues from the capital. The American army was not to obstruct the passage from the surrounding country into the capital of the ordinary supplies of food necessary for the subsistence of the Mexican army and the inhabitants within the city, nor were the Mexican authorities to obstruct the passage of supplies of subsistence from the city or country necessary for the supply of the American army. The armistice was to continue pending negotiations or until the commander of either army should give notice to the other of its cessation;

MAJOR LALLY AT OVEJAS.

and forty-eight hours after such notice General Worth, on the night of the 21st, moved his division to Tacubaya, where he was preceded by General Scott, and established his headquarters in the Bishop's Palace. General Quitman remained at San Augustin, to which point General Shields returned with his command. General Twiggs was at San Angel, and General Pillow at Mexcoac.

Previous to the occurrences just narrated, Major Folliot Thornton Lally had on August 6th marched with a force of about one thousand men from Vera Cruz. He was joined *en route* by a company of mounted Georgia volunteers, one of Louisiana mounted men, and two six-pounders, under command of Lieutenant Henry B. Sears, of the Second Artillery. General Don Juan Soto, Governor of the State of Vera Cruz, organized a force between one thousand and two thousand strong, a part of which were paroled prisoners, with the purpose of attacking Major Lally and capturing his wagon train, which was supposed to carry a large amount of silver coin. An attack was made by this force on Major Lally at the pass of Ovejas, the engagement lasting an hour and a half. Captains James Nelson Caldwell, of the Voltigeurs, and Arthur C. Cummings, Eleventh Infantry, were severely wounded. Nine enlisted men were wounded, one mortally. The Mexican loss is not known. On August 12th the command reached Puente Nacional and found the Mexicans in considerable force, strongly barricaded. An artillery fire was opened on them and they were driven back. The American loss in this affair was sixty killed and wounded. On approaching the battlefield of Cerro Gordo they were again attacked, and sustained a loss of one killed and eight wounded. Several other attacks of a similar character were made, but without success. Major Lally, with his troops and wagon train, arrived at Jalapa thirteen days out from Vera Cruz, when without interruption five days would have been sufficient for the march. Mr. Trist notified the Mexican Minister of Foreign Affairs, August 25th, of the object of his mission, and requested a meeting. He was advised that commissioners would meet him on the 27th at Azapotzalco, which was between the two armies. General Santa Anna, after appointing several persons who declined, named General Herrera, Señor Conto, General Mora y Villamil, Señor Atristain, and Secretary Miguel Arroyo. On the morning of the 27th, before the meeting of the commissioners, a train of wagons sent into the city to obtain supplies for the American army was met by a mob, stoned and driven away. Subsequently an apology was offered for this gross infraction of the armistice, and the wagons returned and secured their stores.

On meeting the commissioners, Mr. Trist exhibited his powers, which were ample, but that of the Mexicans was simply confined to hearing propositions from Mr. Trist. Mr. Trist objected to this limitation, but was assured that when it became necessary to sign the treaty they would exhibit full powers. The American commissioners presented the project of a treaty the leading feature of which related to the boundary line between the two countries. It was also a part of the project that Mexico was to concede to the United States the right of transport across the Isthmus of Tehuantepec free from tolls. These and all else asked by Mr. Trist were refused. The Mexican commissioners asked for further instructions from their Government, which were given —that they should neither exceed nor modify the former instructions given them. They asked to be relieved, as these instructions placed them in an embarrassing position. A council of ministers was called, and their former instructions were changed so as to authorize them "to approximate to them as much as possible, agreeing to some modifications which the circumstances of the country may exact, as well as to things of minor importance which may arise during the discussion."

On September 1st, when the third meeting was held, the Mexican commissioners exhibited plenary powers. No agreement being reached, it was proposed to extend the armistice for forty-five days. But on September 5th the Mexican commissioners were informed that the Government would not consent to the extension or to the cession of New Mexico, which Mr. Trist had insisted on. The Mexican commissioners then submitted a counter project on the 6th, which in effect refused all of the more important concessions asked by the United States. With this the diplomatic conferences terminated. General Scott at once called a conference with his general officers. He stated to them the bad faith of the enemy, who commenced the work of repair on their fortifications. He recited the incident of the mobbing of teamsters. He closed by saying: " I have therefore called you to headquarters to advise upon the propriety of dissolving the armistice, or [after a pause] to inform you that I have dissolved it, and to read to you my letter to General Santa Anna notifying him of the fact." Looking for the letter, he said, "I have torn it up." He at once wrote a note and dispatched it to General Santa Anna, as follows:

"HEADQUARTERS, ARMY OF THE UNITED STATES OF AMERICA,
"TACUBAYA, *September 6, 1847.*

"*To his Excellency the President and General in Chief of the Mexican Republic.*

"SIR: The seventh article, as also the twelfth, that stipulates *that trade* shall *remain unmolested*—of the armistice or military convention which I had the honor to ratify and to exchange with your Excellency the 24th ultimo—has been repeatedly violated, beginning soon after date, on the part of Mexico; and I now have good reasons to believe that within the last forty-eight hours, if not earlier, the third article of that convention has been equally violated by the same party. These direct breaches of faith give to this army the most perfect right to resume hostilities against Mexico, without any notice whatever; but, to allow time for possible apology or reparation, I now give formal notice that, unless full satisfaction on these allegations should be received by me by 12 o'clock meridian to-morrow, I shall consider the said armistice at an end from and after that hour.

"I have the honor to be your Excellency's most obedient servant, WINFIELD SCOTT."

General Santa Anna replied in an insolent note, denying General Scott's charges and making counter charges.

Many newspapers throughout the United States criticised General Scott in the severest terms for being duped by General Santa Anna into an armistice which the latter only desired to recruit his army. There is the strongest evidence—that of Mr. Trist and the Mexican commissioners—that Santa Anna was really desirous to make peace. The manifesto which he issued to the nation is itself sufficient proof on this score; and certainly it reflects the highest credit on General Scott, that when he was at the very gates of the capital, which he could have entered in a few hours, he was willing to spare not only the lives of his own gallant army, but those of the enemy. Santa Anna now called a meeting of the principal officers and governmental civilians to meet him in the palace, and it was agreed to continue resistance.

A force was at once sent out under cover of the guns of Chapultepec to strengthen the position and resist the advance of the Americans. At this point was a number of very large buildings known as Molino del Rey, which had formerly been used for the manufacture of ordnance stores. Chapultepec was a strong, well-fortified and well-armed fort. Molino del Rey was occupied by a brigade of the National Guards, under General Leon. These were re-enforced on the morning of the 7th by a brigade under General Rangel. The Casta Mata, a large storehouse surrounded by a wide ditch and inclosed by a bastioned fort, was occupied by the brigade of General Perez, and between these two positions was posted General Ramirez's brigade with six pieces of artillery. In the rear occupying some woods were the reserves.

The Mexican cavalry, about two thousand strong, under command of General Alvarez, was two miles west from Chapultepec on the right of the line. After a thorough reconnoissance by the American engineer, General Scott on the afternoon of the 7th issued the necessary orders for massing and disposing his army. The general depot was established at Mexcoac. One brigade of Twiggs's division under Colonel Plympton was ordered to move and threaten the city by way of the Niño Perdido road, moving at 6 P. M. Quitman marched from San Augustin on the 8th to Coyoacan. Pillow was to advance with one brigade and take command of the advanced position which was held by Twiggs's division and a part of his own, while Cadwallader was to join Worth. At Molino del Rey was supposed to be a cannon foundry, and it was thought by General Scott that a large quantity of powder was stored there. General Worth was ordered to make the attack, carry the enemy's lines, and destroy the ordnance works and return to his former position. To carry out this order General Worth directed General John Garland's brigade to be posted on the right with two pieces of Simon H. Drum's battery, so as to prevent re-enforcements from Chapultepec, and to be in position to support, if necessary, the assaulting forces; the guns of Captain Benjamin Hugér to be placed on the eminence to Garland's right and rear; a storming party of some five hundred picked men under Brevet Major George Wright, Eighth Infantry, to take post near and to the right of Hugér's battering guns, to attack the battery in the center of the enemy's lines; Clarke's brigade under Colonel James S. McIntosh and Captain James Duncan's battery opposite the enemy's right to support the assaulting column; Cadwallader to be held in reserve; and Major Edwin V. Sumner with his cavalry to be posted on the extreme left. Some changes were made in the disposition of the Mexican forces. Early on the morning of the 8th Hugér with two 24-pounders opened fire, and the assaulting column under Major Wright advanced under a heavy fire of grapeshot from the Mexican center and left. Undismayed, they pushed forward now under fire of musketry, captured a battery, and turned it upon the enemy, who fled in confusion. They were soon re-enforced, and rallied and reopened fire not only from their lines but from the housetops and walls. The storming party was driven back, but Duncan's battery opening fire at this time checked the Mexican advance. The light battalion of Colonel Charles F. Smith, now under command of Captain Edmund Kirby Smith, Fifth Infantry, moved forward, supported by a part of Cadwallader's brigade, and this was followed by a forward movement of Garland's brigade and Drum's battery. This movement was irresistible, and the Mexicans fell back, bravely contesting every inch of ground. Pending the fire of Duncan's battery, one section of the battery, under Lieutenant Henry J. Hunt, opened fire on the enemy's lines between the Casta Mata and Molino del Rey. McIntosh fought in close quarters, and charged and drove the enemy in his front, but received three wounds, one of which proved mortal. General Alvarez, commanding the Mexican cavalry, was held in check by the voltigeur regiment under command of Major E. V. Sumner, and Duncan's battery. The fight was continued obstinately and bravely by the Mexicans from the roofs of houses. The main force of the enemy, having been driven toward Chapultepec, were rallied by General Peña Y. Barragan, and made an advance. Captain Drum was ordered forward, and with a captured six-pounder cleared the road. The battle lasted for more than two hours and was hotly contested by the Mexicans. Those who escaped death or capture retreated to Chapultepec, leaving General Worth in full possession of their lines. Worth's loss was one hundred and sixteen killed and six hundred and seventy-one wounded, a total of seven hundred and eighty-seven. His estimate of the Mexican strength was fourteen thousand.

CHAPTER XI.

General Quitman's movements to San Antonio and Coyoacan—Movements of General Pillow—General reconnoissance by Scott—Chapultepec—Scott announces his line of attack—Surrender of the Mexican General Bravo—Preparations to move on the capital—Entry of General Scott into the City of Mexico—General Quitman made Military Governor—General Scott's orders—Movements of Santa Anna—General Lane—American and Mexican deserters—Orders as to collection of duties and civil government.

GENERAL QUITMAN, who, it will be remembered, was to march from San Augustin to Coyoacan on the 8th, having heard firing in the direction of Tacubaya, moved, early on September 8th, to San Antonio, and from thence on to Coyoacan. A reconnoissance was made in the afternoon by General Pillow as far as the town of Piedad and the Niño Perdido roads, one of which leads to the Belen gate of the city and the other through a gate of the same name. These roads run parallel to each other, about three fourths of a mile apart. On the 9th, General Scott, accompanied by Captain R. E. Lee, made an examination of the works near the San Antonio gate, where they discovered Mexican soldiers busily at work. On the 9th Riley took position to the right of Piedad, and was joined on the 11th by Smith's brigade and Francis Taylor's and Edward James Steptoe's batteries.

An advanced post of the enemy was evacuated on the approach of the Americans on the night of the 9th and occupied; this force was strengthened by both infantry and artillery, and a bridge was thrown over a ditch in front of it for the passage of cannon. Colonel Harvey, on the night of the 10th, occupied Mexcoac with the Second Dragoons for the purpose of protecting the hospitals and stores there. General Scott called a meeting of his general officers and informed them of his plan of attack. He had determined to attack either the San Antonio Garita or Chapultepec and the western gates. After hearing the opinions of his officers, who differed on the place of attack, General Scott determined to make the movement on Chapultepec and the western gate, and he so announced.

A reconnoissance was made on the morning of the 11th, with a view to the location of the batteries. The locations selected by Captain Hugér, who was sent for the purpose, were adopted. The division of Quitman was ordered to unite with Pillow near Piedad in the evening, and after nightfall both divisions were to move to Tacubaya. Twiggs was ordered to remain in front of the southern gates and divert the enemy's attention.

Major Sumner with seven companies was to march at daylight and join Pillow. Chapultepec is a natural fortification, rising one hundred and fifty feet above the valley. A large building, the Military School, is on its summit, and it is bounded on the west by the Molino del Rey. The grounds are surrounded by a thick wall some fifteen feet in height. It is situated two miles from the Belen gate, and was regarded as the key to the city. The officer in com-

ATTACK ON CHAPULTEPEC.

mand was General D. Nicholas Bravo, an officer of skill, distinction, and courage. Second in command was General D. Mariano Monterde. The chief of engineers was D. Juan Cano, and D. Manuel Gamboa commandant of artillery. Generals Noriega and Perez were afterward attached to the command. The orders of the 11th to Quitman and Pillow were to march to Tacubaya, where they awaited further orders.

The attack was begun by the batteries of Drum and Peter Valentine Hagner, and the fire proved to be well directed. The guns at the castle answered promptly and kept up a vigorous cannonade. When there was some cessation of firing from the castle, Captain Lee, under direction of General Scott, using the wall of the aqueduct as a parapet, placed two pieces of artillery under Captain Horace Brooks, which opened fire. Steptoe's battery kept up a continuous firing. Santa Anna, who was deceived at the point of attack, on hearing the guns of Steptoe, moved at once to Candelaria and San Antonio Garita, where he expected the attack. At noon he repaired to Chapultepec, and, taking charge of a battalion, moved to re-enforce a work which was being attacked. The Americans opened fire on this force and compelled it to withdraw. General Bravo, expecting an assault, asked for re-enforcements, which General Santa Anna promised should be furnished in time. In the meantime the Governor of the State of Mexico had arrived with seven hundred men, having reached a point near Tacubaya on the 11th, and his arrival greatly increased the Mexicans' hopes. Not being joined by cavalry as he expected, the Governor remained inactive on the 11th, 12th, and 13th. Quitman's division, with United States Marines and a company of New York volunteers, remained in the rear near the Tacubaya road during the 12th.

It was now determined by General Scott to resume the bombardment early next morning, and to attack with the columns under Quitman and Pillow. In aid of this a storming party was detailed from Worth's division of ten officers and two hundred and sixty men, under command of Captain Samuel McKenzie, Second Artillery, and a like detail from Twiggs's division under Captain Silas Casey, Second Infantry, in support of Pillow's movement, and General P. F. Smith's brigade of Twiggs's division was ordered to the support of Quitman. The bombardment was renewed early on the morning of the 13th. Four companies of the voltigeur regiment, under Lieutenant-Colonel Joseph E. Johnston, were instructed, on the cessation of firing, to move rapidly under cover of the wall and enter the inclosure at its opening. Four companies under Colonel Timothy P. Andrews were ordered to unite with Johnston, deploy as skirmishers, and drive the enemy from his shelter. McKenzie was ordered to move in the rear of Johnston, with orders to follow the latter through the breach and advance rapidly and carry the main work by assault. A force of men carrying scaling ladders were placed with Johnston. Colonel William Trousdale, with the Eleventh and Fourteenth Regiments, and one section of Magruder's battery, under command of Lieutenant Thomas Jonathan Jackson, was placed in position in the road leading on the left of Chapultepec to the city, and ordered to advance and prevent an advance of the enemy in that direction. General Cadwallader was directed by General Pillow to execute the orders.

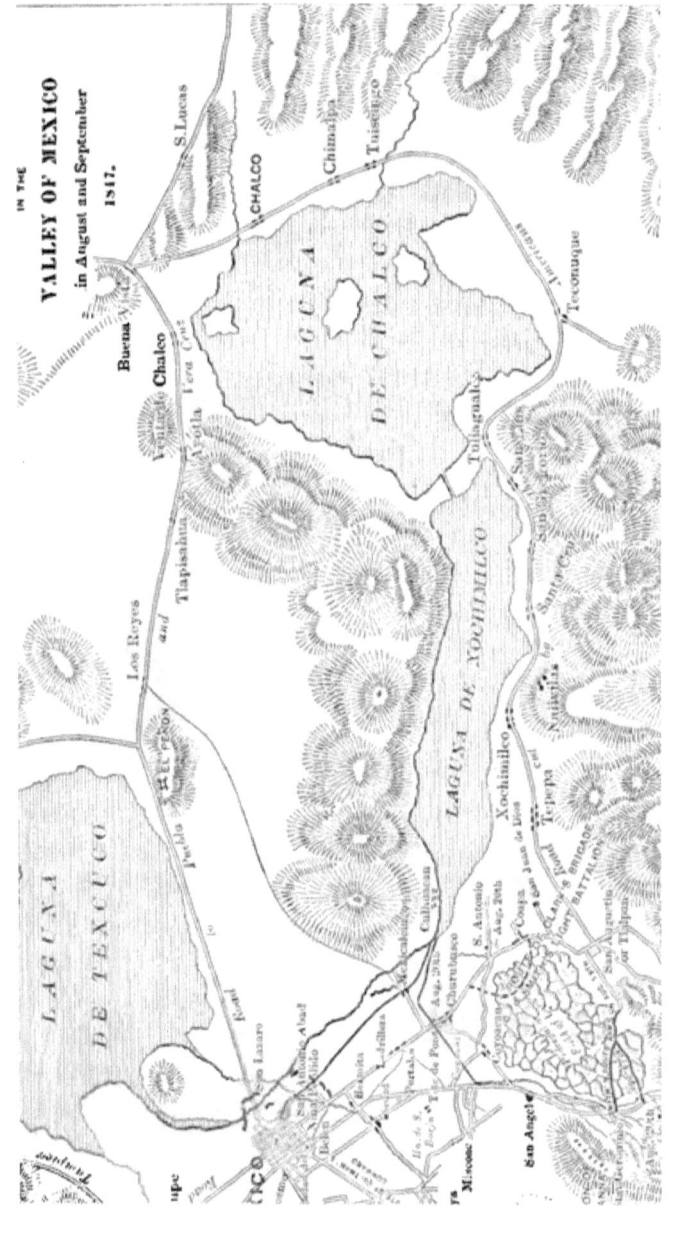

General Smith's brigade had orders to move on the right of the column of attack and cut off the retreat of the enemy in that direction. General Scott now notified the commanding officers of the attacking forces to be ready to move when the signal was given. The troops moved forward promptly at the signal, and after a brave and desperate struggle its gallant defender, General Bravo, surrendered. With the exception of Riley's brigade, Steptoe's battery, and the garrison at Mexcoac, all of the American army were engaged. General Scott's forces engaged amounted to about seven thousand five hundred men. The Mexican authorities state that eight hundred men were in Chapultepec. The brigades of Rangel and Pena were stationed near. The Mexicans engaged did not probably exceed four thousand men.

Among the prisoners captured were Generals Monterde, Saldana, and Norriega, the former superintendent of the military school, and forty of his pupils. On the commencement of the engagement these youths deserted their schoolrooms, and, arming themselves, joined in the defense of Chapultepec and fought with great bravery.

Preparations were now made for an advance and the capture of the capital. The pursuit of the retreating enemy was followed on two roads leading to the city, and there was considerable desultory fighting. At 1 o'clock A. M. on the 14th a deputation of citizens arrived at General Worth's headquarters, who were sent by him, under charge of Major William W. Mackall, to General Scott's headquarters. They reported that General Santa Anna had fled from the city, leaving it with the civil authorities, and they came to ask favorable terms of surrender. General Scott declined to make any terms with them, telling them that the city had practically been in his possession from the day before; that he would levy a moderate tax, and would be governed by no terms except his own and such only as the honor and dignity of the United States would require. Early on the morning of the 14th a white flag was displayed at the Garita de Belen, and General Quitman was requested to take possession, as the city had been evacuated by the Mexican army. Leaving a guard at the Belen gate, General Quitman marched his command and took possession of the citadel. Leaving the Second Pennsylvania Regiment at the citadel, he marched to the Grand Plaza, followed by Steptoe's battery. The Marine Battalion was placed in the National Palace, and the American flag was hoisted from its summit. Lieutenant G. T. Beauregard was dispatched to notify General Scott. About eight o'clock the general in chief, accompanied by his staff, with an escort of cavalry, all in full dress, passed through the northwestern angle into the Grand Plaza. The line of soldiers presented arms, lowered colors, and gave the drum beat. General Scott uncovered in acknowledgment of the salute, dismounted, and passed into the *porte-cochère* of the palace, followed by Generals Quitman and Smith and officers of the staff. He said, "Gentlemen, we must not be too elated with our success." Then turning, he said: "Let me present to you the Civil and Military Governor of the City of Mexico, Major-General John A. Quitman. I appoint him at this instant. He has earned the distinction, and he shall have it." The general then ascended the stairway and at once wrote General Order No. 284, as follows:

OCCUPATION OF THE CAPITAL.

"HEADQUARTERS OF THE ARMY,
"MEXICO, *September 14, 1847.*

"1. Under the favor of God, the valor of this army, after many glorious victories, has hoisted the colors of our country in the capital of Mexico and on the palace of its Government.

"2. But the war is not yet ended. The Mexican army and Government have fled, only to watch an opportunity to turn upon us with vengeance. We must, then, be upon our guard.

"3. Companies and regiments will be kept together, and all stand on the alert. Our safety is in military discipline.

"4. Let there be no drunkenness, no disorders, no straggling. Stragglers will be in great danger of assassination, and marauders shall be punished by courts-martial.

"5. All the rules so honorably observed by this glorious army in Puebla must be observed here. The honor of the army and the honor of our country call for the best behavior on the part of all. To win the approbation of their country, the valiant must be sober, orderly, and merciful. His noble brethren in arms will not be deaf to this hearty appeal from their commander and friend.

"6. Major-General Quitman is appointed Civil and Military Governor of Mexico.

"By command of Major-General Scott.

"H. L. SCOTT,
"*Acting Assistant Adjutant General.*"

Firing having been heard in the street, General Scott said to an officer: "Will you have the kindness to go and say to our volunteer friends that it is unsoldierlike, bad manners, and dangerous to discharge arms in a city, and to say to their officers that it must not occur again. None of us desire, I am sure, to hear more musketry." When the officer returned he informed the general that it was not the volunteers, but Mexicans, who were firing from the roofs of houses. Orders were at once issued to place soldiers in the steeples of churches and on the roofs of houses as sharpshooters, to sweep the streets with artillery if necessary, and to break open and enter all houses from which the troops were fired upon. The prompt execution of this order soon had the effect of putting a stop to the firing and restoring order in the city.

The retreating Mexican infantry on its arrival at Guadalupe received orders from General Santa Anna to move to Tlalnepantla. One of the Mexican battalions having discharged its guns without orders and the sound being heard, Santa Anna, believing it to have proceeded from the American army, gave orders to countermarch. On learning the truth, the order was countermanded and the march resumed. General Herrera was then ordered with artillery and infantry to march to Queretaro, while Santa Anna would move on Puebla and surprise and capture the small garrison left there by General Scott.

General Santa Anna, learning of the street firing in the city, supposed that the Mexicans had rallied and were contesting the possession of the capital by the Americans. He received this information from Prospero Terez, one of the leaders of the mob, who urged him to return. He at once dispatched a staff officer to General Herrera, ordering his return, and took up the line of march for the capital. Learning on his approach that the Mexicans under Alvarez in their attempt on the city were unsuccessful, he revoked his order to Herrera and ordered him to proceed to Queretaro. Very soon he again sent orders to countermarch and move to the capital. Again he ordered Herrera to move on Queretaro, when he marched to Guadalupe and issued a call for a junta to meet on the 16th.

From General Scott's report we learn that the loss in his army in the various engagements around and in the City of Mexico amounted to two thousand seven hundred and three. The whole force engaged in the capture of the capital was less than six thousand. The Mexicans admit that their force for the defense of the capital was about twenty thousand, with one hundred and four cannon. The Mexican army encountered by General Scott on his move to the capital was not less than thirty thousand. In nearly if not quite all of the engagements they were intrenched, and occupied their own chosen positions. Of these, the American army killed or wounded not less than seven thousand officers and men, captured three thousand seven hundred and thirty prisoners, more than twenty colors and standards, seventy-five pieces of ordnance, besides fifty-seven wall pieces, twenty thousand stand of small arms, and a large quantity of ammunition.

Following are orders issued by General Scott after the occupation of the capital:

"HEADQUARTERS OF THE ARMY, NATIONAL PALACE OF MEXICO,
"*September 16, 1847.*
"GENERAL ORDERS No. 286.

"The general in chief calls upon his brethren in arms to return, both in private and public worship, thanks and gratitude to God for the signal triumph which they have recently achieved for their country. Beginning with August 10th and ending the 14th inst., this army has gallantly fought its way through the fields and forts of Contreras, San Antonio, Churubusco, Molino del Rey, Chapultepec, and the gates of San Cosme and Tacubaya, into the capital of Mexico. When the very limited number who have performed these brilliant deeds shall have become known, the world will be astonished and our own countrymen filled with joy and admiration. But all is not yet done. The enemy, though scattered and dismayed, has still many fragments of his late army hovering about us, and, aided by an exasperated population, he may again unite in treble our numbers and fall upon us to advantage if we rest inactive in the security of past victories. Compactness, vigilance, and discipline are therefore our only securities. Let every good officer and man look to these cautions and enjoin them on all others.

" By command of Major-General Scott.
" H. L. Scott,
"*Acting Assistant Adjutant General.*"

" Headquarters of the Army, National Palace of Mexico,
"*September 17, 1847.*
"General Orders No. 287.

" The general in chief republishes, with important additions, his General Order No. 20, of February 19, 1847, declaring martial law to govern all who may be concerned. There are nineteen paragraphs in the order. (See Ex. Doc. No. 1, Thirtieth Congress, first session, Senate.) The last seven will be copied.

" 13. The administration of justice, both in civil

and criminal matters, through the ordinary courts of the country, shall nowhere and in no degree be interrupted by any officer or soldier of the American forces except, first, in case where an officer or soldier, agent, servant, or follower of the army may be a party; and second, in political cases—that is, prosecutions against other individuals on the allegation that they have given friendly information, aid, or assistance to the American forces.

"14. For the care and safety of both parties in all cities and towns occupied by the American army, a Mexican police shall be established and duly harmonized with the military police of said forces.

"15. This splendid capital, its churches and religious worship, its convents and monasteries, its inhabitants and property, are, moreover, placed under the special safeguard of the faith and honor of the American army.

"16. In consideration of the foregoing protection, a contribution of one hundred and fifty thousand dollars is imposed on this capital, to be paid in four weekly installments of thirty-seven thousand five hundred dollars each, beginning on Monday next, the 20th inst., and terminating on Monday, October 11th.

"17. The Ayuntamiento, or corporate authority of the city, is specially charged with the collection and payment of the several installments.

"18. Of the whole contribution to be paid over to this army, twenty thousand dollars shall be appropriated to the purchase of extra comforts for the wounded and sick in hospital, ninety thousand dollars to the purchase of blankets and shoes for gratuitous distribution among the rank and file of the army, and forty thousand dollars reserved for other necessary military purposes.

"19. This order shall be read at the head of every company of the United States forces serving in Mexico, and translated into Spanish for the information of the Mexicans.

"By command of Major-General Scott.
"H. L. SCOTT,
"*Acting Assistant Adjutant General.*"

"HEADQUARTERS OF THE ARMY, NATIONAL PALACE OF MEXICO,
"*September 18, 1847.*
"GENERAL ORDERS NO. 289.

"1. The army by degrees, and beginning as soon as practicable, will be distributed and quartered over the city as follows:

"2. The first division (Worth's) in or near the direct route from the San Cosme toward the cathedral and extending a little beyond the east end of the Alameda. This division will keep a competent guard with two guns of medium caliber at that gate.

"3. The second division (Twiggs's) about the Grand Plaza and extending toward the gate of San Lazaro, or the Penon, at which it will keep a guard and two pieces of artillery, as above.

"4. The third division (Pillow's) on or near the direct route from the gate of Peralvillo, or Guadalupe, toward the cathedral, but not south of the convent of San Domingo, and will keep a guard of two pieces of artillery at that gate.

"5. The volunteer division (Quitman's) on or near the direct route from the gate of San Antonio toward the cathedral, but not north of the Hospital of Jesus, and will keep a guard with two pieces of artillery, as above, at that gate.

"6. The brigade of cavalry (Colonel Harney's) will be quartered in the cavalry barracks near the National Palace (marked on the plan of the city small m). This brigade will furnish daily a detachment of a corporal and six men to the respective gates of division, to serve as couriers between the gates and the commanders of the respective divisions, and for no other purposes.

"7. No private house shall be occupied by any corps or officers until all suitable public buildings within the above ranges shall be first fully occupied, and all officers attached to troops shall be quartered with or near their troops.

"8. No rent shall be paid by the United States for any buildings occupied by troops or officers without a special direction from general headquarters; nor shall any private house be occupied or quartered without the free consent of the owner or orders from general headquarters. No deviations from these injunctions will be tolerated.

"9. The collection of customs or duties at the several gates of the city by the civil authorities of the same will be continued as heretofore until modified by the Civil and Military Governor, Major-General Quitman, according to the views of the general in chief; but supplies belonging to the quartermaster and commissary departments will at once be exempted from all duties.

"By command of Major-General Scott.

"H. L. SCOTT,
"*Acting Assistant Adjutant General.*"

The effect of the strict enforcement of these admirable orders was to bring the American army under a discipline which won for them the confidence of the people of the city, and to revive and restore trade, open up the churches, and, as near as could be done under the circumstances, to place matters in the city *in statu quo ante bellum*. At the meeting of the junta called by General Santa Anna he tendered his resignation as President of the Republic and of the command of the army. Under the Constitution of Mexico the office devolved upon Manuel de la Peña y Peña, who at once assumed it, and Santa Anna set out with a view to the capture of Puebla and the occupation of the road leading to the coast.

Instead of marching on Puebla, Santa Anna turned his forces toward Queretaro, but in a few days countermarched. After two or three maneuvers of this kind, he finally invested Puebla with about fifteen hundred cavalry and four field pieces. He summoned Colonel Childs, who was in command, to surrender on the score of humanity. Santa Anna represented his force at eight thousand men, and threatened assault. Colonel Childs declined to surrender, and made preparations to resist the assault by strengthening his position. The threatened assault was not made. On October 1st Santa Anna raised the siege of Puebla and marched toward El Pinal to intercept a train of wagons with supplies and re-enforcements, leaving General Rea with sufficient force to continue operations against the Americans. The Americans were so annoyed by continuous firing from the housetops that Captain William F. Small, First Pennsylvania Infantry, was ordered to dig through the walls of the houses until he had gained a point which would command a barricade that had been thrown up by the Mexicans. The enemy was driven off, leaving seventeen dead on the ground; the barricade was then burned. Hostile parties were constantly annoying the garrison, until two companies of the First Pennsylvania regiment were sent out and dispersed them. Many skirmishes took place, which invariably resulted disastrously to the enemy.

General Joseph Lane's efforts to exterminate the roving bands of *guerillos* and *rancheros* involved great rapidity of movement, and he had officers and men under his command eminently fit for such service. One of the most pestiferous of the *guerillo* leaders was a Catholic priest called Padre Juarata. He seemed to be everywhere at once, and notwithstanding his party was frequently met by the Americans, sometimes surrounded and always beaten, yet the Padre adroitly managed to get out of every trap and escape. Being a priest, he was always ready and willing to administer the last rites of the Church to friend or foe.

While the army was at Puebla, General Scott organized a company of Mexicans under command of one Dominguez, which was regularly mustered into the service of the United States. A battalion of deserters from the American army, known as the San Patricio Battalion, composed almost wholly of Europeans, was organized under the command of one O'Riley. These two commands met in battle in the convent of Churubusco, and fought each other with great desperation. The Mexicans under Dominguez entered Churubusco with the American army, and met the execration of their countrymen, who denounced them as traitors. The American deserters (the San Patricio Battalion) were captured at Churubusco, tried by court-martial, and all but sixteen sentenced to death and executed. Some were pardoned, and O'Riley, their leader, was branded with the letter D on his cheek and released. This clemency was shown him because he deserted before hostilities commenced.

The number of American troops engaged at Churubusco on August 19th and 20th was four thousand five hundred. The entire force engaged at Churubusco was about seven thousand four hundred. General Scott's estimate of the Mexican force on August 20th, including Contreras, Churubusco, and the road between San Antonio and Churubusco, the Portales, and the road to the Capitol, was thirty-two thousand.

In these battles three thousand prisoners were captured, including eight general officers and two hundred and five other officers. The killed and wounded amounted to over four thousand. Thirty pieces of cannon were taken. The loss to the American army was one hundred and thirty-nine officers, including sixteen killed, and one thousand and fifty-three enlisted men; sixty officers and eight hundred and seventy-six men wounded.

Commodore William B. Shubrick having captured Mazatlan and Guaymas, General Scott wrote him, December 2, 1847: "I have been waiting here for two and a half months to learn the views of the Government at home, or at least for re-enforcements, before undertaking any new and distant operations. The forces I have under my orders in the whole of this republic, except the troops immediately under Major-General Taylor, only give me means of holding Tampico, Vera Cruz, Puebla, Chapultepec, and this capital."

GENERAL SCOTT'S ORDERS.

General Scott had made a careful study of the statistics of Mexican finances, and previous to ordering the occupation of several important districts near the capital, to be followed by a like disposition in more remote departments, issued General Orders No. 376, December 15, 1847:

"(1) This army is about to spread itself over and to occupy the Republic of Mexico until the latter shall sue for peace on terms acceptable to the Government of the United States. (2) On the occupation of the principal point or points in any State the payment to the Federal Government of this republic of all taxes or dues of whatever manner or kind heretofore, say in 1844, payable or collected by that Government, is absolutely prohibited, as all such taxes, dues, etc., will be demanded of the proper civil authorities for the support of the army of occupation. (3) The State and Federal districts being already so occupied, as well as the States of Vera Cruz, Puebla, and Tamaulipas, the usual taxes or dues heretofore contributed by the same to the Federal Government will be considered as due and payable to this army from the beginning of the present month, and will early be demanded of the civil authorities of said States and districts under rules and penalties which shall be duly announced and enforced. (4) Other States of this republic, as the Californias, New Mexico, Chihuahua, Coahuila, New Leon, etc., already occupied by the forces of the United States, though not under the immediate orders of the general in chief, will conform to the prescriptions of this order, except in such State or States where a different system has been adopted with the sanction of the Government at Washington. (5) The internal taxes or dues referred to are: 1, District taxes; 2, Dues on the production of gold and silver; 3, Melting and assaying duties; 4, The tobacco rent; 5, Rent of stamped paper; 6, The rent on the manufacture of playing cards; and, 7, The rent of post offices. (6) The rent of national lotteries is abolished, lotteries being hereby prohibited. (7) Import and export duties at ports of the republic will remain as fixed by the Government of the United States, except that the exportation of gold and silver in bars or ingots— *plata y oro en pasta*—is prohibited until the further instructions of the Government on the subjects. (8) All imported articles, goods, or commodities which have once paid or given sufficient security for the payment of duties to the United States at any port of entry of the republic shall not again be burdened with any tax or duty in any port of this republic occupied by the forces of the United States. (9) The levying of duties on the transit of animals, goods, or commodities, whether of foreign or domestic growth, from one State of this republic to another, or on entering or leaving the gate of any city within the republic, will, from and after the beginning of the ensuing year, be prohibited, as far as the United States forces may have power to enforce the prohibition. Other and equitable means, to a moderate extent, must be resorted to by the several State and city authorities for the necessary support of their respective governments. (10) The tobacco, playing cards, and stamped paper rents will be placed for three, six, or twelve months under the contract with the highest bidders respectively, for the several States, the State and Federal district of Mexico being considered one. Accordingly, offers or bids for those rents within each State, or any of them, are invited. They will be sent in as early as possible, sealed, to the headquarters of departments, except for the Federal District and State of Mexico. For this latter the offers or bids will be addressed to the general in chief. (11) Further details for the execution of the foregoing system, of government and revenue will soon be given in general orders."

General Scott forwarded the above order to Washington, together with a memoir of the precious metals, showing that he had carefully studied and had thorough knowledge of the subject. In his letter forwarding the order he said:

"The Government of the United States proposes that their forces shall occupy the Mexican Republic, and raise in said country the means to meet the expenses of occupation. To obtain this object, it appears convenient that said resources should be raised so as to interfere as little as possible with the existing interests of foreign as well as of native residents; for if any measure calculated to involve the ruin of a part or the whole of said interests was taken, there is little or no doubt that the results would be as injurious to the interest of the United States as to those of this country, for the destiny of both interests in the case of occupation is linked together. It appears that this recommendation, besides being fully justified by a sound policy, will also be the means of facilitating the organization of a financial system, and ultimately lead to increase of revenue.

. . . .

"The tariff given by the United States for the Mexican ports occupied allows the free exportation of gold and silver either in bars or coined. Although it has been done, perhaps, with a liberal view, it would seem that the measure was taken to hostilize the Mexican Government, preventing thus any advance from being made to said Government on future export duties on silver or gold, and depriving it of that resource. However, who would benefit by the free export of gold or silver? It is well known that nothing finds its level, respecting prices, as soon as the precious metals, and therefore as soon as the exportation should be carried into effect there would have been exchange on England, France, and the United States, a difference equivalent to the duties taken off on the precious metals. The free exportation would apparently have been advantageous to none but the miners; apparently is the word, for it is evident that the higher prices obtained by them at first would have gradually come down until they were on a level with those obtained in Europe, and ultimately would have become lower than they are to-day, for it is not to be doubted that the free exportation of bars partially or totally occasioning the ruin of the mints, coined specie would have disappeared from circulation, and that miners would have been for the sale of their product entirely at the mercy of the speculators, while, the exportation being prohibited, the mints are obliged to pay to them at any time a fixed price for their gold and silver which can not be altered.

. . . .

"The exportation of gold and silver in bars has been prohibited in this country by all the tariffs that have existed either under the Spanish or Mexican Government; and though licenses of exportation to a small amount have now and then been granted, the prohibition has been the rule and the exportation has been the exception, until the Mexican Government, having rented all their mines but two to foreign companies, has taken the solemn engagement not to give any more licenses of exportation. As it may easily be supposed, the engagement of giving no more licenses of exportation has been the principal basis on which the companies have relied to make their contracts, and the principal inducement for them to advance the rent as they have done. It is not known what policy will be adopted by the United States respecting neutral interests in Mexico in case the country should be occupied by their armies, but too high an opinion is entertained of the justice of their Government to admit for a moment the possibility of such interests being sacrificed or ruined when no direct benefit could be derived from such a measure for the United States, and when, on the contrary, it might be injurious to them, as may be explained."

On December 17th he again wrote to the Secretary calling his attention to General Orders No. 376, the seventh paragraph of which contained the duties on exported bars of gold and silver, which had been made free by order of the United States Government. Since the publication of the order he had seen a slip cut from a Vera Cruz paper of the 17th, from the Department to him on the subject, which said: "I have taken great pains to obtain correct information in respect to the production and exportation of the precious metals in and from this country. The Mexican policy has been uniform against the exportation of bars and ingots, though, from want or cupidity, special licenses have been given in violation of that sound policy and in gross violation of the rights purchased by the renters of the mints. This army is also interested in some prohibition, for if we permit the exportation of bars and ingots there will be but little domestic coinage, our drafts would soon be under par, and the Mexicans, from want of sufficient circulating medium, be less able to pay the contributions which we propose to levy upon them through their civil authorities."

General Scott, knowing the President's great desire to have the war terminated, embraced every opportunity to keep him advised as to the prospects, more or less remote, of peace, and wrote, December 14th, that he " had received no communication from the Mexican Government, and did not expect any before the Congress and President had been installed, about March 10th. It is believed that both will be inclined to peace." Congress, however, did not meet until May.

General William O. Butler arrived at the capital December 18th with thirty-six hundred men, and the train dispatched November 1st, under Colonel Harney, returned, under command of Lieutenant-Colonel Joseph E. Johnston, of the voltigeurs, with thirteen hundred men in addition to the escort that accompanied it on the trip down. These re-enforcements, with those that recently arrived, made a total of eight or nine thousand for duty.

General Scott was anxious to occupy the mining districts of· San Luis and Zacatecas, maintain communication with the capital, and open one with Tampico, and for that purpose needed two columns of five thousand men each, and to garrison the State capitals within reach of the two columns. It was represented that great embarrassment would result from the movement on Zacatecas, as that column would have to march through Queretaro to reach its destination. It was represented that it would cause the dispersion of the Mexican Government and make its assembling at any other point doubtful. The Department, however, directed the double movement to be made when the re-enforcements known to have left Vera Cruz would arrive, unless in the meantime otherwise instructed.

The commanding general was greatly disappointed when the first train returned from Vera Cruz without bringing a jacket, blanket, or a pair of shoes for the army. That small depot had been exhausted by the troops of Patterson, Butler, and Marshall, who were fresh from home, or the Brazos, and others that arrived without clothing since June; and on December 25th he wrote of his great disappointments, and stated that this want might delay distant expeditions for many weeks, as some of the new volunteers were in want of essential articles of wear. He called attention to the fact that requisitions for clothing made by the regular regiments over a year previous had not been sent, or at any rate had not reached the regiments. No general ever paid more attention or displayed greater interest in the comfort of his men than General Scott. The quartermaster's and commissary departments were his never-ceasing care, and he gave constant personal attention to both.

On the matter of assessments he says: "You perceive I do not propose to seize the ordinary State or city revenue, as that, in my judgment, would be to make war on civilization, as no community can escape absolute anarchy without civil government. I shall take care, however, to see that the means collected within any particular State or city for that purpose are moderate and reasonable."

Order No. 395 was issued December 31st, specifying the States by name and the several sums they would be annually taxed. The duties paid at the gates of the cities, and in passing from one State to another, as well as the tobacco monopoly and lotteries, were abolished. Governors and members of the Legislature of the different States, and all collecting officers then in commission and charged with the collection of Federal duties of any, were held individually responsible in their persons and property for the collection and payment of the assessment. The order, which was a long one and carefully prepared, gave many details. The last two paragraphs say: "The American troops, in spreading themselves over this republic, will take care to observe the strictest discipline and morals in respect to the persons and property of the country, purchasing and paying for all necessaries and comforts they may require, and treating the unoffending inhabitants with forbearance and kindness. The higher honor of the country, as well as the particular honor of the army, must and shall be maintained against the few miscreants in our ranks. The laws of war will also be strictly observed toward all Mexicans who respect those laws. For the treatment of those atrocious bands of *guerillos* and armed *rancheros*, General Order No. 392 of the 12th instant will be rigidly enforced."

To prevent frauds in the payment of dues as assessed, General Orders No. 8, of January 9, 1848, were issued. The orders referred to and quoted in part show that General Scott was eminently qualified to fulfill a position in civil as well as military life. The orders he promulgated were laws to the Mexicans, and show that his administration of the civil affairs of the conquered country was wise, merciful, and judicious. It was here that General Scott's early legal training manifested itself. These orders had anticipated the message of the President which reached him on the 14th in a communication from the War Department, and in which the President's views were given in regard to the future prosecution of the war. He was urged to endeavor to lessen expenses by compelling Mexico to contribute, and see the necessity of making a peace honorable alike to both countries. Says the Secretary: "Our object being to obtain acceptable terms, which it is apprehended can not be speedily obtained without making the enemy feel he is to bear a considerable part of the burden of war.

"Should there not be at this time a government in Mexico of sufficient stability to make peace, or should the authority which there exists be adverse to it, and yet a large and influential portion of the people be really disposed to put an end to hostilities, it is desirable to know what prospect there is that the latter could, with countenance and protection of our arms, organize a government willing to make peace and sustain relations of peace with us. It is presumed that your opportunities of knowing the disposition of the people of Mexico will enable you to furnish your Government with correct information on the subject, and the President desires to be furnished with your views."

On January 6, 1848, General Scott reported to the Department that his total force in the Valley of Mexico was fourteen thousand nine hundred and sixty-four, with only eleven thousand one hundred and sixty-two fit for duty, measles prevailing mainly among the volunteers. Half of General Marshall's force at Jalapa was sick, and he reported, December 22d, that he had sent his wagons back to Vera Cruz for medicines and other supplies. Pachuca was occupied without opposition by Colonel Jones M. Withers, Ninth Infantry, and General Cadwallader marched, December 22d, for Lerma and Toluca, the latter the State capital and thirty-eight miles from the City of Mexico.

On January 13th General Scott reported the unsuccessful efforts of Colonel Wynkoop's First Pennsylvania Volunteers to capture the Padre Jaruata, but the same colonel, learning of General Valencia's whereabouts, made a night march, surprised and captured him and a colonel of his staff. Colonel Jack Hays made efforts to capture Jaruata, but also failed. He had an engagement with the band, killing and wounding many of them.

On January 12, 1848, a letter was dispatched by the Secretary of War to General Scott informing him that he had been relieved from the command of the army by order of the President of the United States, and was to be brought before a court of inquiry to be convened in the Castle of Peroté, Mexico, on the 18th of February.

On February 2, 1848, General Scott acknowledged receipt of the Secretary's letters of November 8th and 17th and December 14th. The system of finance—prohibiting the export duties on coins and the prohibition of export in bars, inaugurated by the general—differed materially from the instructions in the Secretary's letter of November 17th, and the general hoped, for the reasons suggested in his letter of December 17th, that the President would consent to adopt his views in respect to the precious metals. He informed the Secretary that the ayuntamiento of the capital had charged itself with the payment on account of the Federal district of four hundred thousand dollars of the six hundred and sixty-eight thousand three hundred and thirty-two dollars imposed per year on the State of Mexico; that General Cadwallader would soon begin to collect through the ayuntamiento of Toluca a large part of the remainder. Colonel Clarke, of the Sixth Infantry, had been ordered into the Cuernavaca Valley, forty-three miles south, with a force amply sufficient to enforce a thorough collection.

General Scott says: "The *war of masses* ended with the capture of the enemy's capital; the *war of detail*, including the occupation of the country and the collection of revenue, requires a large additional force, as before suggested." Referring to the fact that he had learned it was thought in Washington that "he had thirty thousand men under his command, while in truth, including the forces at Tampico, Vera Cruz, on the line from that port, and in the valley and vicinity, he had a total of twenty-four thousand eight hundred and sixteen; the sick, necessary, and indispensable garrisons deducted would leave an available force for distant service of only four thousand five hundred, and he did not know of the approach of any considerable re-enforcements. Seven thousand he deemed a minimum number with which the important line from Durango through Zacatecas and San Luis to Tampico could be opened and maintained. Many of the volunteers were sick with measles, mumps, and erysipelas, common among all classes of soldiers."

A treaty of peace had been agreed upon and signed and was to be forwarded at once. Referring to the fact, he says: "In about forty days I may receive an acknowledgment of this report, and by that time, if the treaty of peace be not accepted, I hope to be sufficiently re-enforced to open the commercial line between Zacatecas and Tampico. The occupation of Queretaro, Guanajuato, and Guadalajara would be the next in importance, and some of the ports of the Pacific third. Meanwhile the collection of internal revenue dues on the precious metals and direct assessments shall be continued."

The following is the organization of the army in its march from Puebla to the City of Mexico:

GENERAL STAFF.

Lieutenant-Colonel Ethan Allen Hitchcock, Assistant Inspector General.
Captain Henry Lee Scott, Acting Adjutant General.
First-Lieutenant T. Williams, Aid-de-camp.
Brevet First-Lieutenant George William Lay, Aid-de-camp.
Second-Lieutenant Schuyler Hamilton, Aid-de-camp.
Major J. P. Gaines, Volunteer Aid-de-camp.

ENGINEER CORPS.

Major John Lind Smith, Chief; Captain Robert Edward Lee; Lieutenants Pierre Gustave Toutant Beauregard, Isaac I. Stevens, Zealous Bates Tower, Gustavus Woodson Smith, George B. McClellan, John Gray Foster.

ORGANIZATION OF THE ARMY. 251

ORDNANCE DEPARTMENT.

Captain Benjamin Hugér, Chief, with siege train.
First-Lieutenant Peter Valentine Hugner.
Second-Lieutenant George Thom.
Brevet Second-Lieutenant E. L. F. Hardcastle.

QUARTERMASTER'S DEPARTMENT.

Captains James R. Irwin, Chief; Abraham C. Myers, Robert Allen, Henry Constantine Wayne, Justus McKinstry, George W. F. Wood, J. Daniels, O'Hara, Samuel McGowan.

SUBSISTENCE DEPARTMENT.

Captain John Breckinridge Grayson, Chief.
Captain Thomas P. Randle.

PAY DEPARTMENT.

Major Edmund Kirby, Chief.
" Abraham Van Buren.
" Albert Gallatin Bennett.

MEDICAL DEPARTMENT.

Surgeon-General Thomas Lawson; Surgeons Benjamin Franklin Harney, Richard Smith Satterlee, Charles Stuart Tripler, Burton Randall, James Meck Cuyler; Assistant Surgeons Alexander F. Suter, Josiah Simpson, David Camben De Leon, Henry H. Steiner, James Simons, Joseph K. Barnes, Levi H. Holden, Charles Carter Keeney, James Frazier Head, John Fox Hammond, Josephus M. Steiner, Charles P. Deyerle, Ebenezer Swift. Surgeons J. M. Tyler, volunteer; McMillan, volunteer; Courtney J. Clark, volunteer; W. B. Halstead, volunteer. Assistant Surgeons R. Hagan, volunteer; H. L. Wheaton, volunteer. Surgeons R. Ritchie, First Volunteers; J. Barry, First Volunteers; Edwards, First Volunteers; L. W. Jordan, First Volunteers; R. McSherry, First Volunteers; Roberts, First Volunteers.

CORPS.

Colonel Harney's Brigade.

Detachment of First Light Dragoons, Captain James Kearny.
Detachment of Second Light Dragoons, Major Edwin Vose Sumner.

Detachment of Third Light Dragoons under Major Andrew Thomas McReynolds.

I. Brevet Major-General Worth's Division.

1. Colonel John Garland's Brigade.

Second Regiment of Artillery, serving as infantry.
Third   "   "   "   "   "
Fourth   "   " Infantry.
Duncan's Field Battery.

2. Colonel Andrew Clark's Brigade.

Fifth, Sixth, and Eighth Regiments of Infantry.
A Light Battery.

II. Brevet Major-General Twiggs's Division.

1. Brevet Brigadier-General Persifor F. Smith's Brigade.

Rifle Regiment.
First Regiment of Artillery, serving as infantry.
Third Regiment of Infantry.
Taylor's Light Battery.

2. Colonel Bennet Riley's Brigade.

Fourth Regiment of Artillery, serving as infantry.
First Regiment of Infantry.
Seventh Regiment of Infantry.

III. Major-General Gideon J. Pillow's Division.

1. Brigadier-General G. Cadwallader's Brigade.

Voltigeurs.
Eleventh and Fourteenth Infantry.
A Light Battery.

2. Brigadier-General Franklin Pierce's Brigade.

Ninth, Twelfth, and Fifteenth Infantry.

IV. Major-General John A. Quitman's Division.

1. Brigadier-General Shields's Brigade.

New York Volunteers.
South Carolina Volunteers.

ORGANIZATION OF THE ARMY.

2. Lieutenant-Colonel Watson's Brigade.
A detachment of Second Pennsylvania Volunteers.
A detachment of United States Marines.

List of Officers of the Battalion of Marines under Command of Lieutenant-Colonel Watson.

Brevet Lieutenant-Colonel Samuel E. Watson, Major Levi Twiggs, Major William Dulany.

Staff.—First Lieutenant and Adjutant D. D. Baker, First Lieutenant and Acting Quartermaster John S. Devlin.

Captains.—John G. Reynolds, George H. Terrett, and William Lang.

First Lieutenants.—Jabez C. Rich, Robert C. Caldwell, William L. Young, Thomas A. Brady, John D. Simms, and Daniel J. Sutherland.

Second Lieutenants.—George Adams, E. McD. Reynolds, Thomas Y. Field, Charles G. McCawley, Freeman Norvell, Charles A. Henderson, John S. Nicholson, Augustus S. Nicholson, and Henry Welsh.

CHAPTER XII.

Scott's care for the welfare of his army—Account of the money levied on Mexico—Last note to the Secretary of War while commander in chief in Mexico—Army asylums—Treaty of peace—Scott turns over the army to General William O. Butler—Scott and Worth—Court of inquiry on Worth—The "Leonidas" and "Tampico" letters—Revised paragraph 650—Army regulations—General Worth demands a court of inquiry and prefers charges against Scott—Correspondence—General belief as to Scott's removal command—The trial—Return home of General Scott.

As an army commander General Scott had frequent occasion to use money for which vouchers or even ordinary receipts could not be taken and the nature of the service could not be specified; he styled them "secret disbursements." In a letter to the War Department of February 6, 1848, he stated that he "had made no report of such disbursements since leaving Jalapa, (1) because of the uncertainty of our communications with Vera Cruz, and (2) the necessity of certain explanations which, on account of others, ought not to be reduced to writing," and added, " I have never tempted the honor or patriotism of any man, but have held it as lawful in morals as in war to purchase valuable information or services voluntarily tendered me."

He charged himself with the money he received in Washington for "secret disbursements," the one hundred and fifty thousand dollars levied upon the City of Mexico for the immediate benefit of the army, and of the captured tobacco taken from the Mexican Government, with other small sums, all of which were accounted for. He then charged himself with sixty-three thousand seven hundred and forty-five dollars and fifty-seven cents expended in the purchase of blankets and shoes distributed gratuitously to enlisted men, for ten thousand dollars extra supplies for the hospitals, ten dollars each to every crippled man discharged or furloughed, some sixty thousand dollars for secret services, including the native spy company of Dominguez, whose pay commenced in July, and which he did not wish to bring into account with the Treasury. There remained a balance of one hundred thousand dollars, a draft for which he inclosed, saying: "I hope you will allow the draft to go to the credit of the army asylum, and make the subject known in the way you may deem best to the military committees of Congress. The sum is, in small part, the price of American blood so gallantly shed in this vicinity; and considering that the army receives no prize money, I repeat the hope that its proposed destination may be approved and carried into effect. . . . The remainder of the money in my hands, as well as that expended, I shall be ready to account for at the proper time and in the proper manner, merely offering this imperfect report to explain, in the meantime, the character of the one hundred thousand dollars draft."

On February 9, 1848, General Scott addressed what seems to have been his last note to the War Department as commander in chief of the army of Mexico. It is brief. He adverted to the fact of his not receiving any communication from the War Department or adjutant general's office, and says: "But slips from newspapers and letters from Washington have come to interested parties here, representing, I learn, that the President has determined to place me before a court for daring to enforce necessary discipline in this army against certain of its high officers. I make only a passing comment upon these unofficial announcements, learning with pleasure, through the same sources, that I am to be superseded by Major-General William O. Butler." The admirable recommendation in regard to the draft was adopted and carried out, and the money applied to the purchase of asylums for soldiers.

There was not any general engagement of the armies after the capture of the City of Mexico. General Lane, always vigilant, kept his force in constant motion, pursuing, engaging, when possible, and dispersing the numerous predatory bands that infested his flanks and rear.

The first efforts to agree upon a treaty of peace failed. Active operations were resumed, and so weakened Mexico that she was left no alternative but to make " peace such as her powerful and successful enemy might dictate." By the Constitution of Mexico the office of President in case of a vacancy devolved upon the president of the Supreme Court provisionally; but there was no president of the Supreme Court in September, 1847, the last incumbent having died, and no successor having been elected when Santa Anna resigned. Congress, whose duty it was to elect this officer, could only be convened by proclamation of the President, but, as is seen, there was no President. In this unfortunate state of affairs, the most influential of the *Moderado* party, with the hope of preventing anarchy, then greatly threatened, if it had not already raised its head, and conclude terms of peace, prevailed upon Peña y Peña, an able and enlightened jurist, statesman, and patriot, and senior judge of the Supreme Court, to assume the provisional presidency. He was recognized by the State authorities, and pledges were given that they would uphold and defend it against all intriguers opposed to peace, through the non-existence of a government competent to make it. It was known that Peña was not averse to peace.

Mr. Nicholas P. Trist, the commissioner on the part of the United States, upon the formation of the new Government, made propositions for a conference of representatives. Owing to the fact that the Mexican Congress had to be called together to elect a President *ad interim* to serve until January 8, 1848, the overtures of Mr. Trist could not be entertained. By a combination between the Puro party and the adherents of Santa Anna and other factions, the *Moderado* party came very near being defeated, but the latter were successful and elected General Don Pedro Maria Anaya *ad interim* President; and Peña y Peña and General Mora y Villamil, both in favor of peace, were made respectively Minister of Foreign Relations and Minister of War.

Negotiations were now again formally undertaken. The Mexican Government was represented by Señores Conto, Atristain, and Cuevas. The commissioners of the respective countries met at Guadalupe Hidalgo, three miles from the City of Mexico. After many meetings, long conferences, and discussions, a treaty of peace, friendships, and limits between Mexico and the United States was concluded and signed February 2, 1848.

A synopsis of the treaty is given. Some of the articles are given in full, as the fifth, which secured to the United States the great State of California with its incalculable wealth in mineral and agriculture resources, and the territory of New Mexico, also rich in all that Nature can yield.

Treaty of Guadalupe Hidalgo, concluded February 2, 1848. Ratifications exchanged at Queretaro, May 30, 1848. Proclaimed July 4, 1848.

The United States was represented by Nicholas P. Trist, and the Republic of Mexico was represented by Don Louis Gonzaga Cuevas, Don Bernardo Conto, and Don Miguel Atristain.

"ARTICLE I. There shall be firm and universal peace between the United States of America and the Mexican Republic, and between respective countries, territories, cities, towns, and people, without exception of places or persons.

"ART. II provides that, immediately upon the signature to this treaty, commissioners shall be appointed by the commander in chief of the American forces and the Mexican Government for the provisional suspension of hostilities and the re-establishment of the political, administrative, and judicial branches so far as this shall be permitted by the circumstances of the case.

"ART. III. Immediately upon the ratification of this treaty by the United States orders shall be issued to the commanders of the land and naval forces, requiring the latter (provided this treaty has been ratified by Mexico and ratifications exchanged) to immediately desist from blockading any Mexican ports, and requiring the former (under the same conditions) to withdraw all troops of the United States then in the interior of the Mexican Republic to a distance from the seaport not exceeding thirty leagues—this to be done with the least possible delay; and to deliver up all customhouses at all ports occupied by the forces of the United States to persons authorized by the Mexican Government to receive it, with all bonds and evidences of debt for duties on importations and exportations. An exact account to be rendered of all duties on imports and exports, after the ratification of this treaty by Mexico, deducting only the cost of collection. The City of Mexico to be evacuated within one month after the orders there stipulated shall be received by the commander of said troops.

"ART. IV. Immediately after the ratifications of the present treaty all castles, forts, territories, places, and possessions shall be definitely restored to Mexico; the final evacuation of the territory of Mexico shall be completed within three months, or sooner if possible, the Mexican Government engaging to use all means in its power to facilitate the same. All prisoners of war taken on sea or land to be restored, and all Mexicans held by savage tribes within the United States to be exacted from such tribes and restored to their country.

"ART. V is given in full:

"The boundary line between the two republics shall commence in the Gulf of Mexico, three leagues from land, opposite the mouth of the Rio Grande, otherwise called Rio Bravo del Norte, or opposite the mouth of its deepest branch, if it should have more than one branch emptying directly into the sea; from thence up the middle of that river, following the deepest channel, where it has more than one, to the point where it strikes the southern boundary of New Mexico; thence westwardly along the southern boundary of New Mexico (which runs north of the town called Paso) to its western termination; thence northward along the western line of New Mexico until it intersects the first branch of the Rio Gila (or if it should not intersect any branch of that river, then to a point on said line nearest to said branch, and thence in a direct line to the same); thence down the middle of the said branch of said river until it empties into the Rio Colorado; thence across the Rio Colorado, following the division line between Upper and Lower California to the Pacific Ocean. The southern and western limits of New Mexico mentioned in this article are those laid down in the map entitled '*Map of the United Mexican States, as organized and defined by various acts of Congress of said republic, and constructed according to the best authorities. Revised edition. Published in New York, in 1847, by J. Disturnell*'; of which map a copy is added to this treaty, bearing the signatures and seals of the undersigned plenipotentiaries. And in order to preclude all difficulty in tracing upon the ground limit separating Upper from Lower California, it is agreed that the said limit shall consist of a straight line drawn from the middle of the Rio Gila, where it unites with the Colorado, to a point on the coast of the Pacific Ocean distant one marine league due south of the southernmost point of the port of San Diego, according to the plan of said port made in 1782 by Don Juan Pantoja, second sailing master of the Spanish fleet, and published at Madrid in the year 1802, in the atlas to the voyage of said schooners Sutil and Mexicana; of which plan a copy is hereunto added, signed and sealed by the respective plenipotentiaries.

"In order to designate the boundary line with due precision upon authoritative maps, and to establish upon the ground landmarks which shall show the limits of both republics, as described in the present article, the two governments shall each appoint a commissioner and surveyor, who, before the expiration of one year from the date of the exchange of ratifications of this treaty, shall meet at the port of San Diego and proceed to run and mark the said boundary in its whole course to the mouth of the Rio Bravo del Norte. They shall keep journals and make out plans of their operations; and the result agreed upon by them shall be deemed a part of this treaty, and shall have the same force and effect as if inserted therein. The two governments will amicably agree regarding what may be necessary to these persons, and also as to their respective escorts, should such be necessary.

"The boundary line established by this article shall be religiously respected by each of the two republics, and no change shall ever be made therein, except by the express and free consent of both nations lawfully given by the General Government of each in conformity with its own constitution.

"Art. 6 gives citizens of the United States free navigation of the Gulf of California and the Rio Colorado below its confluence with the Gila.

"Art. 7. The Rio Gila and the part of the Rio Bravo del Norte are made free for the navigation of vessels of both countries without tax.

"Art. 8. Mexicans to remain in the ceded territory if they choose to do so, or to remove at any time to the Mexican republic, retaining the property they possess in said territories, or disposing of the same and removing the same wherever they please. Those who remain in said territories may either retain the title and rights of Mexican citizens or acquire those of citizens of the United States; but they shall be under the obligation to make their election within one year from the date of the exchange of ratifications of this treaty; and those who shall remain in said territories after the expiration of that year, without having declared their intention to retain the character of Mexicans, shall be considered to have elected to become citizens of the United States. Property in those territories belonging to Mexicans shall be inviolably respected, and the present owners and their heirs and those who have acquired the same shall enjoy the same, as if it belonged to citizens of the United States.

"Art. 9. Mexicans who do not declare themselves citizens of Mexico shall be incorporated in and become citizens of the United States under such regulations as shall be provided by law.

"Art. 10 of the treaty was stricken out.

"Art. 11. The United States undertakes to deliver up, if possible, any Mexicans that may be captured by any of the savage tribes within the ceded territory; and to prevent purchasing any property from any Mexican while in capture by the Indians; nor to purchase any property of any kind stolen within Mexican territory by such Indians.

"Art. 12. In consideration of the extension acquired by the boundaries of the United States, as defined by the fifth article of the present treaty, the Government of the United States engages to pay to that of the Mexican republic the sum of fifteen millions of dollars, and prescribes the manner and times of payment.

"Art. 13. The United States assumes the payment of all claims now due and those hereafter to become due by reason of claims already liquidated against Mexico under the treaties of April 11, 1839, and January 30, 1843.

"Art. 14. The United States discharges Mexico from all claims of citizens of the United States against said republic.

"Art. 15 provides for the appointment of a board of commissioners to adjudicate all claims against Mexico, the United States assuming the payment of such as may be allowed; the Mexican Government agreeing to furnish such books, papers, etc., as may be deemed necessary as evidence.

"Art. 16. The right of both parties to fortify any point in its territory it may deem proper.

"Art. 17. The treaty of April 5, 1831, and its provisions not inconsistent with this treaty, revived.

"Art. 18. All supplies for troops of the United States shall be exempt from duties or charges of any kind; the United States engaging to prevent merchandise and goods from being landed, under cover of this article, not intended for the army.

"Art. 19. General provisions in regard to merchandise imported into Mexico during hostilities.

"Art. 20 provides what disposition shall be made of merchandise arriving in Mexico, if the customhouses shall be delivered up less than sixty days from the signatures to this treaty.

"Art. 21. If disagreements should arise between the two countries, every effort will be made to adjust the same peaceably; and failing in that, the subject-matter of dispute shall be referred to arbitration.

"Art. 22 provides what shall be done with the citizens of either country residing in the other, should war unhappily break out between the two republics."

The treaty was given to a trusty messenger, dispatched to Vera Cruz, and the general commanding at that point was ordered to forward it immediately by the swiftest steamer in the harbor. The general requested, in case the treaty was accepted and ratified, that he be instructed as early as practicable in regard to evacuating Mexico, and the disposition to be made of the wagons, artillery, and cavalry horses, and the points in the United States to which the troops should be ordered, and hoped the troops could leave Mexico before the return of the *vomito*, which would probably be in May.

It had been rumored in the army for several weeks that General Scott was to be superseded in command, and he announced the fact in the following order:

"Headquarters of the Army,
"Mexico, *February 18, 1848*.
"General Orders No. 59.

"By instruction from the President of the United States just received, Major-General Scott turns over the command of the army to Major-General Butler, who will immediately enter upon duty accordingly. In taking leave of the troops he has so long had the command of in an arduous campaign, a small part of whose glory has been from position reflected on the senior officer, Major-General Scott is happy to be relieved by a general of established merit and distinction in the service of his country.

"By command of General Scott.

"H. L. Scott,
"Acting Assistant Adjutant General."

There was nothing for General Butler to do but wait the action of the United States on the treaty that had been forwarded, and then evacuate the Mexican territory. As has been seen, ratifications of the treaty were exchanged at Queretaro May 30, 1848, and proclaimed July 4, 1848.

Although General Worth had served with General Scott as his aid, and the most friendly relations had heretofore existed between them, circumstances occurred in May and June, 1847, that caused an estrangement between them which was never healed. On June 16, 1847, General Worth issued a circular at Peublo of the following purport: "Intelligence has come to the headquarters of this division, in a form and from sources entitled to consideration, that food exhibited, and, in tempting form, for sale to the soldiers, is purposely prepared to cause sickness and ultimately death"; and he appealed to every soldier to forbear the procurement or use of such food, as ample rations were issued, and added: "Doubtless there are among those with whom we are situated many who will not hesitate, as is the habit of cowards, to poison those from whom they habitually fly in battle—a resource familiar in Spanish history, legitimately inherited and willingly practiced in Mexico."

General Scott had animadverted upon the terms granted by Worth to the functionaries of the city of

Puebla, about May 15, 1847, and strongly censured the circular referred to. These reproofs induced General Worth to call for a court of inquiry, which was ordered to convene June 17, 1847, at 10 o'clock A. M. The court met, and General Worth submitted a statement of the matters in which he deemed himself wronged by the general in chief, and to which he invited investigation. The court gave the matters before it careful consideration on the evidence adduced and the documents submitted, and pronounced their opinions. The court found nothing in the remarks of the general in chief in regard to General Worth's terms to the functionaries of Puebla to which he [Worth] could take exception; "that the terms or stipulations granted by Brevet Major-General Worth to the functionaries of the city of Puebla upon his entrance with his advance of the army on the 15th of May last were unnecessarily yielded, improvident, and in effect detrimental to the public service," and continues: "The court, as required, further declares its opinion that the 'circular' published by Brevet Major-General Worth to his division, dated Puebla, June 16, 1847, was highly improper and extremely objectionable in many respects, especially as it might tend, by exasperating the whole Mexican nation, to thwart the well-known pacific policy of the United States, and, in view of the high source from which it emanated, to disturb the friendly relations of our Government with Spain, or at least give occasion to that power to call for explanations or apologies. The barbarous offense against which that 'circular' warned the soldiers of the First Division, if it exists at all, equally affected the whole army. The information obtained by General Worth, if worthy of notice, should therefore have been communicated to the general in chief, that he might have exercised his discretion on the means to be adopted for correcting the evil. With these views of the 'circular' alluded to the court is of the opinion that it called for the 'emphatic admonition' and rebuke of the general in chief."

About two months after the occupation of the City of Mexico by the United States forces a mail arrived from the States. It was found that two letters written from the valley a few days after the battles of Contreras and Churubusco had been published in the newspapers. One of them, published in the New Orleans Delta, was known as the "Leonidas letter," and gave to General Pillow nearly all the credit for winning these important battles, and placed him on a plane of military genius far above the facts, as was understood by parties present. Among other things the letter said: "He [Pillow] evinced on this, as he had on other occasions, that masterly military genius and profound knowledge of the science of war which has astonished *the mere martinets of the profession.* His plan was very similar to that by which Napoleon effected the reduction of the fortress of Ulm, and General Scott was so perfectly well satisfied with it that he could not interfere with any part of it, but left it to the gallant projector to carry into glorious and successful execution."

The "Tampico letter," as the other letter was called, is given in full:

"TACUBAYA, MEXICO, *August 27, 1847.*

"The whole force which moved from Puebla, amounting to ten thousand, more or less, marched in four columns on successive days, in the following order, viz.: Twiggs, Quitman, Worth, and Pillow. In approaching the City of Mexico by the main highway you go directly on to Penon, which is a strong position, exceedingly well fortified. Before leaving Puebla, it had been considered whether the main road can not be avoided and El Penon turned by passing around to the south and left of Lakes Chalco and Xochimilco. The engineer officers serving immediately at general headquarters had questioned a number of persons, including spies and agents sent expressly to examine the route, and the mass of testimony was entire to the boggy, mucky, and perfectly impracticable character for wagons and artillery of the road leading in that direction. It was therefore in contemplation to turn Penon by forcing Mexicalcinzo, although the ground was difficult and the batteries known to be numerous. This route, you will observe, is to the north and right of the lakes. The reconnoissances of the engineers were consequently directed to this end. In the meantime General Worth, whose division had been left at Chalco, while General Scott, with Twiggs, had gone to Ayotla, sent Colonel Duncan with a large party to examine the denounced route.

"Colonel Duncan found it just the reverse of what it had been pronounced to be; it was firm, rocky, and quite practicable, requiring, to be sure, a little labor here and there. General Worth instantly sent Colonel Duncan with this information to General Scott, and urged the movement of the whole army to the left of Lake Chalco. The direct attack was abandoned, and on the morning the whole army was in motion."

Owing to a letter written by General Taylor to General Gaines, which was intended to be private and confidential, finding its way into the New York Morning Express, the Secretary of War issued the following:

"WAR DEPARTMENT, WASHINGTON, *January 28, 1847.*

"The President of the United States directs that paragraph 650 of the General Regulations of the Army, established the 1st of March, 1825, and not included among those published January 25, 1841, be now published, and its observance, as a part of the general regulations, be strictly enjoined upon the army.

"By order of the President.

"W. L. MARCY, *Secretary of War.*"

The following is the paragraph referred to and ordered to be "published":

"Private letters or reports relative to military movements and operations are frequently mischievous in design, and always disgraceful to the army. They are therefore strictly forbidden, and any officer found guilty of making such report for publication, without special permission, or of placing the writing beyond his control, so that it finds its way to the press within one month after the termination of the campaign to which it relates, shall be dismissed from the service.'

Upon the appearance in print of the two letters referred to, the commanding general issued the following:

"Headquarters of the Army,
"Mexico, *November 12, 1847.*
"General Orders No. 349.

"The attention of certain officers of this army is recalled to the foregoing—650th paragraph, 1,825 regulations—a regulation prohibiting officers of the army from detailing in private letters or reports the movements of the army, which the general in chief is resolved to enforce so far as it may be in his power. As yet but two echoes from home of the brilliant operations of our army in this basin have reached us—the first in a New Orleans and the second through a Tampico newspaper.

"It requires not a little charity to believe that the principal heroes of the scandalous letters alluded to did not write them, or especially procure them to be written; and the intelligent can be at no loss in conjecturing the authors, chiefs, partisans, and pet familiars. To the honor of the service, the disease—pruriency of fame not earned—can not have seized upon half a dozen officers present, all of whom, it is believed, belonged to the same two coteries.

"False credit may no doubt be attained at hand by such despicable self-puffings and malignant exclusion of others, but at the expense of the just esteem and consideration of all honorable officers who love their country, their profession, and the truth of history. The indignation of the great number of the latter class can not fail in the end to bring down the conceited and envious to their proper level."

The day after the publication of the above General Orders General Worth forwarded to army headquarters a communication in which he said:

"I learn with much astonishment that the prevailing opinion in this army points the imputation of 'scandalous' contained in the third, and the invocation of the 'indignation of the great number' in the fourth paragraph of Orders No. 349, printed and issued yesterday, to myself as one of the officers alluded to. Although I can not suppose those opinions to be correctly formed, nevertheless, regarding the high source from which such imputations flow, so seriously affecting the qualities of a gentleman, the character and usefulness of him at whom they may be aimed, I feel it incumbent on me to ask, as I do now most respectfully, of the frankness and justice of the commander in chief, whether in any sense or degree he condescended to apply, or designed to have applied, the epithets contained in that order to myself, and consequently whether the general military opinion or sentiment in that matter has taken a right or intended direction. I trust I shall be pardoned for pressing with urgency an early reply to this communication."

On the day General Worth addressed his communication to General Scott, Brevet Lieutenant-Colonel James Duncan wrote to the editor of the North American (a newspaper published in the City of Mexico in English), in which he avowed that the substance of the "Tampico letter" was communicated by him to a friend in Pittsburg from Tacubaya soon after the battles, and added: "The statements in the letter are known by very many officers of this army to be true, and I can not but think that the publication of the truth is less likely to do violence to individuals or to the service than the suppression of it." He states that justice to General

Worth, who was evidently one of the persons pointed at in Orders No. 349, requires him [Duncan] to state that he [General Worth] knew nothing of the writer's purpose in writing the letter in question; that General Worth never saw it, and did not know, directly or indirectly, even the purport of one line, word, or syllable of it until he saw it in print; that this letter was not inspired by General Worth, but that both the "Tampico letter"—or rather the private letter to his friend which formed the basis of that letter—and this were written on his own responsibility.

On November 14, 1847, General Scott acknowledged General Worth's letter of the 13th, and said: "The General Order No. 349 was, as is pretty clearly expressed on its face, meant to apply to the letter signed 'Leonidas' in a New Orleans paper, and to the summary of two letters given in the Washington Union and copied into a Tampico paper, to the authors, aiders, and abettors of those letters, be they who they may."

It may be well questioned if an officer has a right to demand of his superior in command whether or not certain expressions used in written orders apply to him. If one officer could claim this privilege another also could, until every officer in the command had interrogated the commanding officer as to the intention of words used in general orders. To comment upon and disapprove or censure the official acts of his subordinates is not only a privilege of the commanding general, but an obligation, for the maintenance of discipline and the *morale* of the army.

But any officer aggrieved by any censure or disapproval may demand a court of inquiry, which General Worth did in a letter dated November 14,

1847, addressed to General Scott, in which he says: "I have the honor to receive your letter in reply, but not in answer to mine of yesterday, handed in this morning. The General Order is too clearly expressed on its face to admit of any doubt in regard to papers, and, in public military opinion, in regard to persons. The object of my letter, as I endeavored clearly to express, was to seek to know distinctly, and with a view to further measures to protect myself, if, as is supposed, I was one of the persons referred to. Regretting the necessity for intrusion, I am compelled again respectfully to solicit an answer to that question. I ask it as an act of simple justice, which it is hoped will not be denied."

To this General Scott replied through his assistant adjutant general [H. L. Scott], November 14, 1847, "that he [General Scott] can not be more explicit than in his reply through me already given; that he has nothing to do with the suspicions of others, and has no positive information as to the authorship of the letters alluded to in General Orders No. 349. If he had valid information he would immediately prosecute the parties before a general court-martial."

The correspondence on this subject was terminated by General Worth in the following letter:

"HEADQUARTERS FIRST DIVISION,
"MEXICO, *November 14, 1847.*

"SIR: It is due to official courtesy and propriety that I acknowledge your letter No. 2, in answer to mine of this date; and in doing so, and in closing this correspondence with the headquarters of the army, I beg permission to say, and with regret, that I have received no satisfactory answer to the just and rightful inquiries which I have addressed to the general in chief; but inasmuch as I know myself to be deeply aggrieved and wronged, it only remains to go by appeal, as I shall do through the prescribed channels, to the constitutional commander in chief.

"The general in chief is pleased to say through you that he has nothing to do with the suspicion of others, and that he has no positive information as to authorship, etc., granted. But has not the manner in which the general in chief has been pleased to treat the case established—whether designedly or not remains to be seen—an equivocal public sentiment on the subject? There are always enough of that peculiar pestilential species who exist upon the breath of authority to catch up the whisperings of fancy and infect a whole military community. I do not design to be stifled under the miasma of such, nor stricken down in my advanced age, without an effort to convince my friends that I scorn to wear 'honor not earned.' Your obedient servant,

"W. J. WORTH, *Brevet Major General.*"

Following this, General Worth prepared the following communication, and sent it to army headquarters:

"HEADQUARTERS FIRST DIVISION, *November 16 1847.*
"*To the Honorable Secretary of War, Washington:*

"SIR: From the arbitrary and illegal conduct, the malice and gross injustice, practiced by the general officer, commanding in chief, this army, Major-General Winfield Scott, I appeal (as is my right and privilege) to the constitutional commander in chief, the President of the United States. I accuse Major-

General Winfield Scott of having acted in a manner unbecoming an officer and a gentleman. He has availed himself of his position to publish by authority to the army which he commands, and of the influence of his station to give the highest effect to an order bearing date November 12, 1847, and numbered 349—official printed copy herewith—calculated and designed to cast odium and disgrace upon Brevet Major-General Worth; to bring that general officer into disrepute with the army, to lessen, if not destroy, his just influence and proper authority with those officers over whom he is placed in command; that he has, without inquiry or investigation, in the said order published to the army and the world, falsely charged Brevet Major-General Worth with having written, or connived at the writing, a certain letter published in the United States, and to which he has been pleased to apply the epithet of 'scandalous,' 'malignant,' etc.; that he has made these statements to the world, giving to them the sanction of his high authority and the influence of his position, while he has had no information as to the authorship of the letters in question; and when respectfully and properly addressed upon the subject by the undersigned appellant, he has declined to reply whether or not he intended to impute to Brevet Major-General Worth conduct which he had characterized as 'scandalous,' 'malignant,' etc.; be pleased to refer to correspondence herewith marked from A to E. I do not urge present action on these accusations, because of their inconvenience to the service in withdrawing many officers from their duties, but I do humbly and respectfully invoke the President's examination into the case, and such notice thereof and protection from arbitrary conduct of said Major-General Scott as he may deem suitable.

"I have the honor to be, etc.,
"W. J. WORTH,
"*Brevet Major General, United States Army.*"

Upon receipt of the above communication at General Scott's headquarters, General Worth was placed under arrest and charged "with behaving with contempt and disrespect toward his commanding officer," or words to that effect; and the specification to the charge was to the following effect: "Under pretext of appeal he charged his commanding officer to be actuated by malice toward him [Worth] and conduct unbecoming an officer and a gentleman."

It must have been under a painful stress of duty that General Scott preferred charges against General Worth; they had been friends for over thirty years, and the latter had been aid-de-camp to the former. Worth was the first general officer ordered from General Taylor's army to report to General Scott on his arrival in Mexico.

It was shown that General Pillow had given a written account of the battles of Contreras and Churubusco to the correspondent of a newspaper about August 25th, expressing a desire that it should go off with first impressions and form a part of the correspondent's letter. The general told the correspondent he had prepared it for him. The latter examined the paper submitted by the general, found it incorrect in many details, and did not send it as requested. When, however, the mail from New Orleans brought the newspaper with the "Leonidas letter," the correspondent compared the letter with the memorandum or statement given him by Pillow and pronounced them almost identical.

The arrest of General Pillow was ordered. He was charged: 1. With a violation of a general regulation or standing order of the army. 2. With conduct unbecoming an officer and a gentleman.

The specification to the first charge was, that he [Pillow] wrote or caused to be written an account of military operations between the United States forces and those of the Republic of Mexico, August 19, 1847, in and about Contreras and Churubusco, in which operations said Pillow bore a part, and which account was designed by said Pillow and in due time, over the signature of "Leonidas," partially printed and published in the New Orleans Delta of September 10, 1847, and reprinted entire in the Bulletin and the Daily Picayune of the 15th and 16th of the same month, all this pending the campaign between the forces before mentioned. There were eight different specifications to the second charge, and under the first there were eight different items or headings. The specifications cover eleven printed pages. Their substance and effect was that General Pillow's account was not correct in the very many particulars specified.*

Colonel Duncan was charged: 1. With violation of the 650th paragraph (revised), General Regulations of the Army; and the specification cited the "Tampico letter," which he confessed to have written. The second charge had relation solely to matters of fact set forth in the "Tampico letter."

On January 13, 1848, the Secretary of War ad-

---

* See Ex. Doc. No. 65, Thirtieth Congress, first session.

dressed a communication to General Scott in which he said: "The President has determined to relieve you from further duty as commanding general in Mexico. You are therefore ordered by him to turn over the command of the army to Major-General Butler, or, in his absence, to the officer highest in rank with the column under you, together with all instructions you have received in relation to your operations and duties as general in chief command, and all records and papers properly belonging or appertaining to general headquarters.

"Desirous to secure a full examination into all matters embraced in the several charges which you have presented against Major-General Pillow and Brevet Colonel Duncan, as well as the charges or grounds of complaint presented against you by Brevet Major-General Worth, and deeming your presence before the court of inquiry which has been organized to investigate these matters indispensably necessary for this purpose, you are directed by the President to attend the said court of inquiry wherever it may hold its sittings; and when your presence before or attendance upon the court shall no longer be required, and you are notified of that fact by the court, you will report in person at this department for further orders."

General Scott while in Puebla had asked to be relieved from command of the army because of the want of sympathy and support of the home Government. He thought active operations would cease in November, and the passage through Vera Cruz would be safe by that date. The Secretary, in reply to this request of General Scott, said:

"Regarding the inducement you have assigned

for begging to be recalled as deserving to have very little influence on the question, it will be decided by the President with exclusive reference to the public good. When that shall render it proper in his opinion to withdraw you from your present command, his determination to do so will be made known to you."

And further:

"The perusal of these communications by the President has forced upon his mind the painful conviction that there exists a state of things at the headquarters of the army which is exceedingly detrimental to the public service, and imperiously calls upon him to interfere in such a way as will, he sincerely hopes, arrest and put an end to the dissensions and feuds which there prevail. . . . The documents show that General Worth felt deeply aggrieved by your General Order No. 349. . . . With this view of the import and object of the order, his attempt by all proper means to remove from himself the ignominy of these imputations can not be regarded as an exceptionable course on his part. If he was actually aggrieved in this matter, or believed himself to be so, he had an unquestionable right to have the subject brought to the consideration of his and your common superior—the President. He prepared charges against you, for his letter of November 16th to the Secretary of War can be viewed in no other character, and endeavored to send them through you, the only channel he could use without violating established regulations to his common superior. . . . General Worth having preferred charges against General Scott before the latter preferred charges against him, both law and natural justice require that the order of events should be pursued in such cases. The charges which he prefers against you should be first disposed of before proceedings can be instituted against him for malice in preferring charges, or for presenting such as he did know or believe to be well founded."

The President was evidently laboring under a misapprehension in regard to the condition of affairs at the headquarters of the army. Everything was quiet, industry prevailed, and constant watchfulness for the comfort of the men of his command was being observed by the general in chief. The public interests under his charge received his constant care. No feuds were known to the army, and it was expected that if there was anything done by the President it would be to sustain the commanding general. At the time the order was issued relieving General Scott, both Generals Quitman and Shields were in Washington, but they were not consulted by the President or Secretary of War. General Quitman wrote from Washington to his aid, Lieutenant Christopher S. Lovell: "You are long since informed of the course the War Department has thought fit to pursue in relation to the difficulties between some of the generals. Though General Shields and myself were at Washington when the information came, we were not consulted."

It was believed by a large number of persons both in and out of the army that considerations of public good had not in themselves caused the President to relieve General Scott from command of the army. It was well known that his political opinions were not in harmony with the Administration, while those of his successor were. There had been anything but that amenity which should exist between a commissioner to negotiate a treaty of peace and the commanding general. General Scott did not think that Mr. Trist treated him with the consideration his position required — rejecting all overtures on the part of the general. General Scott ascribes Trist's conduct to sickness, which is throwing the mantle of charity over a series of slights amounting almost to insults, which a general less solicitous for the cause he was engaged in, and less regardful of his country's good, would have resented in a manner that would have produced a crisis detrimental to the interests of the Government.

General Scott, commander in chief, being the accuser, and Pillow, Worth, and Duncan the defendants, the duty devolved upon the President to appoint the court, which he did, composed of Brigadier-General Nathan Towson, paymaster general, Brigadier-General Caleb Cushing, and Brevet Colonel William G. Belknap, with Captain S. C. Ridgely, judge advocate and recorder.

The court organized and adjourned to the City of Mexico, where it met March 16, 1848, all the members present, the judge advocate and recorder. General Pillow was also in attendance. No objection being made to any member of the court, they were duly sworn. General Scott then read a paper, from which the following extracts are made:

"Having, in the maintenance of what I deemed necessary discipline, drawn up charges and specifications against three officers then under my command, I transmitted the papers November 28, 1847, to the Secretary of War, with a request in each case that the President, under the act of May 29, 1830, would appoint a general court-martial for the trial of the same. This court of inquiry is the result. I am stricken down from high command; one of the arrested generals is pre-acquitted and rewarded, and of the other parties, the judge and his prisoners, the accuser and the accused, the innocent and the guilty, with that strange exception, all thrown before you to scramble for justice as we may.

"In the case of Major-General Pillow I preferred two charges: the first with one specification, respecting a prohibited publication in the newspapers of the United States, and the second embracing a great number of specifications.

"Considering, Mr. President, that I asked for a general court-martial to try and definitely determine cases specifically defined and set out, and that this preliminary court has no power beyond the mere collection of facts and giving an inoperative opinion thereon; considering that, if we now proceed, the whole labor must be gone over again at least by the parties and witnesses; considering that the court will be obliged to adjourn to the United States in order to have the least hope of obtaining the testimony of these important witnesses, now retired to civil life, and therefore not compellable to attend a military court even at home, or to testify before a commission duly appointed by such courts, and the parties will not be able to leave this country for home without peril of life. Considering that there is a near prospect of peace between the United States and Mexico, which may be consummated in time to enable this whole army to return home at once in safety; considering immediately, on such consummation, that Major-General Pillow would, by express terms of the law under which he holds his commission, be out of the army, and therefore no longer amenable for his acts to any military tribunal; considering that, in preferring the charges against that officer, I was moved solely by the desire to preserve the discipline and honor of the army, not having even had the slightest personal quarrel or difficulty with him, and that the time had probably gone by for benefiting the service by a conviction and punishment—in view of these circumstances, I shall, Mr. President, decline prosecuting the charges and specifications against Major-General Pillow before this preliminary court, without its special orders, or further orders from the President of the United States."

In total disregard of the charges preferred against General Worth by the commanding general, the President ordered him to be released from arrest and restored to his command. General Worth, considering that the President had done him "full and ample justice," withdrew his charges against General Scott; to which the latter said that he "felt strong in conscious rectitude, strong in all the means of defense, defied his accusers, and would not plead the letter withdrawing the accusations against him in bar of trial; that he challenged the writer of that letter to come forward and do his worst."

Colonel Duncan having admitted that he had written the "Tampico letter," thus pleading guilty to violating the army regulations, and the President having ordered a court of inquiry and not a court-martial, General Scott declined to prosecute him before this court or a court-martial without express orders from the President. General Scott considered that it was not for him to attempt to uphold a regulation which the President had revived and then disregarded. While Colonel Duncan no doubt believed all he had written to be true, the evidence of Colonel H. L. Scott, assistant adjutant general of the army, Colonel Hitchcock, and Captain Lee shows that the direct attack, or that by Mexicalcingo, was never decided upon.

General Scott was informed that the court of inquiry would probably adjourn to await further orders from the Government. To prevent this delay, he [Scott] consented to prosecute the case of General Pillow. With a probability of peace and the disbanding of the army, it was almost certain that there never would be a trial by court-martial should such a court be recommended.

On March 21st the investigation before the court of inquiry commenced in the City of Mexico and continued until April 21st, when the court, as General Scott had predicted, adjourned to the United States for the purpose of obtaining further testimony, and reassembled in Frederick, Md., May 29, 1848. General Pillow did not appear until June 5th, when General Scott was also present. The latter had been detained by sickness, and General Pillow had stopped in Tennessee to visit his family.

On July 1st General Scott submitted the following paper to the court, and withdrew the charges against Colonel Duncan:

"The reason given for withdrawing the first charge was, that the President seemed indisposed to enforce the revised paragraph 650, which he had ordered to be published, and enjoined all to obey and enforce.

"In regard to the second charge and specification,

relating to matters of fact set forth in the 'Tampico letter,' and which Colonel Duncan had acknowledged over his own signature he had written, General Scott, believing that Colonel Duncan had fallen undesignedly into erroneous statements of fact in the letter, sent an officer to ask him if he was not ignorant, at the time of writing the letter,

"1. That before the army left Pueblo for the valley his [Scott's] bias and expectation were that the army would be obliged to reach the enemy's capital by the left or south around Lakes Chalco and Xochimilco.

"2. That after his headquarters were established at Ayotla, August 11th, he [Scott] had shown equal solicitude to get additional information of that route, as well as that of Penon or Mexicalcingo.

"3. That besides sending from Ayotla, August 12th, oral instructions to Brevet Major-General Worth to push further inquiries from Chalco as to the character of the southernmost route around the two lakes, he [Scott] had sent written instructions to General Worth to the same effect from his quarters at Ayotla.*

"4. That while at Ayotla, from the 11th to the 15th of August, he [Scott] sent a Mexican from Ayotla, independent of General Worth, all around the village of Xochimilco to report to him [Scott] whether there had been any recent change in the

---

* General Worth wrote to Colonel Duncan from Tacubaya, March 31, 1848: "General Scott evinced a disposition to gather information as respected this route (Chalco) on the 12th. . . . As I have said, General Scott directed me to send and examine the Chalco route," etc.

route, either in the matter of fortifications or from overflowing of the lakes.

"5. That in the evening of the 13th he [Scott] had ordered Captain Mason, of the engineers, to report to General Worth the next morning, to be employed in reconnoitering that same southern route, in which service he had already been anticipated by the reconnoitering party under himself — Colonel Duncan."

The officer was authorized to say that if Colonel Duncan would state that he was ignorant of these facts, he would withdraw and abandon, upon his word, the second charge and specification.

To this Colonel Duncan replied that he "believed the facts therein ("Tampico letter") set forth to be substantially true, and still believed so; had no desire to detract directly or indirectly from the merits of any officer, and no one could regret more than himself if he had done so. If the statements of General Scott were facts, he learned them for the first time, and was ignorant of them when he wrote the 'Tampico letter.'" General Scott's reply was that "ample evidence, both oral and written, was at hand to substantiate his averments in respect to the route around Lakes Chalco and Xochimilco." He then withdrew the second charge against Colonel Duncan.

Following is the opinion of the court of inquiry in General Pillow's case:

"On reviewing the whole case, it will be seen that the points on which the conduct of General Pillow has been disapproved by the court are his claiming in certain passages of the paper No. 1" (the letter he gave Mr. Freuner, correspondent of the New Orleans Delta, and which had been pronounced a twin brother to the "Leonidas letter"), "and in his official report of the battles of Contreras and Churubusco, a larger degree of participation in the merit of the movements appertaining to the battle of Contreras than is substantiated by the evidence, or he is entitled to, and also the language above quoted, in which that claim is referred to in the letter to General Scott.

"But as the movements actually ordered by General Pillow at Contreras on the 19th were emphatically approved by General Scott at the time, and as the conduct of General Pillow in the brilliant series of military operations carried on to such triumphant issue by General Scott in the Valley of Mexico appears by the several official reports of the latter, and otherwise, to have been highly meritorious, from these and other considerations the court is of the opinion that no further proceedings against General Pillow in this case are called for by the interests of the public."

On July 7, 1848, the President, through the Secretary of War, issued an order approving the findings of the court of inquiry, and adds:

"The President, finding, on a careful review of the whole evidence, that there is nothing established to sustain the charge of 'a violation of the general regulation or standing order of the army,' nothing in the conduct of General Pillow, nor in his correspondence with the general in chief of the army, 'unbecoming an officer and a gentleman,' concurs with the court in their conclusion that 'no further proceedings against General Pillow in the case are called for by the interests of the public service,' and he accordingly directs that no further proceedings be had in the case."

As has been seen, General Scott had defied his enemies, whoever they were, to do their worst. The charges against him were withdrawn, and the court only investigated the charges against General Pillow, with the result as given above. The court was then dissolved. It is probably fortunate for all the parties against whom General Scott had brought charges that a peace had been consummated, after a campaign in which all participants from the highest in rank to the private had borne such a brilliant part.

When General Scott arrived at Vera Cruz on his journey home he found several fast steamers in port, any one of which he could have taken passage in, but, with a consideration for the comfort of his men, which throughout his career he never failed to evince, he left them for the troops soon to embark, and taking a small sailing brig, loaded down with guns, mortars, and ordnance stores, started on his voyage to New York. On Sunday morning, May 20th, at daylight, the health officer boarded the brig, and the general landed and proceeded to Elizabeth, N. J., to join his family. He had the Mexican disease (diarrhœa) upon him, and required rest and good nursing. He was not long permitted to enjoy his much-needed repose, for deputations from New York tendered him one of the most magnificent civic and military receptions ever extended to any hero in this country up to that time.

CHAPTER XIII.

General Taylor nominated for the presidency—Thanks of Congress to Scott, and a gold medal voted—Movement to revive and confer upon Scott the brevet rank of lieutenant general—Scott's views as to the annexation of Canada—Candidate for President in 1852 and defeated—Scott's diplomatic mission to Canada in 1859—Mutterings of civil war—Letters and notes to President Buchanan—Arrives in Washington, December 12, 1861—Note to the Secretary of War—"Wayward sisters" letter—Events preceding inauguration of Mr. Lincoln—Preparation for the defense of Washington—Scott's loyalty—Battle of Bull Run—Scott and McClellan—Free navigation of the Mississippi River—Retirement of General Scott and affecting incidents connected therewith—Message of President Lincoln—McClellan on Scott—Mount Vernon—Scott sails for Europe—Anecdote of the day preceding the battle of Chippewa—The Confederate cruiser Nashville—Incident between Scott and Grant—Soldiers' Home—Last days of Scott—His opinion of noncombatants.

GENERAL TAYLOR had been nominated by the Whigs as their candidate for President, and at the instance of General Scott he [Scott] was put in command of the Eastern Department and the former the Western Department. This was considered a compliment to General Taylor. March 9, 1848, the following joint resolution, unanimously passed by Congress, was approved by the President:

" 1. That the thanks of Congress be and they are hereby presented to Winfield Scott, major general commanding in chief the army in Mexico, and through him to the officers and men of the regular and volunteer corps under him, for their uniform gallantry and good conduct, conspicuously displayed at the siege and capture of the city of Vera Cruz and castle of San Juan de Ulloa, March 29, 1847; and in the successive battles of Cerro Gordo, April 18th; Contreras, San Antonio, and Churubusco, August 19th and 20th; and for the victories achieved in front of the City of Mexico, September 8th, 11th, 12th, and 13th, and the capture of the metropolis, September 14, 1847, in which the Mexican troops, greatly superior in numbers and with every advantage of position, were in every conflict signally defeated by the American arms.

"2. That the President of the United States be and he is hereby requested to cause to be struck a gold medal with devices emblematical of the series of brilliant victories achieved by the army, and presented to Major-General Winfield Scott, as a testimony of the high sense entertained by Congress of his valor, skill, and judicious conduct in the memorable campaign of 1847.

"3. That the President of the United States be requested to cause the foregoing resolutions to be communicated to Major-General Scott in such terms as he may deem best calculated to give effect to the objects thereof."

On February 24, 1849, a joint resolution was offered in the United States Senate to confer upon General Scott the brevet rank of lieutenant general, which went only to its second reading, an objection being interposed to a third reading and passage of the resolution. On July 29, 1850, Mr. Jere Clemens, of Alabama, submitted a resolution instructing the Committee on Military Affairs to inquire into the expediency of conferring by law the brevet rank of lieutenant general on Major-General Scott, "with such additional pay and allowances as might be deemed proper, in consideration of the distinguished services rendered to the republic by that officer during the late war with Mexico." The resolution was eight days after referred to the Committee on Military Affairs.

On September 30, 1850, Senator Jefferson Davis, of Mississippi, Chairman of the Military Committee, reported a resolution requesting the President to refer to a board of officers, to be designated by him, the following questions:

"Is it expedient or necessary to provide for additional grades of commissioned officers in the army of the United States; and, if so, what grades, in addition to the present organization, should be created?"

Mr. Davis's opposition to conferring the brevet rank of lieutenant general upon General Scott was well known at the time. In pursuance of this request by the Senate, the following officers were appointed on the board: Generals Jesup, president, Wool, Gibson, Totten, Talcott, Hitchcock, and Colonel Crane. The unanimous report was:

"Under the first inquiry referred to it, the board is of opinion that it is expedient to create by law for the army the additional grade of lieutenant general, and that when, in the opinion of the President and Senate, it shall be deemed proper to acknowledge eminent services of officers of the army, and in the mode already provided for in subordinate grades, it is expedient and proper that the grade of lieutenant general may be conferred by brevet."

Several efforts were subsequently made to pass joint resolutions similar in purport to those quoted and referred to, but it was not until 1852 that the joint resolution was passed creating the brevet rank of lieutenant general, and General Scott succeeded to that dignity in the army. The law did not in terms carry with it the pay and emoluments of the brevet rank, and Mr. Davis, who had become Secretary of War under President Pierce, referred the question to the Attorney-General, Mr. Caleb Cushing; but before that officer rendered an opinion Congress inserted a declaratory provision in the military appropriation bill, which, becoming a law, gave the pay proper and all that went with it to a veteran who had by his services well earned it. General Scott was thenceforward until he died the second officer of the American army (General Washington being the first) who held the office of lieutenant general.

After the inauguration of General Taylor as President, General Scott, between whom and the President there was no very good feeling, continued his headquarters in New York; but when President Fillmore succeeded, in 1850, he removed to Washington, and continued to reside in the latter city until the accession of President Pierce, when, by General Scott's request, there was another change back to New York, where until 1861—with the exception of ten months of hard duty—he remained and maintained headquarters of the army.

In 1849 there were evidences of discontent which almost assumed the attitude of threats in the Canadas growing out of political agitation, and General Scott was interrogated on the question of the advisability of annexation by John C. Hamilton, Esq., of New

York. General Scott replied from West Point, June 29, 1849, in which he expressed the opinion that the news from the British Parliament would increase the discontent of the Canadas, and that those discontents might in a few years lead to a separation of the Canadas, New Brunswick, etc., from England. He thought that, instead of those provinces forming themselves into an independent nation, they would seek a connection with our Union, and that thereby the interests of both sides would be promoted, the provinces coming into the Union on equal terms with the States. This would secure the free navigation of the St. Lawrence River, which would be of immense importance to at least one third of our population, and of great value to the remainder. Although opposed to incorporating with us any district densely populated with the *Mexican* race, he would be most happy to fraternize with our Northern and Northeastern neighbors.

In 1852 General Scott became a candidate a second time for the presidency, having been nominated by the Whig Convention that met at Baltimore in June of that year, his competitors being Mr. Webster, and Mr. Fillmore, who succeeded President Taylor. William A. Graham, Mr. Fillmore's Secretary of the Navy, was put on the ticket for Vice-President. General Franklin Pierce and William R. King, a Senator from Alabama, were respectively put forward for President and Vice-President by the Democrats. The campaign was a heated one. The Democratic orators, however, on all occasions accorded to the Whig candidate that meed of praise for his gallantry as an army officer and commander to which his services to the country had entitled him, and accorded with the universal sentiment that his services to the country had been of inestimable benefit and shed ineffaceable luster on the American arms in the wars since 1800; but still, being in all essentials but a military man, it was contended he was not fit to be intrusted with the exalted office of President. These speakers had doubtless never read, or had forgotten, the orders published by General Scott upon his capturing the City of Mexico, which show a wonderful insight into civil as well as military command. It was left to the lower portion of the opposition to indulge in caricature, and garbled and distorted paragraphs in reports and published letters, such as a "hasty plate of soup" already mentioned, and his reference to "a fire in the rear," which had reference to the weak sympathy and support he had experienced from the Administration during the war with Mexico. The Democratic candidate was overwhelmingly elected, only four States—Massachusetts, Vermont, Kentucky, and Tennessee—casting their votes for Scott. In his autobiography General Scott thanks God for his political defeats. It detracted none from his reputation that the people chose some one else for the chief Executive.

The expedition set on foot in 1857 to bring the hostile Mormons to terms met with General Scott's censure, and he made no concealment of his belief that it was a scheme got up for the benefit of army contractors, whose peculations would involve the country in great expense. It is true the cost in hardship and privation to the army, as well as the money involved, was very great, but the results were very beneficial. During the late civil war the inhabitants of Utah had it in their power to greatly embarrass the Federal Government, but they did not, as a people, commit one disloyal act. At the time of the expedition they had put themselves in such defiance of the Federal Government that it was necessary that strong measures should be resorted to, and the result was as has been stated.

In 1859 General Scott was again called upon to exercise his powers as a diplomat. Commissioners were at that time engaged in running the boundary line between the British possessions and the United States. Differences sprang up as to which of the two countries the San Juan Island in Puget Sound belonged to. This question should have been referred to the two Governments for amicable settlement. General Harvey, an impetuous officer then in command of the United States forces in that country, took forcible possession of the island, endangering the friendly relations between the two countries. The situation was critical, but President Buchanan requested General Scott to go to the scene of operations and settle the matter without conflict, if possible. The general had recently been crippled from a fall, but, suffering as he was, he sailed September 20, 1859, from New York in the Star of the West for Panama, and thence to his destination. The British governor was at Victoria. The few friendly notes that passed between General Scott and the governor restored the island to its former condition, the joint possession of both parties, and thus averting what might have led to great and serious complications.

Nothing of particular public importance attracted the attention of the general until the mutterings of civil war gave utterance to sound. That he knew the feeling and determination of the Southern people better than those in high authority is shown by his suggestions to prevent, if possible, the secession of the Southern States. He was a native of Virginia, and every effort was made by persuasion to induce him to link his fortunes with his State, but without avail. Even his old friends—the friends of his early youth and manhood, to say nothing of those of maturer years—brought to bear upon him every argument to swerve him, but to no purpose. He remained true to the Government he had served and that had honored him, and if his suggestion had been carried out, the war would not perhaps have attained the proportions it did.

On October 29, 1860, General Scott addressed the following note to the President [Buchanan]: "The excitement that threatens secession is caused by the near approach of a Republican's election to the presidency. From a sense of propriety as a soldier, I have taken no part in the pending canvass, and, as always heretofore, mean to stay away from the polls. My sympathies, however, are with the Bell and Everett ticket. With Mr. Lincoln I have no communication whatever, direct or indirect, and have no recollection of ever having seen his person; but can not believe any unconstitutional violence or breach of law is to be apprehended from his administration of the Federal Government.

" From a knowledge of our Southern population, it is my solemn conviction that there is some danger of an early act of secession, viz.: The seizure of some or all of the following posts: Forts Jackson and St. Philip, on the Mississippi below New Orleans, both without garrisons; Fort Morgan, below Mobile, without garrison; Forts Pickens and McKee, Pensacola

Harbor, with an insufficient garrison for one; Fort Pulaski, below Savannah, without a garrison; Forts Moultrie and Sumter, Charleston Harbor, the former with an insufficient garrison and the latter without any; and Fort Monroe, Hampton Roads, without a sufficient garrison. In my opinion, all these works should be immediately so garrisoned as to make any attempt to take any one of them by surprise or *coup de main* ridiculous.

"With the army faithful to its allegiance and the navy probably equally so, and a Federal Executive for the next twelve months of firmness and moderation, which the whole country has a right to expect—*moderation* being an element of power not less than *firmness*—there is good reason to hope that the danger of secession may be made to pass away without one conflict of arms, one execution, or one arrest for treason. In the meantime it is suggested that exports might be left perfectly free, and, to avoid conflicts, all duties on imports be collected outside of the cities in forts or ships of war."

Again, October 31st, the general suggested to the Secretary of War that a circular should be sent at once to such of those forts as had garrisons to be on the alert against surprises and sudden assaults; but no notice seems to have been taken of the judicious and wise suggestion.

On December 12th General Scott arrived in Washington. He had been confined to his bed for a long time and was physically very much depleted. He again personally urged upon the Secretary of War the views expressed in his note from West Point of October 29th as to strengthening the forts in Charleston Harbor, Pensacola, Mobile, and the Mississippi River below New Orleans. The Secretary did not concur in these views. Finally General Scott called on the President, on December 15th, in company with the Secretary, and urged upon the chief Executive the importance of re-enforcing the forts mentioned; but no action was taken. After the Secretary of War [Floyd] had resigned his position in the Cabinet he was given a reception in Richmond, which called out the remark from the Examiner, of that city, that if the plan invented by General Scott to stop secession had been carried out, and the arsenals and forts put in the condition he wanted them to be, " the Southern Confederacy would not now exist."

On December 28th he wrote a note to the Secretary expressing the hope: 1. That orders may not be given for the evacuation of Fort Sumter [this was after Major Anderson had withdrawn his forces from Fort Moultrie and concentrated at Sumter]. 2. That one hundred and fifty recruits may be instantly sent from Governor's Island to re-enforce that garrison, with ample supplies of ammunition and subsistence, including fresh vegetables, as potatoes, onions, turnips, etc. 3. That one or two armed vessels be sent to support the said fort. In the same communication he calls the Secretary's attention to Forts Jefferson (Tortugas) and Taylor (Key West). On December 30th he addressed the President and asked permission, "without reference to the War Department, and otherwise as secretly as possible, to send two hundred and fifty recruits from New York Harbor to re-enforce Fort Sumter, together with some extra muskets or rifles, ammunition, and subsistence," and asked that a sloop of war and cutter might be ordered for the same purpose as early as the next day. The documents show that from General Scott's first note, referred to and quoted herein, down to the inauguration of Mr. Lincoln, he was persistent in his efforts to have the Southern forts, or as many of them as the means at hand would permit, re-enforced and garrisoned against surprise and capture; but little heed was paid to his importunities.

On the day before the inauguration of Mr. Lincoln General Scott addressed William H. Seward, who, it was known, would become Secretary of State in Lincoln's Cabinet, what is called the "Wayward sisters" letter, and which is quoted in full:

"WASHINGTON, *March 3, 1861.*

"DEAR SIR: Hoping that in a day or two the new President will have happily passed through all personal dangers and find himself installed an honored successor of the great Washington, with you as the chief of his Cabinet, I beg leave to repeat in writing what I have before said to you orally, this supplement to my printed 'Views' (dated in October last) on the highly disordered condition of our (so late) happy and glorious Union.

"To meet the extraordinary exigencies of the times, it seems to me that I am guilty of no arrogance in limiting the President's field of selection to one of the four plans of procedure subjoined:

"I. Throw off the old and assume the new designation, the Union party; adopt the conciliatory measures proposed by Mr. Crittenden or the Peace Convention, and my life upon it, we shall have no new case of secession; but, on the contrary, an early return of many, if not of all, the States which have already broken off from the Union. Without some equally benign measure the remaining slaveholding States will probably join the Montgomery Confederacy in less than sixty days, when this city, being included in a foreign country, would require a permanent garrison of at least thirty-five thousand troops to protect the Government within it.

"II. Collect the duties on foreign goods outside the ports of which the Government has lost the command, or close such ports by act of Congress and blockade them.

"III. Conquer the seceded States by invading armies. No doubt this might be done in two or three years by a young and able general—a Wolfe, a Desaix, a Hoche—with three hundred thousand disciplined men, estimating a third for garrisons and the loss of a yet greater number by skirmishes, sieges, battles, and Southern fevers. The destruction of life and property on the other side would be frightful, however perfect the moral discipline of the invaders.

"The conquest completed at the enormous waste of human life to the North and Northwest, with at least $250,000,000 added thereto, and *cui bono?* Fifteen devastated provinces! not to be brought into harmony with their conquerors, but to be held for generations by heavy garrisons at an expense quadruple the net duties or taxes, which it would be possible to extort from them, followed by a protector or emperor.

"IV. Say to the seceded States: 'Wayward sisters, depart in peace.'

"In haste, I remain very truly yours,

"WINFIELD SCOTT."

The two months preceding the inauguration of Mr. Lincoln were fraught with great responsibility to General Scott. He had moved his headquarters to Washington, as he thought, temporarily; but from the threatening aspect of the political troubles it soon became apparent that his stay there would be, if not permanent, prolonged a greater length of time than was at first expected. As March 4th approached, rumors thick and fast filled the atmosphere of attempts to resist Mr. Lincoln's taking the oath. It was said that bodies of men were drilling in Maryland, Virginia, and even in the District of Columbia, for that purpose. There is no doubt men were being put through military exercise within a few miles of the capital, which was known at the War Department; but if the object was violence of any kind it never developed. Great apprehension was felt, and not without reason, for the general's daily mail contained letters—mostly anonymous, a few signed doubtless with fictitious names—threatening him and Mr. Lincoln with assassination if the latter should attempt to be inaugurated. Some idea of the difficulty may be gathered when it is known that the militia of the District was but poorly equipped either in officers or otherwise to cope successfully with the situation should an outbreak or invasion of armed men from Maryland or Virginia be attempted. The military force of the District showed large *on paper*, but the actual force consisted of two or three companies tolerably well drilled. In this emergency Captain (afterward Brigadier-General) Charles P. Stone, a graduate from West Point, offered his services, which were accepted, and about January 1, 1861, he was mustered into the United States service as colonel and inspector general of the militia of the District of Columbia, and assigned to the command of the District, with authority to organize volunteers. Some members of the companies already in existence left the ranks, but Colonel Stone soon succeeded in organizing a small compact force with those that remained loyal, and a number of recruits, which did good service. In addition to these, a light battery, under Captain John B. Magruder, First Artillery; Captain (afterward General) William Farquhar, Barry's Battery of the Second Artillery; and a battery made up at West Point and commanded by Captain (afterward General) Charles Griffin, arrived. With these, some infantry ordered from distant points, and the District militia, which had been very much increased in numbers, General Scott had about three thousand men under his command for the defense of Washington, the preservation of order, and to guard the approaches to the city. It is but due to the citizens of Washington to state that, when trouble was apprehended and an intimation went out that there was a possibility of trouble, they came in great numbers to offer their services in defense of their city and the Government. Companies were organized, and persons in all positions and callings, from the highest in social life to the humblest resident, were not backward in asserting their allegiance and giving proof of it by entering the ranks. By marching and maneuvering the men on the streets frequently they made the impression that a greater force was present than really was.

Many efforts were made to induce General Scott to resign, but he never once wavered in his devotion to the Union. On one occasion Judge Robertson, a small, thin, but venerable-looking man, who had filled the office of chancellor in Virginia and was a man of high character and standing, came to Washington with two other Virginia gentlemen to offer Scott the command of the Army of Virginia if he would abandon the United States service and go with his State. The general listened in silence as Robertson feelingly recalled the days when they were schoolboys together, and then spoke of the warm attachment Virginians always cherished for their State, and of their boasted allegiance to it above all other political ties. But when he began to unfold his offer of a commission, General Scott stopped him, exclaiming: "Friend Robertson, go no further. It is best that we part here before you compel me to resent a mortal insult!" It is needless to say that this ended the interview, and Judge Robertson and his companions departed, looking and doubtless feeling very much discomfited. No man stood higher in the esteem of the people of Virginia than Judge Robertson, and it is not probable that he and his friends would have taken it upon themselves to make the offer they did upon a contingency. If, however, they had any authority to act on the part of the Commonwealth of Virginia, no act of the Convention to that effect can be discovered.

Hon. Stephen A. Douglas, a Senator from Illinois and one of the unsuccessful candidates for the presidency in 1860, made a speech in Ohio early in 1861, in which, in alluding to a question that had been asked, or rather suggested, as to General Scott's loyalty to the Government, said: "Why, it is almost profanity to ask such a question. I saw him only last Saturday. He was at his desk, pen in hand, writing his orders for the defense and safety of the American capital."

On April 30, 1861, Alexander Henry, Horace Binney, William M. Meredith, a former Secretary of the Treasury, and others of Philadelphia, addressed a letter to General Scott, in which they said: "At a time like this, when Americans distinguished by the favor of their country, intrenched in power, and otherwise high in influence and station, civil and military, are renouncing their allegiance to the flag they have sworn to support, it is an inexpressible source of consolation and pride to us to know that the general in chief of the army remains like an impregnable fortress at the post of duty and glory, and that he will continue to the last to uphold that flag, and defend it, if necessary, with his sword, even if his native State should assail it."

The Charleston (South Carolina) Mercury of April 22, 1861, contained the following statement: "A positive announcement was made at Montgomery, Ala. (then the capital of the Southern Confederacy), "that General Scott had resigned his position in the army of the United States and tendered his sword to his native State—Virginia. At Mobile one hundred guns were fired in honor of his resignation." This shows in some measure the high estimation in which General Scott's influence was held throughout the South.

The ceremonies of the inauguration passed off without incident. There was no attempt to prevent it, or any show of violence. Apprehension was shown in every countenance. General Scott rode in front of the President's carriage with the company of Sappers and Miners from West Point, commanded by Captain (afterward General) James Chatham Duane, of the engineers. During the ceremonies the general, in order to be more free in case of emergency, remained outside the Capitol square (which was at that time surrounded by a strong iron fence) with the batteries. The precautions thus taken were, like all of General Scott's plans, wise, and possibly saved the city from one of those scenes incident to the French Revolution, and, it may be, saved the country. At the conclusion of the ceremonies the march back to the White House was made, and Mr. Lincoln was President of the United States.

From long association in military and private life a warm personal friendship had existed between General Scott and General Robert E. Lee. At the outbreak of the war the latter, then a colonel in the army, was at his residence, Arlington, near Washington, in Virginia, on leave of absence. General Scott sent for him, and after an interview Lee tendered his resignation, which was accepted, and he entered the service of his own State as major general of State troops, and subsequently became commanding general of the armies of the Confederate States.

Soon after this, and when it was apparent that war would come, General Scott's first care was to provide for the safety of the city, the Capitol, and public buildings. He caused large quantities of army supplies, flour, provisions, etc., to be stored in the Capitol building, and quartered companies in the public buildings with stores and ammunition. A signal was agreed upon at sound of which the troops could assemble. These companies were all put under command of regular officers. There was a company of citizens from different States organized, and quartered at night at the President's house, under command of General Cassius M. Clay, of Kentucky. By the action of the seceded States the war was commenced by firing on the steamer Star of the West, January 13, 1861, in an effort to re-enforce Fort Sumter, Charleston Harbor, and subsequently bombarding that fort April 12, 1861. On April 15th the President issued his proclamation calling on the governors of the States for seventy-five thousand volunteers for three months. Troops soon began to assemble at the national capital. The first to arrive was the famous New York Seventh Regiment. There was also a Massachusetts and Rhode Island regiment present, when, on April 26th, General Orders No. 4 were issued from Headquarters of the army at Washington. It was as follows:

"I. From the known assemblage near this city of numerous hostile bodies of troops, it is evident that an attack upon it may be soon expected. In such an event, to meet and repel the enemy, it is necessary that some plan of harmonious co-operation should be adopted on the part of all the forces, regular and volunteer, present for the defense of the capital—that is, for the defense of the Government, the peaceable inhabitants of the city, their property, the public buildings and public archives.

"II. At the first moment of attack every regiment, battalion, squadron, and independent company will promptly assemble at its established rendezvous (in or out of the public buildings), ready for battle and wait for orders.

"III. The pickets (or advance guards) will stand fast until driven in by overwhelming forces; but it is expected that those stationed to defend the bridges, having every advantage of position, will not give way till actually pushed by the bayonet. Such obstinacy on the part of pickets so stationed is absolutely necessary, to give time for the troops in the rear to assemble at their places of rendezvous.

"IV. All advance guards and pickets driven in will fall back slowly, to delay the advance of the enemy as much as possible, before repairing to their proper rendezvous.

"V. On the happening of an attack, the troops lodged in the public buildings and in the navy yard will remain for their defense respectively, unless specially ordered elsewhere, with the exception that the Seventh New York Regiment and Massachusetts regiment will march rapidly toward the President's Square for its defense; and the Rhode Island regiment (in the Department of the Interior), when full, will make a diversion by detachment, to assist in the defense of the General Post-Office Building, if necessary."

From this time on General Scott, old and infirm, suffering from wounds received in early service and from accidents which befell him in maturer life, continued, from his bed or couch on which he was compelled often to recline, to direct the movements and disposition of the troops and provide for the defense of the city. The pressure for an onward movement of the army was such that it could not be withstood. Brigadier-General Irvin McDowell, who had served several years on General Scott's staff, was assigned to command the forward movement. He prepared his plans carefully, under the advice and direction of General Scott, which involved a possible battle. These plans were frequently gone over with General

Scott, and finally submitted to and approved by the President at the White House, his Cabinet, General Scott and staffs, and others, of whom General John C. Fremont was one. The result of the advance is well known. The Union troops were driven back in great disorder; confusion reigned in Washington, and grave apprehensions were felt as to the safety of the city if the Confederates should follow up their advantage. The battle of Bull Run was fought July 21, 1861. On the day following a telegram was sent to General George B. McClellan, then at Beverly, Virginia, directing him to turn over his command to General William S. Rosecrans and come to Washington. In the meantime, however, General Scott had taken measures to gather the straggling officers and men from the streets and place them in quarters, that discipline might be again asserted and maintained. Upon the arrival of McClellan the work of reorganizing the army was intrusted to him, and he was put in command of the Army of the Potomac. He was not General Scott's first choice for that command, the latter preferring General Henry W. Halleck, then on his way from California to Washington, for that responsible position. When McClellan took command he at once commenced making his reports directly to the Secretary of War, instead of through the lieutenant general. This was resented by the commander in chief, who, September 16, 1861, issued General Orders No. 17 by way of admonition, in which he said: "It is highly important that junior officers on duty be not permitted to correspond with the general in chief, or other commander, on current official business, except through intermediate commanders; and the same rule applies to correspondence with the President direct, or with him through the Secretary of War, unless it be by special invitation or request of the President." This gentle reminder of his duty to his superior officer did not have the desired effect, and so, on October 4th, General Scott addressed a letter to Hon. Simon Cameron, wherein he quotes his General Orders No. 17, in which he says: "I hailed the arrival here of Major-General McClellan as an event of happy consequence to the country and to the army. Indeed, if I did not call for him, I heartily approved of the suggestion, and gave it the most cordial support. He, however, had hardly entered upon his new duties when, encouraged to communicate directly with the President and certain members of the Cabinet, he in a few days forgot that he had any intermediate commander, and has now long prided himself in treating me with uniform neglect, running into disobedience of orders of the smaller matters—neglects, though in themselves grave military offenses." He complains that General McClellan, with the General Orders No. 17 fresh in his mind, had addressed several orders to the President and Secretary of War over his [Scott's] head. On the same day of the issuance of General Orders No. 17 General Scott addressed a letter to McClellan directing that officer to report to the commanding general the position, state, and number of troops under him by divisions, brigades, and independent regiments or detachments, which general report should be followed by reports of new troops as they arrived, with all the material changes which might take place in the Army of the Potomac. Eighteen days had elapsed between his letter to McClellan and his communication to the Secretary of War, and no response had been received. He says: "Perhaps he will say in respect to the latter that it has been difficult for him to procure the exact returns of divisions and brigades. But why not have given me the proximate returns, such as he so eagerly furnished the President and certain secretaries? Has, then, a senior no corrective power over a junior officer in case of such persistent neglect and disobedience?" He remarks that arrest and trial by court-martial would soon cure the evil, but feared a conflict of authority over the head of the army would be highly encouraging to the enemies and depressing to the friends of the Union, and concludes: "Hence my long forbearance; and continuing, though but nominally, on duty, I shall try to hold out till the arrival of Major-General Halleck, when, as his presence will give me increased confidence in the safety of the Union, and being, as I am, unable to ride in the saddle, or to walk, by reason of dropsy in my feet and legs and paralysis in the small of my back, I shall definitely retire from the command of the army." Thus the crippled, illustrious old hero asserted his power and authority to command the respect of his subordinates to the last. Owing, as has been seen, to his physical condition, it was not possible for General Scott to take active command of the army. In fact, but comparatively few of the army assembled here had ever seen him, and they only when they were passing in review.

The defense of Washington and the organization of the army for that purpose and aggressive movements from that point did not alone command the attention of General Scott. He was solicitous about the free and uninterrupted navigation of the Mississippi River, and to prevent obstructions by the Confederates, or to remove any that might have been placed on shore or in the water, he addressed a confidential letter to General McClellan, then commanding in the West, dated May 3, 1861, in which he informed that general that the Government was to call for twenty-five thousand additional regulars, and sixty thousand volunteers to serve for two years.

An act of Congress approved March 3, 1861, provided:

SECTION 15. "That any commissioned officer of the army, or of the marine corps, who shall have served as such for forty consecutive years, may, upon his own application to the President of the United States, be placed upon the list of retired officers, with the pay and allowances allowed by this act.

SECTION 16. . . . "*Provided*, That should the lieutenant general be retired under this act, it shall be without reduction in his current pay, subsistence, and allowances."

On October 31, 1861, General Scott addressed Hon. Simon Cameron, Secretary of War, the following communication:

"SIR: For more than three years I have been unable, from a hurt, to mount a horse or to walk more than a few paces at a time, and that with much pain. Other and new infirmities—dropsy and vertigo—admonish me that repose of mind and body, with the appliances of surgery and medicine, are necessary to add a little more to a life already protracted much beyond the usual space of man. It is under such circumstances, made doubly painful by the unnatural and unjust rebellion now raging in the

Southern States of our lately prosperous and happy Union, that I am compelled to request that my name be placed on the list of army officers retired from active service. As this request is founded on an absolute right, granted by a recent act of Congress, I am at liberty to say that it is with deep regret that I withdraw myself in these momentous times from the orders of a President who has treated me with much distinguished kindness and courtesy, whom I know upon much personal intercourse to be patriotic, without sectional prejudices; to be highly conscientious in the performance of every duty, and of unrivaled activity and perseverance; and to you, Mr. Secretary, whom I now officially address for the last time, I beg to acknowledge my many obligations for the uniform high consideration I have received at your hands, and I have the honor to remain, sir, with the highest respect, etc."

The following day, November 1st, a special meeting of the Cabinet was convened, and it was decided that the request, under the circumstances set forth in the letter, should be complied with. At four o'clock of that day the President and his Cabinet proceeded to the residence of General Scott. The scene is well described by General Edward Davis Townsend, a member of the general's staff, who was an eye-witness, and who says: "Being seated, the President read to the general the following order:

"'On the 1st day of November, A. D. 1861, upon his own application to the President of the United States, Brevet Lieutenant-General Winfield Scott is ordered to be placed upon the list of retired officers of the Army of the United States, without reduction in his current pay, subsistence, or allowance. The American people will hear with sadness and deep emotion that General Scott has withdrawn from the active control of the army, while the President and unanimous Cabinet express their own and the nation's sympathy in his personal affliction, and their profound sense of the important public services rendered by him to his country during his long and brilliant career, among which will be gratefully distinguished his faithful devotion to the Constitution, the Union, and the flag when assailed by parricidal rebellion.   ABRAHAM LINCOLN.'

"General Scott thereupon arose and addressed the Cabinet, who had also risen, as follows:

"'President, this honor overwhelms me. It overpays all the services I have attempted to render my country. If I had any claims before, they are all obliterated by this expression of approval by the President, with the remaining support of the Cabinet. I know the President and his Cabinet well. I know that the country has placed its interests in this trying crisis in safe keeping. Their counsels are wise, their labors as untiring as they are loyal, and their course is the right one.

"'President, you must excuse me. I am unable to stand longer to give utterance to the feelings of gratitude which oppress me. In my retirement I shall offer up my prayers to God for this Administration and for my country. I shall pray for it with confidence in its success over all enemies, and that speedily.'

"The President then took leave of General Scott,

giving him his hand, and saying that he hoped soon to write him a private letter expressive of his gratitude and affection. . . . Each member of the Administration then gave his hand to the veteran and retired in profound silence."

The Secretary of the Treasury and the Secretary of War accompanied Generel Scott to New York the next morning. On the same day (November 1st) Secretary Cameron addressed the lieutenant general the following letter in response to the latter's of the day previous:

"GENERAL: It was my duty to lay before the President your letter of yesterday, asking to be relieved on the recent act of Congress. In separating from you, I can not refrain from expressing my deep regret that your health, shattered by long service and repeated wounds received in your country's defense, should render it necessary for you to retire from your high position at this momentous period of our history. Although you are not to remain in active service, I yet hope that while I continue in charge of the department over which I now preside I shall at all times be permitted to avail myself of the benefits of your wise counsels and sage experience. It has been my good fortune to enjoy a personal acquaintance with you for over thirty years, and the pleasant relations of that long time have been greatly strengthened by your cordial and entire co-operation in all the great questions which have occupied the department and convulsed the country for the last six months. In parting from you I can only express the hope that a merciful Providence that has protected you amid so many trials will improve your health and continue your life long after the people of the country shall have been restored to their former happiness and prosperity. I am, general, very sincerely,

"Your friend and servant."

In his first annual message to Congress, Mr. Lincoln deplores the physical necessity that compelled the retirement of Scott in the following language:

"Since your last adjournment Lieutenant-General Scott has retired from the head of the army. During his long life the nation has not been unmindful of his merits; yet, in calling to mind how faithfully and ably and brilliantly he has served his country, from a time far back in our history, when few now living had been born, and thenceforward continually, I can not but think we are still his debtors. I submit, therefore, for your consideration what further mark of consideration is due to him and to ourselves as a grateful people."

In virtue of this act and in pursuance of the foregoing request on November 1, 1861, the lieutenant general having been retired from active service, General Orders No. 94 announced that "the President is pleased to direct that Major-General George B. McClellan assume command of the Army of the United States." On assuming the important command to which he had been designated, General McClellan on the same day issued his General Orders No. 19, in which he gracefully and feelingly alludes to the retiring commander:

"The army will unite with me in the feeling of regret that the weight of many years and the effect of increasing infirmities, contracted and intensified in his country's service, should just now remove from our head the great soldier of our nation—the hero who in his youth raised high the reputation of his country on the fields of Canada, which he hallowed with his blood; who in more mature years proved to the world that American skill and valor could repeat, if not eclipse, the exploits of Cortez in the land of the Montezumas; whose life has been devoted to the service of his country; whose whole efforts have been directed to uphold our honor at the smallest sacrifice of life; a warrior who scorned the selfish glories of the battlefield when his great abilities as a statesman could be employed more profitably to his country; a citizen who in his declining years has given to the world the most shining instances of loyalty in disregarding all ties of birth and clinging to the cause of truth and honor—such has been the career, such the character, of WINFIELD SCOTT, whom it has long been the delight of the nation to honor, both as a man and a soldier. While we regret his loss, there is one thing we can not regret—the bright example he has left for our emulation. Let us all hope and pray that his declining years may be passed in peace and happiness, and that they may be cheered by the success of the country and the cause he has fought for and loved so well. Beyond all that, let us do nothing that can cause him to blush for us; let no defeat of the army he has so long commanded embitter his last years, but let our victories illuminate the close of a life so grand." General Scott lived to see the fulfillment of this devout prayer in a restoration of the union of the States.

General Scott held in great reverence the fame and memory of the Father of his Country, and was desirous that Mount Vernon should be left undisturbed during the trouble arising from the civil war. A report was sent abroad that the bones of Washington had been removed. This report was wholly without foundation, but it created a great deal of excitement in both sections of the country. Through the efforts of the lady regent who resided there, an understanding was arrived at by which it should be regarded by both sides as neutral ground. The general, however, issued General Orders No. 13, July 31, 1861, from which is quoted: " Should the operations of the war take the United States troops in that direction, the general in chief does not doubt that each and every man will approach with due reverence and leave uninjured not only the tombs, but also the house, the groves, and walks which were so loved by the best and greatest of men." It is true that neither party ever invaded the sacred precincts where repose the remains of the illustrious Washington, but they were found when the war closed to be in as fair a state of preservation as was possible under the circumstances, and of partial suspension of husbandry. No act of vandalism was attemped.

In the fall of 1861 Brigadier-General Charles P. Stone obtained permission from General Scott to take a brigade and make a demonstration along the line of the Chesapeake and Ohio Canal toward Harper's Ferry in order to afford an outlet for the fine wheat that had been harvested about Leesburg, Virginia, to the large flouring mills at Georgetown, adjoining Washington. This led to the battle of Ball's Bluff, or Leesburg, October 21st, the death of Colonel Edward D. Baker, of the Seventy-first Pennsylvania Infantry, and at the time a senator in Congress from the State of Oregon, and the subsequent arrest and close confinement of the unfortunate commander for several months without charges of any nature having been preferred against him.*

On November 9, 1861, General Scott sailed for Europe in the steamer Arago for Havre to join his wife, who was in Paris. Mr. Thurlow Weed, a thorough loyalist and prominent politician, was a passenger on the same ship. He and General Scott had been on terms of intimacy for over thirty years. During the passage over the general gave Mr. Weed the true version of how he came near being made a prisoner in 1814. After apologizing in advance for the question about to be put and receiving permission to propound it, Mr. Weed said: "General, did anything remarkable happen to you on the morning of the battle of Chippewa?" The general answered: "Yes, something did happen to me—something very remarkable. I will now for the third time in my life repeat the story:

"The fourth day of July, 1814, was one of extreme heat. On that day my brigade skirmished with a British force commanded by General Riall from an early hour in the morning till late in the afternoon. We had driven the enemy down the river some twelve miles to Street's Creek, near Chippewa, where we encamped

---

* General Stone (1824-1887) was arrested by order of the Secretary of War and confined in Fort Lafayette, New York Harbor, from February 9 to August 16, 1862. The general impression that it was done through the influence of Senator Sumner is denied by his biographer, Mr. Henry L. Pierce. *Vide* Life of Sumner, vol. iv, pp. 67, 68; Boston, 1893. Generals Grant and Sherman both stated to the editor of this series, that it was an exceedingly arbitrary and unjust act.

for the night, our army occupying the west, while
that of the enemy was encamped on the east side of
the creek. After our tents had been pitched I noticed
a flag borne by a man in a peasant's dress approaching my marquee. He brought a letter from a lady
who occupied a large mansion on the opposite side of
the creek, informing me that she was the wife of a
member of Parliament who was then in Quebec; that
her children, servants, and a young lady friend were
alone with her in the house; that General Riall had
placed a sentinel before her door; and that she ven-
tured, with great doubts of the propriety of the request, to ask that I would place a sentinel upon the
bridge to protect her against stragglers from our
camp. I assured the messenger that the lady's request should be complied with. Early the next morning the same messenger, bearing a white flag, reap-
peared with a note from the same lady, thanking me
for the protection she had enjoyed, adding that, in
acknowledgment for my civilities, she begged that I
would, with such members of my staff as I chose to
bring with me, accept the hospitalities of her house
at a breakfast which had been prepared with considerable attention and was quite ready. Acting upon
an impulse which I never have been able to analyze
or comprehend, I called my two aids, Lieutenants
Worth and Watts, and returned with the messenger.

"We met our hostess at the door, who ushered
us into the dining room, where breakfast awaited us
and where the young lady previously referred to
was already seated by the coffee urn, our hostess
asking to be excused for a few minutes, and the
young lady immediately served our coffee. Before
we had broken our fast, Lieutenant Watts rose from

the table to get his bandanna (that being before the days of napkins), which he had left in his cap on a side table by the window, glancing through which he saw Indians approaching the house on one side and redcoats approaching it on the other, with an evident purpose of surrounding it and us, and instantly exclaimed, 'General, we are betrayed!' Springing from the table and clearing the house, I saw our danger, and, remembering Lord Chesterfield had said, 'Whatever it is proper to do it is proper to do well,' and as we had to run and as my legs were longer than those of my companions, I soon outstripped them. As we made our escape we were fired at, but got across the bridge in safety."

After the battle of Chippewa the mansion described, being the largest near by, was used as a hospital for the wounded officers of both armies. The general went there to visit his officers, whom he found on the second floor. On going there he met the hostess, who, by her flurried and embarrassed manner, impressed the general with the belief that she had endeavored to entrap him. But years after General Scott was inclined to give her the benefit of the doubt and think that the presence at the house of himself and staff was accidentally discovered by the Indians and British.

The Arago touched at Southampton to discharge the English mail and passengers, and here an exciting incident occurred. When the anchor had been cast, a vessel steamed up, flying the Confederate colors, which proved to be the cruiser Nashville. All was astir on the Arago, as an attack was expected as soon as that vessel had cleared port and got into neutral waters. The general asked the captain of the vessel what means of defense he had. It was found that thirty muskets and two cannon were available. The crew and those of the passengers who were fit for duty were formed upon the forward deck and the business of drilling was commenced, the general advising and in great measure directing the preparations for defense. It turned out, however, that the Nashville had put into Southampton for repairs, and the Arago proceeded on her voyage in safety. After remaining one day at Havre General Scott proceeded to Paris. The steamer that followed the Arago brought news of the "Trent affair." On November 8, 1861, Commodore Charles Wilkes, in command of the United States steamer San Jacinto, on his return from the coast of Africa, put into Havana. On the same day the British mail steamer Trent sailed from that port, having on board as passengers James M. Mason, of Virginia, and John Slidell, of Louisiana, Confederate plenipotentiaries to France and England. The San Jacinto overhauled the Trent in the Bahama Straits, brought her to by a shot across the bow, arrested and removed the Confederate commissioners and their secretaries from the mail steamer, and brought them to Fortress Monroe, where Commodore Wilkes awaited instructions from Washington. They were subsequently removed to Fort Warren, in Boston Harbor. The arrest and removal of these Confederate diplomats created great excitement in England, and for a time it was feared that hostilities between the countries would ensue. The affair was commented upon severely by the press, and the subjects of Her Britannic Majesty were at fever heat. Eight thousand British soldiers were immediately dispatched to Canada, and the shipyards were put to their utmost capacity. When the news and the excitement reached the old hero, who had hoped that he would find some rest in Paris after his long and eventful career, he determined at once to return to his native country and be on the spot should his counsel and advice be needed. He took the same steamer that he had gone out on and returned home. The Trent affair was settled by surrendering the Confederate commissioners, and war was happily averted.

During the years that followed, his advice was frequently sought by the President and others high in authority. It was at West Point that the general received the Prince of Wales when he visited this country, and at the same place the interview occurred between Scott and Grant when the former presented the latter a gift "from the oldest to the greatest general." In December, 1865, General Scott went to Key West, Fla., and remained there a portion of the winter. On returning, he spent a few weeks in New York city, and then went to West Point. It was then the incident mentioned took place between him and General Grant.

As early as February 27, 1829, a report was made to Congress by the Committee on Military Affairs upon the subject of establishing an "army asylum fund," and letters were submitted from the major general commanding and other officers of the army expressive of their views on the subject. In February, 1840, General Robert Anderson (then a captain in the adjutant general's department) addressed a letter to Hon. John Reynolds, giving his views upon the benefits and advantages which would result from establishing such an institution, with suggestions for a plan for one. This letter formed the basis of a report, January 7, 1841, by the Committee on Military Affairs, submitting a bill in which the measures suggested therein were embraced, and urging the necessary legislation as commending itself "by every attribute and motive of patriotism, benevolence, national gratitude, and economy." General Scott was deeply interested in the subject, and in 1844 gave it special prominence in his annual report, which led to a report as theretofore from the military committee. On March 5, 1846, a report was also made on a memorial of the officers of the army stationed at Fort Moultrie and the petition of officers of the Second United States Infantry, and later (on January 19, 1848) upon the memorial of the officers of the army then in Mexico. The committee in each case approved and recommended the passage of the bill reported January 7, 1841. The plan, however, did not assume practical shape until the transmission by General Scott of the draft for one hundred thousand dollars, a part of the tribute levied on the City of Mexico for the benefit of the army, requesting that it might be allowed to go to the credit of the asylum fund. He says in a letter dated November, 1849, referring to the same matter: "The draft was payable to me, and, in order to place the deposit beyond the control of any individual functionary whatever, I indorsed it. The Bank of America will place the within amount to the credit of the army asylum, subject to the order of Congress." This fund, together with a balance of eighteen thousand seven hundred and ninety-one dollars and nineteen cents remaining from the same levy, was subsequently appropriated to found the asylum. By the act those who are entitled to the benefits of the asylum were soldiers of twenty years' service and men, whether pensioners or not, who have been disabled by wounds or disease in the service in the line of duty. An honorable discharge is a preliminary requisite to admission. The inmates are all thus civilians. At first the general in chief, the generals commanding the Eastern and Western military divisions, the chiefs of the quartermaster's, commissary, pay, and medical departments, and the adjutant general of the army composed the board of commissioners *ex officio* to administer the affairs of the institution. An unexpended balance of fifty-four thousand three hundred and nineteen dollars and twenty-three cents was appropriated " for the benefit of discharged soldiers disabled by wounds." A perpetual revenue was provided from " stoppages and fines imposed by court-martial," " forfeitures on account of desertion," a certain portion of the hospital and post fund of each station, moneys belonging to the estates of deceased soldiers not claimed for three years; also a deduction of twenty-five cents per month with his consent from the pay of each enlisted man. The act of Congress of March 3, 1859, changed the provisions of the original act and reduced the number of commissioners to three—the commissary general of subsistence, the surgeon general, and the adjutant general of the army, substituted the name of " Soldiers' Home " for " Military Asylum," and extended the benefits of the Home to the soldiers of the War of 1812. The act of Congress of March 3, 1883, added the general in chief commanding the army, the quartermaster general, the judge advocate general, and the governor of the Home to the board of commissioners; these officers, together with those already named, compose the board. By the same act pensioners who are inmates of the Home may assign their pension and have the same or any portion thereof paid to a wife, child, or parent if living; otherwise the pension is paid to the treasurer of the Home and held by him in trust for the pensioner, who may, while an inmate, draw upon it for necessary purposes, and receive whatever balance may remain upon his discharge.

In 1851 temporary asylums were established at New Orleans, La., Greenwoods Island, Miss., and Washington, D. C. The one at New Orleans continued about one year. A tract of land was purchased in Mississippi comprising one hundred and ten acres in 1853, and was occupied until 1855. At this date the inmates were removed to a branch asylum near Harrodsburg, Mercer County, Ky. This latter asylum was discontinued in 1858 under the act of March 3, 1857, and the inmates transferred to the Home near Washington, which was established in 1851–'52. This Home is situated about three miles due north of the Capitol of the nation. At first it comprised two hundred and fifty-six acres of land. Subsequent acquisitions by purchases have been added, so that now the grounds comprise five hundred acres and three quarters. The largest part of the grounds are woodland, a portion being cultivated for the benefit of the Home, and through it nearly ten miles of graded, macadamized roads have been constructed, winding through the groves of native and foreign selected trees. The park is open to the public at proper hours, and forms a favorite drive and walk for the residents of and visitors to

Washington. The principal building for the inmates is of white marble, the south part being called the Scott Building, after the founder of the institution, and the addition on the north is called the Sherman Building, after General W. T. Sherman. The old homestead building to the west of and not far from the Scott Building is called the Robert Anderson Building, in commemoration of the early advocacy of and interest in the establishment of the Home by that officer. This building was the home of the first inmates, and has frequently been used as the summer residence of the Presidents. It has been occupied by Presidents Buchanan, Lincoln, Hayes, and Arthur. There is a building to the east called the King Building, after Benjamin King, U. S. A., who was the surgeon in charge for thirteen years. Brick quarters were erected to the northeast of the Sherman Building in 1883, and, in honor of General Philip H. Sheridan, is named the Sheridan Building. There is a neat chapel built of red sandstone, which was completed in 1871, where religious services, both Protestant and Roman Catholic, are regularly held. The officers in immediate charge of the Home are a governor, a deputy governor, a secretary and treasurer, and a medical officer detailed from the army. The inmates who are not pensioned receive one dollar a month pocket money, and twenty-five cents a day for such labor as they are detailed for and willing to perform. Some beneficiaries who have families receive a small monthly stipend and reside elsewhere than at the Home. The whole number of permanent inmates admitted up to September 30, 1892, was 8,086. The number on the rolls January 31, 1893, was 1,196; of these, 824 were present at the Home, some receiving outside assistance, and some being absent on furlough.

A heroic statue in bronze of Lieutenant-General Winfield Scott, by Launt Thompson, was erected in 1874 on the most commanding point of the grounds. Aside from the artistic finish of the statue, it is a wonderful likeness of the subject. There is also a perfectly designed hospital for the sick and an infirmary for the aged and helpless, which was completed in 1876. No grander or more lasting monument could be erected to perpetuate the memory of the illustrious general than the Soldiers' Home near Washington.

General Scott, in his later years, was very impatient of contradiction, but when convinced that he was in error was always ready to acknowledge it. In a diary of Colonel (now General) James Grant Wilson, who was at that time aid-de-camp to General Banks, occurs the following:

"On the morning of the 19th of February, 1864, I spent an hour with Scott at his quarters, Delmonico's, corner Fourteenth Street and Fifth Avenue. During our conversation he mentioned that he was engaged in writing his Memoirs, and that he experienced a great deal of annoyance from his difficulty in obtaining dates relating to events in the southwest. He expressed regret that Gayarre, whom he knew and had met before the war, had not published the third volume of the History of Louisiana, which he [Scott] knew was in manuscript. I remarked that I thought I had seen the work in three octavo volumes. 'No, you have not seen three volumes. There are only two published, and the first is a small 18mo volume,' was the old gentleman's answer. I further added that it was my impression that I had seen three, when the old soldier settled the matter by saying, 'Your impressions are entirely wrong, colonel.' An hour later I purchased the third volume at a Broadway bookseller's, and sent it to him with the following note:

"'FIFTH AVENUE HOTEL, *February 19, 1864.*

"'MY DEAR GENERAL: I have much pleasure in sending you the third volume of Gayarre's History of Louisiana, which I trust may contain the desired information. Should you wish to refer to the first volume of his work, you will find it at the Astor Library. It is an octavo volume of about five hundred pages, published by Harper & Brothers, of this city. I have the honor to be, general, very truly yours,

(Signed) "'JAS GRANT WILSON.,
"'*Col., A. D. C.*

"'*Lieutenant-General* WINFIELD SCOTT.'

"Called on Scott soon after my arrival from New Orleans (early in October, 1864), and had a very pleasant interview. Almost the first thing he said was thanking me most kindly for the third volume of Gayarre's History, and apologizing for his mistake. Told me his Memoirs were completed and in press; that he had closed them abruptly, as he was fearful that his end was near, during the early part of the summer—about June, I think he said."

General Scott's health continuing bad, he was conveyed in a quartermaster's boat from New York to West Point by General Stewart Van Vliet, accompanied by several personal friends. He died at the West Point Hotel a few minutes after eleven o'clock, May 29, 1866. The last words which he spoke were to his coachman: "Peter, take good care of my horse." He was buried, in accordance with his oft-expressed wish, in the West Point Cemetery, on June 1st, his remains being accompanied to the grave by some of the most illustrious men of the country, including General Grant and Admiral Farragut. The horse mentioned above was a splendid animal, seventeen hands high and finely formed. The last time that General Scott mounted him was in the latter part of 1859, which he did with the aid of a stepladder, for the purpose of having an equestrian portrait painted for the State of Virginia. The war coming on, the picture passed into possession of the Mercantile Library of New York.

The author received a letter from the late Rutherford B. Hayes in January, 1892, in which he said: "On my Southern tour in 1877 I repeated two or three times something like this, purporting to be quoted from General Scott: 'When the war is over and peace restored, there will be no difficulty in restoring harmonious and friendly relations between the soldiers of the sections. The great trouble will be to restore and keep the peace between the non-belligerent combatants of the war.' I did not hear the remark of General Scott. My recollection is that I heard it from General Rosecrans." . . .

On submitting President Hayes's letter to General Rosecrans, he made the following statement: "I heard that story about General Scott from General Charles P. Stone. General Stone was on the staff of General Scott. At the beginning of the war, in the spring of 1861, he was directed to organize the militia of the District of Columbia, and was present when the following occurred, as he told me personally. Shortly after the fall of Sumter and the President's call for troops, Secretaries Seward, Chase, and Cameron came to General Scott's residence in Washington one evening and found him at the dinner table. One of them said: 'General, our duties as members of the Cabinet make it very desirable for us to have some idea of what the probable range and course of the war will be, that we may guide ourselves accordingly. We have therefore come to you to get your judgment on the situation.' On the general's invitation, they sat down at his dinner table, and he went on to explain his idea of how the war would progress from year to year. While he was talking, Mr. Seward seemed to be somewhat impatient, and put in several little interruptions, but finally subsided and allowed General Scott to proceed. The general gave an outline of a war probably lasting from three and one half to four years, but resulting in favor of the Union.

"On the general's announcement of his opinion that the Union would triumph, Mr. Seward, rubbing his hands, inquired, 'Well, general, then the troubles of the Federal Government will be at an end.' To which General Scott replied, 'No, gentlemen, for a long time thereafter it will require the exercise of the full powers of the Federal Government to restrain the fury of the noncombatants.'"

To a young army officer he gave the following advice: "You are now beginning life; you are ignorant of society and of yourself. You appear to be industrious and studious enough to fit yourself for high exploits in your profession, and your next object should be to make yourself a perfect man of the world. To do that you must carefully observe well-bred men. You must also learn to converse and to express your thoughts in proper language. You must make acquaintances among the best people, and take care always to be respectful to old persons and to ladies." General Scott was always extremely gallant and courteous to ladies and greatly enjoyed the society of intelligent and refined women. As stated in the early part of this work, General Scott had been an industrious student of the law, and the knowledge thus acquired was of great service to him throughout his eventful career. He was well read in the standard English authors—Shakespeare, Milton, Addison, Pope, Johnson, Goldsmith, Dryden, Hume, Gibbon, and the early English novelists. He was a constant reader of the best foreign and American periodicals and the leading newspapers of the day. He was of the opinion that wars would never cease, and therefore took little interest in peace societies.

He held the opinion that the study of the higher mathematics had a tendency to lessen the ability to move armies in the field, yet expressed regret that he had not in his youth given more study to the subject. He was very fond of whist, but was quite irritated when he was beaten and generally had a ready excuse for his defeat. On one occasion he was playing a very close game, in the midst of which he left the table to expectorate in the fireplace. He lost the game and said to one of the party, "Young gentleman, do you know why I lost that game?" "No, sir," was the response. "It was because I got up to spit." Scott was also a good chess player.

He used tobacco somewhat excessively until the close of the Mexican War, after which time he renounced its use entirely. He was exceedingly vain of his accomplishments as a cook and specially prided himself on the knowledge of how to make good bread. He spent several days in instructing the cook at Cozzens' Hotel, West Point, in this art, and did not desist until the bread was made according to his standard. He had a great aversion to dining alone, and rather than do so would cheerfully pay for the meal of any pleasant friend whom he would invite to dine with him. General Scott openly professed himself a Christian and was a regular attendant at the services of the Episcopal Church. He was broad and liberal in his views and condemned no man who differed with him in religious opinion. He usually carried a large, stout, gold-headed cane, and after entering his pew would rest both hands on its head and bow his head, praying in silence. It was difficult for him to kneel on account of his size. He scrupulously joined with the greatest decorum and seriousness in all the services of the church, responding in a distinct, loud voice.

He was impatient with persons who could not recollect or did not know of dates and events which were conspicuous in his life. He was asked at one time the date of the battle of Chippewa. He answered blandly, "July 5, 1814." Turning to a friend, he remarked, "There is fame for you." The same party inquired in what State he was born. He answered, "Virginia." "Ah," said the questioner, "I thought you were a native of Connecticut." This left him in a bad humor for the remainder of the evening. The editor of this series has said of him: "General Scott was a man of true courage—personally, morally, and religiously brave. He was in manner, association, and feeling courtly and chivalrous. He was always equal to the danger—great on great occasions. His unswerving loyalty and patriotism were always conspicuous, and of such a lofty character that had circumstances rendered the sacrifice necessary he would have unhesitatingly followed the glorious example of the Swiss hero of Sempach, who gave his life to his country six hundred years ago. . . . He was too stately in his manners and too exacting in his discipline—that power which Carnot calls 'the glory of the soldier and the strength of armies.' A brief anecdote will illustrate the strictness of his discipline. While on duty he always required officers to be dressed according to their rank in the minutest particular. The general's headquarters in Mexico comprised two rooms, one opening into the other. In the rear room General Scott slept. One night after the general had retired a member of his staff wanted some water. The evening was warm and the hour late, being past midnight. The officer rose to go in his shirt sleeves. He was cautioned against the experiment as a dangerous one, for if Scott caught him in his quarters with his coat off he would punish him. The officer said he would risk it—that the general was asleep, and he would make no noise. He opened the door softly and went on tiptoe to the water pitcher. He had no time to drink before he heard the tinkle of the bell, and the sentinel outside the door entered. 'Take this man to the guardhouse,' was the brief order, and the coatless captain spent the night on a hard plank under guard."* He did not conceal his opinions of

---

* Wilson's Sketches of Illustrious Soldiers: New York, 1874.

men or measures, and hence he very often gave offense. It should be borne in mind that the public men of the age when General Scott came on the stage, both military and civil, were as a rule dignified, formal, and to some extent dogmatic. They held themselves with great dignity, and their magnetism was the result of their commanding abilities and high character, and they did not rely for popularity upon the methods of modern times.

General Grant, in mentioning General Scott's Mexican campaign, says: "Both the strategy and tactics displayed by General Scott in the various engagements of August 20, 1847, were faultless, as I look upon them now after the lapse of so many years." And further: "General Scott enjoys the rare distinction of having held high and successful command in two wars, which were a full generation apart. In 1847 he commanded, in Mexico, the sons of those officers who aided in his brilliantly successful campaign against the British on the borders of Canada in 1814." Daniel Webster, in a speech delivered in the United States Senate February 20, 1848, said: "I understand, sir, that there is a report from General Scott, a man who has performed the most brilliant campaign on recent military record, a man who has warred against the enemy, warred against the climate, warred against a thousand unpropitious circumstances, and has carried the flag of his country to the capital of the enemy—honorably, proudly, humanely—to his own permanent honor and the great military credit of his country. And where is he? At Pueblo—at Pueblo, undergoing an inquiry before his inferiors in rank, and other persons without military rank, while the high powers he has exercised and executed with so much distinction are transferred to another—I do not say to one unworthy of them, but to one inferior in rank, station, and experience to himself." No more fitting close to this sketch of his life can be given than to quote the words of his friend, General Wilson: "He has bequeathed to his country a name pure and unspotted—a name than which the republic has few indeed that shine with a brighter luster, and a name that will go down to future generations with those of the greatest captains of the nineteenth century."

INDEX.

ABADIE, Captain, Louisiana volunteers, 101.
Aberdeen, Lord, British Minister, 151.
Abraham, negro, Indian interpreter, 74.
Adams, George, Lieutenant, 253.
Adams, John Quincy, ex-President, 153.
Adams, the British vessel, captured, 13.
Allen, Captain, 17.
Alvarez, Mexican General, 219, 221, 231.
Amatha, Charley, 79.
American forces surrender to General Sheaffe, 18.
Ampudia, Pedro de, Mexican General, surrenders, 155, 156.
Anaya, Don Pedro Maria, General, elected President of Mexico, 257.
Andrews, Timothy P., Colonel, 226.
Anderson, Robert, General, 135, 322, 326.
Anecdote of Colonel Scott and a Roman Catholic priest, 19.
Armistice violated; General Scott's letter to President of Mexican Republic, 218.
Arnold, Ripley A., Lieutenant, attacked by Indians, 115.
Arista, Mariano, Mexican General, 155.
Arthur, President, 326.
Assiola, Indian Chief, 88.
Atkinson, T. P., letter from General Scott to, 153.
Atristain, Señor, 216, 257.
Azapotzalco, the place of meeting of the commissioners, 216.

Baker, D. D., Lieutenant, 253.
Baker, Edward D., Colonel, killed at Ball's Bluff, 317.
Bankhead, James, Colonel, 112.
Barcelona, the steamer, 146.
Barker, Captain, 16.
Barr, Captain, Louisiana volunteers, 101.
Barragan, Peña y, 221.
Barron, Major, 109.
Basinger, William E., Lieutenant, 88.
Battle on the Ouithlacoochee, 90-92.
Beall, Benjamin Lloyd, Major, 172.

Beard, Joseph, Major, 95.
Beauregard, P. T., Lieutenant, 203.
Beckwith, J. C., letter to, from General Scott, 154.
Belknap, William G., 281.
Benton, Thomas H., 159.
Biddle, Richard, speech in Congress, 124–127.
Binney, Horace, letter to General Scott, 304.
Black Hawk War, the, 52, 55.
Blockade of Southern ports, 296, 297.
Board of Army Officers, 47.
Boerstler, Charles G., Colonel, 27.
Bolton, Commodore, 97.
Bones, George, Captain, 110.
Botts, Benjamin, 5.
Boyd, John Parker, General, attack on Fort Niagara, 24.
Brady, Hugh, Major, 33; sketch of, 39.
Brady, Thomas A., First-Lieutenant, 253.
Brant, Indian, attacks Colonel Scott, 18, 19.
Bravo, D. Nicholas, Mexican General, 225, 227.
Brazos Santiago, 159.
Brisbane, Abbott H., Colonel, 112.
Brooks, Horace, Captain, 225.
Brown, Jacob, General, 27, 38–40.
Bryant, Thomas S., Captain, 96.
Buchanan, James, President, 296, 326.
Bull Run, 308.

Burlington Heights, 28.
Burnett, Ward B., Colonel, 209.
Burnham, Major, 185.
Burr, Aaron, 5–8.
Burt, Captain, Louisiana volunteers, 101.
Butler, Pierce M., Colonel, 112, 115, 209.
Butler, William O., General, 244, 245, 256, 264.
Cadwallader, George, General, 193, 206, 209, 210, 221, 226, 249.
Caldwell, James N., Captain, 215.
Caldwell, Robert C., First-Lieutenant, 253.
Caledonia, British brig, 13.
Calhoun, John C., 151.
Call, Richard Keith, General, 89.
Cameron, Simon, 309, 314, 315, 330.
Canada political agitation, 2,2.
Cano, D. Juan, Mexican General, 225.
Caroline, the steamboat, 145.
Casey, Silas, Captain, 207, 226.
Cass, Lewis, 59, 66, 67, 76, 77.
Cerro Gordo, the battle of, 176, 190.
Chandler, John, Colonel, attack on Fort George, 24.
Chapultepec, battle of, 223, 228.
Charleston, S. C., furnishes troops and supplies, 94.
Chase, Secretary, 330.
Chauncey, Isaac, Commodore, 24, 28.

INDEX.

Cherokee Indians, removal of, from Georgia, 129.
Chesapeake, the, boarded by the Leopard, 6.
Chesnut, Colonel, 95.
Childs, Thomas, Lieutenant-Colonel, 176, 194, 236.
Chippewa, battle of, 32.
Cholera among troops at Chicago, 56, 57.
Chrysler's Farm, engagement at, 29.
Chrystie, John, Colonel, 14, 17.
Cincinnati, Society of the, 42.
City of Mexico, 195, 228.
Civil war, beginning of, 295, 296.
Clarke, Henry Francis, Colonel, 212, 249.
Clay, Cassius M., 306.
Clay, Henry, 145, 151.
Clinch, Duncan L., General, 82, 88, 93.
Clinton, Governor, 42.
Clifton, Captain, 112.
Coffin, Captain, 19.
Congress declares war against Great Britain, 13.
Congress votes a medal to General Scott, 42.
Conner, Commodore, 165.
Conto, Señor, 216, 257.
Cooper, Mark A., Major, 112, 119.
Coto, Señor, 216.
Crane, Ichabod B., Colonel, 136.
Crawford, William H., 40.
Cuevas, Señor, 257.
Cummings, Arthur C., Captain, 215.

Cunningham, Captain, 94.
Cushing, Caleb, General, 281.

Dade, Francis Langhorne, Major, killed, 88.
Dallas, Commodore, 97.
Davis, Edward, General, 312.
Davis, Jefferson, 291.
Dearborn, Henry, General, 14, 23, 24.
Dennis, Colonel, 29.
Devlin, John S., acting quartermaster, 253.
Dominguez commands Mexicans in American army, 237.
Douglas, Stephen A., 303.
Douglass, John M., Major, 112.
Drum, Simon H., Captain, 220, 225.
Drummond, Lieutenant-General Sir Gordon, 34.
Duane, James Chatham, General, 305.
Duel between Burr and Hamilton, 5.
Dulaney, William, Major, 253.
Duncan, James, Lieutenant-Colonel, 108, 221, 271, 277, 283, 286.
Duval, William P., Governor, 82.

Eaton, J. H., Secretary of War, 49, 50, 76, 82.
Edson, Alvin, Captain, 165.
Elliott, Lieutenant, plans destruction of British brigs, 13.
Eustis, Abram, Brigadier-General, 111, 113, 114.
Expedition of Aaron Burr, 5, 6.

Fagan, John, Major, 75.
Fanning, Alexander C. W., Major, 88.
Farquhar, William, Captain, 302.
Farragut, Admiral D. G., 329.
Fenwick, John R., Colonel, 16.
Field, Thomas Y., Lieutenant, 253.
Fillmore, Millard, President, 293.
Finances of Mexico, 239.
Finlay, Captain, 94.
Florida War, 72, 87, 97-99, 112.
Florida, army of, 115.
Floyd, John B., 136, 298.
Floyd, Robertson R., Captain, 96.
Fort Brooke, the army concentrate there, 118.
Fort Brown occupied by General Taylor, 154.
Fort Erie surrenders, 30; invested, 37.
Fort George, attack on, 16, 17; storming of, 24.
Fort Niagara, defeat of the British at, 26.
Foster, William Sewell, Lieutenant-Colonel, 102.
Frazer, William, Captain, 88.
Freeman, Norvell, Lieutenant, 253.
Fremont, John C., General, 308.
Frontera, Mexican General, 207, 208.

Gadsden, James, Colonel, 75.
Gaines, Edmund, General, 48, 103.

Gaines, J. P., Major, 250.
Gamboa, D. Manuel, Mexican General, 225.
Gardiner, George, 88.
Gardner, Charles K., Lieutenant, 11.
Gardner, Franklin, 175.
Garland, John, General, 220, 221.
Gatlin, John Slade, Dr., 88.
Georgia troops, 95, 96, 110.
Gibson, Captain, 18.
Giles, William B., 5-7.
Goodwyn, Robert H., Colonel, 112-116.
Graham, Captain, 110.
Graham, William A., Secretary of the Navy, 293.
Grant, Ulysses S., General, 322, 329, 334.
Great Britain, war declared against, 11.
Greenway, James, Dr., 3.
Griffin, Charles, Captain, 302.
Guadalupe Hidalgo, text of treaty of, 257, 264.

Hagner, Peter V., Captain, 225.
Halleck, Henry W., General, 308.
Hamilton, Alexander, 5.
Hamilton, John C., 292.
Hamilton, Schuyler, Lieutenant, 250.
Hampton, Wade, General, 7, 9-12, 28.
Hardy, Sir Thomas, 6.
Hargrave, James, 4.
Harney, John, Governor, 142-144.

INDEX.

Harney, William S., Colonel, 186, 224.
Harris, Captain, 33.
Harris, Joseph W., Lieutenant, 83.
Harrison, William Henry, General, 152.
Haskell, William T., Colonel, 166.
Hayes, Rutherford B., President, 326, 329.
Heileman, Julius Frederick, Major, 65, 66.
Henderson, Charles A., Lieutenant, 253.
Henderson, Richard, Lieutenant, 88.
Henry, Alexander, letter to General Scott, 304.
Henry, George, Captain, 115.
Hernandez, John M., General, 96.
Herrera, General, 216.
Hetzel, Abner R., Captain, 135.
Hindman, Jacob, Major, 30, 39.
Hitchcock, Ethan A., Captain, 100, 164, 284.
Holata, Amathla, 75, 77, 78, 79.
Huger, Benjamin, Captain, 220, 224.
Hull, William, General, 13.
Hunt, Henry J., Lieutenant, 221.

Ingersoll, Charles J., 153.
Irish prisoners, 20.
Irving, Washington, 5.
Izard, George, Colonel, 13.
Izard, James Farley, Lieutenant, 101, 102.

Jackson, Andrew, General, 5, 40, 42, 46, 63, 151.
Jackson, Thomas J., Lieutenant, 226.
Jacobs, Captain (Indian), attacks General Scott, 18, 19.
Jefferson, Thomas, President, 7.
Jesup, Thomas S., General, 31, 33, 39, 122, 123.
Johnston, Joseph E., Colonel, 226.
Juarata, Padre, leader of guerrillas, 237.
Judd, Henry, Jr., Lieutenant, 172.

Kearney, Philip, Captain, 211.
Keayes, J. S., Lieutenant, 88.
Ke-o-Kuck, Indian chief, 58.
Ker, Croghan, Captain, Louisiana volunteers, 107.
Ker, William H., Captain, 101.
Keyes, Erastus D., Lieutenant, 135.
King, William R., 293.
Kirby, Reynold M., Major, 94, 115.

Lally, Follict T., Major, 215, 216.
Landero, José Juan de, Mexican General, 169, 170.
Lane, Joseph, General, 237, 256.
Lang, William, Captain, 253.
Lawson, Thomas, Lieutenant-Colonel, 101.
Leavenworth, Henry, Major, 31, 33.
Lee, Robert E., Captain, 101,

164, 175, 203, 208, 223, 225, 284, 305.
Leigh, Benjamin Watkins, 10, 70.
Lendrum, Thomas W., 88.
Leon, Mexican General, 219.
"Leonidas letter," the, 267, 287.
Leopard, British frigate, 6.
Lewis, Morgan, General, 26.
Lincoln, Abraham, President, 296, 301, 312, 313, 315, 316, 326.
Lindsay, William, Colonel, 111, 135.
Lobas Island, 161.
Loring, William W., Major, 206, 212.
Louisiana troops. 119.
Lovell, Christopher H., Lieutenant, 280.
Lundy's Lane, battle of, 34-36.

McCauley, Charles G., Lieutenant, 253.
McClellan, George B., General, 178, 206, 308.
McClure, Brigadier-General, New York militia, 28.
McComb, Alexander, Colonel, 24, 29, 50, 153.
McDonald, Adjutant, 146.
McDowell, Irwin, General, 307.
McDuffie, George, 61-63.
McFeely, George, Lieutenant-Colonel, 24.
McIntosh, James S., Colonel, 193, 220.
McKenzie, Colonel, 226.
McLemore, Captain, 110, 112.

McNeill, John, Jr., General, 31, 33, 39.
McRee, William, Colonel, 39.
McTavish, Carroll, 41.
Mackall, William W., Major, 227.
Madison, James, President, 22.
Magee, Captain, Louisiana volunteers, 101.
Magruder, John B., Lieutenant, 206, 226, 302.
Malone, Captain, 119.
Mansfield, Mr., British Minister, 11.
Marcy, William L., 146, 158, 159, 269.
Marks, George H., Captain, 113.
Marks, Samuel F., Captain, 101.
Marshall, General, 245-248.
Marshall, John, Chief-Justice, 136.
Martin Luther, 5.
Mason, Captain, 286.
Mason, Daniel, 3.
Mason, James M., 321.
Mason, Winfield, 3.
Massacre of General Thompson and others, 89.
May, James F., 5.
Mayo, John, Colonel, 41.
Mendoza, Mexican General, 205, 207.
Mico, Indian chief, 78.
Miconopy, Indian chief, 78.
Miller, James, Colonel, 25.
Mississippi River, free navigation of, 310.
Molino del Rey, battle of, 219-222.
Monroe, James, President, 22.

INDEX. 343

Monterde, D. Mariano, Mexican General, 225.
Morales, Mexican General, 168, 169.
Morgan, George W., Colonel, 208.
Mormon expedition, 294.
Morris, Charles T., Captain, 207.
Mount Vernon, 316, 317.
Mudge, Robert Richard, Lieutenant, 88.
Mullaney, James Robert, Lieutenant-Colonel, 16.

Nashville, Confederate steamer, 320.
Negroes engaged in Dade massacre, 111.
Nicholson, Augustus S., Lieutenant, 253.
Nicholson, John S., Lieutenant, 253.
Nueva de Villa Gutierrez, Colonel, 170.
Nullification in South Carolina, 61-64.

Ogilvie, James, Captain, 4-17.
O'Riley, commander of deserters, captured, 237, 238.

Pachuca occupied, 248.
Packenham, Sir Richard, 151.
Paez, General, 48.
Page, Captain, 135.
Palo Alto, battle of, 155.
Parish, Richard C., Colonel, 90.
Patterson, Robert, General, 245.
Payne, Matthew M., Major, 135.
Payne's Landing, treaty of, 74.
Peña y Peña, 236, 257.

Perez, Mexican General, 208-219.
Perry, Matthew C., Commodore, 169.
Perry, Oliver Hazard, Captain, 14, 24.
Pierce, Franklin, General, 207, 214, 292, 293.
Pike, Zebulon, General, 24.
Pillow, Gideon J., General, 170, 176, 193, 211, 224, 226, 276, 281.
Plympton, Joseph, Lieutenant-Colonel, 208, 220.
Porter, Captain, 25.
Porter, Moses, General, 24, 30.
Porter, W., Secretary to General Gaines, 108.
Prevost, Sir George, 26, 27.
Puebla, occupation of, 197.
Putnam, Benjamin A., Major, 93.
Putnam, General, 5.

Queenstown Heights, storming of, 15.
Quijano, Benito, Mexican commissioner, 214.
Quitman, John A., General, 172, 204, 206, 224, 226, 228, 280.

Randolph, John, 5.
Rangel, Mexican General, 219.
Rea, Mexican General, 236.
Read, Leigh, Colonel, 90, 113.
Resaca de la Palma, battle of, 155.
Ravenel, Captain, 94.
Reynolds, E. McD., Lieutenant, 253.

Reynolds, John G., Captain, 253.
Riall, General, moves to Burlington Heights, 33.
Rich, Jabez L., Lieutenant, 253.
Ridgely, S. C., Captain, 281.
Riley, Bennet, General, 206, 208, 209.
Ripley, Eleazer W., 39.
Ripley, R. S., Lieutenant, 185.
Roach, Isaac, Jr., Lieutenant, 13, 16.
Robertson, Judge, 302, 303.
Robinson, David, Judge, 4.
Robinson, Edward B., Captain, 110.
Robles, Mexican Lieutenant-Colonel, 170.
Rogers, A. P., Lieutenant, 166.
Rogers, Captain Louisiana volunteers, 101.
Rosecrans, William S., General, 308, 329.
Ruffin, Thomas, 5.

Sacs and Fox Indians, treaty with, 58.
Sackett's Harbor, landing of the British, 27.
Sanders, William G., Captain, 107.
Sands, Richard M., Major, 101.
San Jacinto, steamer, 321.
San Pablo, convent of, 212.
San Patricio Battalion, 237.
Santa Anna, Antonio Lopez, General, 156, 173, 175, 190, 206, 209, 225, 230, 231, 236, 256, 257.
Scott, Ann, 3.
Scott, Camilla, 41.
Scott, Cornelia, 41.
Scott, Henry L., Colonel, 135, 164, 178, 284.
Scott, James, death of, 1, 2.
Scott, Winfield, birth and parentage, 1; runs away from Sunday school, 2; defends his teacher; at William and Mary College, 4; enters on the practice of law; present at the trial of Aaron Burr, 5; attacks British camp at Lynn Haven Bay; goes to South Carolina to practice law; returns to Petersburg, Va., to practice law; joins Petersburg cavalry company, 6; receives commission as Captain in the U. S. army; recruits his company and embarks for New Orleans, 7; arrested and tried by court-martial for words spoken of General Wilkinson, 8; tenders his resignation, 8; finding of the court, 9; letter to Lewis Edwards, 10; rejoins the army at Baton Rouge, La.; embarks for Washington; vessel gets aground, 11; appointed Colonel; visits the Secretary of War with General Hampton; an unpleasant incident, 12; war with Great Britain; ordered to the Niagara frontier, 13; volunteers to cross the Niagara; marches to Lewiston, 16; the attack on Fort George, 17; a flag of truce, 18; a prisoner, and attacked by Indians; embarks

INDEX. 345

for Boston, 19; addresses Irish prisoners; letter to Secretary of War, 20; selects hostages in retaliation for Irish prisoners, 21; returns to Washington, 22; ordered to Philadelphia; appointed Adjutant General; promoted Colonel of his regiment; joins General Dearborn, and appointed chief of staff, 23; assault on Fort George; Scott leads the advance, 24; struck by a piece of timber and collar bone broken, 25; anecdote of a British officer, 26; resigns the office of Adjutant General, 27; joins General Wilkinson, 28; marches for Sackett's Harbor; appointed to command of a battalion; preparing new levies of troops, 29; appointed Brigadier General; ordered to join General Jacob Brown; establishes camp of instruction at Sackett's Harbor; assigned to a new command; moves toward Chippewa, 30; wins the battle of Chippewa; report of General Brown, 32; moves to mouth of the Niagara, 33; battle of Lundy's Lane, 34, 35; General Scott disabled, 37-39; in command for defense of Philadelphia and Baltimore, 39; reception at Princeton; declined to act as Secretary of War; ordered to Europe, 40; receives attention in Europe; return home; headquarters in New York; married to Miss Mayo, of Richmond; names of his children, 41; Congress passes resolutions complimenting him; present at the death of President Monroe; thanked by Legislatures of Virginia and New York; honorary member of the Society of the Cincinnati; order of General Jackson, 42; letter of General Jackson to General Scott; his reply, 43; letter to General Jackson, 44; General Jackson's reply; Scott calls on General Jackson, 45; tribute to General Jackson; his work on general regulations for the army, 46; president of board of army and militia officers; publication of his work on infantry tactics; the temperance reform; his views on, 47; controversy with General Gaines; tenders his resignation; not accepted, 48; letter to Secretary of War; the Secretary's reply, 49; assigned to command of Eastern Department; treaty with Sac Indians, 50; ordered to Illinois; Asiatic cholera, 53; letter to Governor Reynolds, 54; newspaper extracts in regard to General Scott's action in the cholera epidemic, 55–57; commissioner to treat with Indians; result of the treaty, 58; arrives in New York, and ordered to Washington; the tariff act of 1828 and excitement in South Carolina, 60; ordered to South Carolina, 66; letter of instruction from Secretary of War; arrival in Charleston, 66, 67; detained by accident, 68; success of his mission, 71; ordered to immediate command in Florida, 98; disposition of troops, 110–112; movement of troops, 114; the army arrives at Tampa Bay, 117; arrival at Fort Brooke, 118; embarks on St. John's River, 120; complaint against General Jesup; court of inquiry on Florida campaign, 122; finding of the court; letter to Secretary of War, 123; defense in Congress, 124; tendered dinner in New York; declines, 127; ordered to remove the Creek Indians, 129; addresses to troops and Indians, 130, 132, 133; the Indians move West, 135; ordered to look after Canada insurgents, 139; ordered to Maine, 140; meets Governor Everett; proceeds to Portland, 141; settlement of the troubles, 143, 144; uprising in Upper Canada; affair of the Caroline, 144, 145; ordered to the scene of the troubles; meets Governor Marcy, 146; letter to commanding officer of British vessels, 147; the affair settled, 147, 148; his name presented to Whig Convention as candidate for the presidency, 152; effort in Congress to reduce his pay; letter to T. P. Atkinson on slavery, 153; letter to peace convention, 154; the War with Mexico; the "hasty plate of soup," 157; his opinion of General Taylor; ordered to Mexico; goes *via* New Orleans, 158; arrives at Brazos Santiago, 159; fails to meet General Taylor, 161; landing of the troops at Vera Cruz, 162; investment and surrender of Vera Cruz, 164–170; advances on Jalapa, 173; Cerro Gordo, 178, 179, 187; occupation of Puebla, 193; movement toward the City of Mexico; criticism by the Duke of Wellington, 195, 196; address to Mexican people, 198; movement on and capture of Padierna, 204–207; Churubusco, 211; arrival of Nicholas P. Trist, U. S. Commissioner, 213; cessation of hostilities by armistice, 214; the armistice ended, 218; Molino del Rey, 219–222; attack on and capture of Chapultepec, 226, 227; occupation of the capital; orders for government of the city, 229; additional orders, 231–234; orders for obtaining revenue in Mexico, 240–242; letter to Secretary of War, 243; his civil administration of Mexico, 246, 247; reports his total force, January 6, 1848; ordered before a court of inquiry; relieved from command of the army, 248; money levied on City of Mexico, 255; turns over command of the army, 264; General Orders No. 349, 270; letter to General Worth, 272; relieved from duty, 277, 278; reads a paper before the court of inquiry, 281, 282; submits paper to court of inquiry, 284; embarks at Vera Cruz for home, 288; receives thanks of Congress, 289; discontent in Canada, 293; candidate for the presidency (1852), 293; on commission to settle boundary line with Great Britain, 295; letter to President Buchanan, 296, 297; letter to Secretary of War, 297, 298; letter to Secretary of War, December 28, 1861, 298; letter to Secretary Seward, March 3, 1861, 299; firing of guns at Mobile on announcement that he had resigned, 304; order of April 26, 1861, at Washington, D. C., 306; issues General Orders No. 17, 308; complains of General McClellan, 309; request to be placed on retired list, 311, 312; addresses the President and Cabinet on his retirement, 313; sails for Europe, November 9, 1861, 318; army asylum fund, 323; statue of, at Soldiers' Home, 327; his death and last words, 329; his acquaintance with English authors, 331; advice to young army officer, 330, 331; anecdote of battle of Chippewa, 332; vain of his accomplishments; regular attendant at the Episcopal Church, 332; goes to West Point, 328; his loyalty, his strict ideas of discipline; anecdote, 333.

Sears, Henry B., Lieutenant, 215.

Secretary of War to General Gaines, 100.

Seminole council, 85.

Seward, Secretary, anecdote of General Scott, 330.

Shannon, Samuel, Captain, 102.

Shaw, H. B., Major, 135.

Sheaffe, General Sir Roger Hale, 17–19.

Shelton, Joseph, General, 116.

Sheridan, Philip H., General, 326.

Sherman, William T., General, 326.

Shields, James, General, 176, 207, 209, 280.

Shubrick, William B., Commodore, 238.

Sibley, Henry H., Captain, 212.

Simms, John D., Lieutenant, 253.

Slidell, John, 321.
Small, William F., Captain, 236.
Smith, Charles F., Captain, 221.
Smith, Colonel, Louisiana volunteers, 101, 118.
Smith, Constantine, Lieutenant, 89.
Smith, E. Kirby, Captain, 221.
Smith, Gustavus W., Lieutenant, 207.
Smith, Persifor F., Colonel, 101, 112, 206, 208, 209, 211, 214, 227.
Smyth, Alexander, General, 14.
Soldiers' Home at Washington, 323, 324, 326.
Soto, Don Juan, Governor of Vera Cruz, 215.
Steptoe, Edward J., Captain, 223.
Stone, Charles P., General, 301, 318.
Strahan, Captain, 17.
Sumner, Edwin V., Major, 175, 211, 220, 221, 224.
Sutherland, David J., Lieutenant, 253.
Swift, Joseph G., Colonel, 28.

Tampico letter, the, 267, 268.
Tariff of 1828 and trouble in South Carolina, 60.
Taylor, Francis, Captain, 135, 223.
Taylor, Governor, of South Carolina, 61.
Taylor, Zachary, General, 154, 289.
Tazewell, Littleton W., 5.
Temperance reform, 47.

Terrett, George H., Captain, 253.
Texas, causes which led to annexation, 149, 154.
Thistle, Captain, Louisiana volunteers, 101.
Thomas, James H., Colonel, 173.
Thompson, General, Indian agent, 79.
Thompson, Launt, 327.
Thurston, Charles Myron, Captain, 110.
Timrod, Captain, 94.
Totten, Joseph G., Colonel, 17, 18, 28, 164.
Towson, Captain, ordered to report to St. Elliott, 13, 16, 33, 37.
Towson, Nathan, General, 281.
Trent, affair of the, 321.
Tripp, T. S., Captain, 115.
Trist, Nicholas P., commissioner, 213, 216, 257, 281.
Trousdale, William, Colonel, 226.
Truxton, Commodore, 5.
Tweedale, Marquis of, crosses the Chippewa, 30.
Twiggs, David E., General, 101, 173, 176, 193, 206, 220.
Twiggs, Levi, Major, 253.
Tyler, John, President, 152.

Upshur, Abel P., Secretary of State, 151.

Valencia, Mexican General, 204, 211, 248.
Van Buren, Martin, President, 145.

INDEX. 349

Van Rensselaer, Colonel, 144.
Van Rensselaer, Solomon, General, 14, 17.
Van Rensselaer, Stephen, General, 14, 16, 18.
Van Vliet, Stewart, General, 328.
Vera Cruz, 161, 162, 167, 171.
Villamil, Mora y., General, 214, 216, 257.
Vincent, General, 27.
Vinton, John R., Colonel, 166.
Volunteer American officers paroled, 19.

Wadsworth, Decius, General, 15.
Walker, Robert J., 159.
Washington, George, General, 5.
Watson, Samuel E., Lieutenant-Colonel, 253.
"Wayward Sisters" letter, 299, 300.
Webb, Captain, U. S. N., 97.
Webster, Daniel, 293.
Weed, Thurlow, 318.
Wellington, Duke of, 195.
Welsh, Henry, Lieutenant, 253.
Wheelock, Eleazer, General, 30.
Wilkes, Charles, Commodore, 321.

Wilkinson, James, General, 7, 8, 28.
William and Mary College, 4.
Williams, Captain, Louisiana volunteers, 101.
Williams, T., A.-D.-C., 250.
Wilson, Henry, Colonel, 173.
Wilson, James Grant, General, 327, 328, 335.
Winder, William Henry, General, 24, 27.
Winfield, Elizabeth, 3.
Winfield, John, 3.
Wirt, William, 5.
Withers, Jones M., 248.
Wood, Major, 37.
Wool, John E., Captain, 15–17.
Worth, W. J., General, 136, 170, 174, 193, 265–267, 270, 271, 273, 274–276, 285.
Wright, George, Major, 220.
Wynkoop, Francis M., Colonel, 166, 248.

Young, William L., Lieutenant, 253.

Zacatepetl, Barreiro, Colonel, 205.

THE END.

www.ingramcontent.com/pod-product-compliance
Lightning Source LLC
Chambersburg PA
CBHW020301240426
43673CB00039B/670